D1201006

International
Business Policy

MODERN MANAGEMENT SERIES

International
Business Policy

▶▶▶▶▶▶▶▶▶▶▶▶▶▶▶▶▶▶▶▶▶

Richard D. Robinson

LECTURER ON INDUSTRIAL MANAGEMENT
MASSACHUSETTS INSTITUTE OF TECHNOLOGY

LECTURER ON HISTORY AND ECONOMICS
HARVARD UNIVERSITY

HOLT, RINEHART AND WINSTON

NEW YORK • CHICAGO • SAN FRANCISCO • TORONTO • LONDON

▶ ▶ ▶ ▶

To Marion Hamlin Robinson

A gentle lady of patience and
compassion, who challenged her sons
when faced with setback "to rise above
it," an admonition often remembered
in the preparation of this volume

▶ ▶ ▶ ▶

Preface

International business as a proper subject for research, theory, education, and specialization by practitioners is relatively new. Perhaps for that reason there have been few attempts to define the field.

The Field of International Business

As do international economics, international politics, and international law, the international business field lies within the broader field of international relations. For reasons not entirely clear, most studies of international relations seem to have vastly underplayed the role of international business. The writers write as though the enormous web of transnational pipelines of men, goods, services, and institutions representing the totality of international business enterprise is of only peripheral importance.[1] They fail to recognize that this web is the very guts of international relations.

The truth is that the foreign policy of at least a modern *liberal* state is very largely designed to service private international business interests that have developed — or are anticipated. The modern state struggles to maintain its sovereignty and expand its power vis-à-vis other nations in order to enhance the position of its people in their relations with the rest of the world. Otherwise, the struggle has no meaning for a modern man. The point is that the state itself

[1]In Quincy Wright's impressive work, *The Study of International Relations* (New York: Appleton-Century-Crofts, 1955), the word "business" is not even listed in the index.

exists as a collective means for expanding the opportunity for more people to live more fruitful and meaningful lives. Such is the purpose of politics and political institutions — be they national or international — even though presidents, kings, and chiefs are prone to overlook this fact and to view politics as an end process, which it is not. The basic prerequisite for a fruitful and meaningful life is the wherewithal to live in the first place. In the more liberal West, that wherewithal is very largely provided through private business enterprise, albeit controlled in the public interest and supported by public services. Indeed, it is very difficult to conceive of a *liberal* society in which the individual is not sufficiently free (1) to choose his own profession from many alternatives, (2) to retain a substantial part of the profits of his own labors, (3) to purchase goods and services that he himself selects from among many alternatives, and (4) to organize and join groups of his own choosing for these same purposes. We have thus defined the private business system, which lies within the broader general field of business. The fact that the tools of production — including land — are owned by some collective agency (government or corporation) may really be irrelevant. The distinguishing feature of a liberal society is the relative mobility and freedom of choice enjoyed by individuals.

Both the international economists and the international politicians seemed to assume that international business is included within the field labeled "international economics." This assumption is unwarranted. The problem is that the word "economics," at least in its academic context, is inadequate, for it relates only to what is in men's minds, to ideas, to theory, to schematized relations drawn on paper. "Business" relates to reality, to activity, to operating institutions, to human effort directed toward achieving some human satisfaction. Business may have a theory, but it is a theory that relates to operating institutions *as they are*, or might be, not in the highly stylized form of the economist's never-never world. Economic theory makes little mention of the social-psychological impact inherent in each business transaction — the induced shifts in preferences, in skills, in understanding, in opinions, in values, in organization, in law, in political relations. Business theory does precisely that. So likewise does the theory of *international* business. In this way, our calculus is quite different from that of the economist, or the politician, or the lawyer. Hence, the fields are distinct. The relationship is pictured here.

The researcher, theorist, teacher, and practitioner of international business is concerned with the relationship among business activities operating within different national political systems, and also with the operational problems of a local branch of a foreign firm. That is, these relationships and operational problems fall within the field of international business so long as they relate to *both* domestic and foreign persons or institutions. For example, a domestic business problem generated by reason of a feedback from an overseas activity is included. So likewise is an overseas organizational problem generated by reason of a feedback from a domestic activity. So likewise is an overseas organizational problem, the resolution of which is ultimately the responsibility of a foreign-based management — or which affects that foreign management in some respect. Also, variables introduced from outside the international business field, such as governmental policy, but which affect business entities in more than one nation, lie within the compass of international business. Such externally generated variables may be considered environmental factors influencing the flow or structure of business relations across an international, territorial, or colonial frontier.

A field of study, theory, and practice may likewise be defined by the social purpose of such activity. I suggest that the unifying purpose (or concept) in the international business field is to enhance the likelihood of mutually profitable, international business transactions, which purpose is the basis upon which the practice of international business must rest in the long run (bearing in mind that profit refers to something more than mere financial return).[2] Corollary to that unifying purpose is the belief that the reduction of the area of conflict in the organizational and personal relationships worked out to effect these transactions is socially desirable.

Some critics have contended that the analytical tools, concepts, and bodies of knowledge relevant to domestic business problems are universally valid — that international business is a simple continuity of the domestic. Of course, in a sense, everything is a continuity. But I believe that the word is generally used in the sense of a sequence; that is, if one knew enough about the domestic experience and the analytical tools that make that experience meaningful, one could make valid predictions about experience elsewhere. In other words, the system continues to operate by the same rules. This implies that

[2]Business relates to organized human effort directed toward achieving some human satisfaction through the transfer of goods or services from one condition to another; or from one person to another, for a mutual profit stated in explicit terms on a *quid pro quo* basis. (For instance, the production and sale of goods by a government agency may be business, but payment of social security benefits or foreign aid is not.) The "explicit terms" need not imply a *financial* profit. I have deliberately chosen not to identify business with a mercantile pursuit or transaction, a definition implying a financial profit incentive. I have merely stipulated an explicit price (perhaps one should add, "at least on a financially self-sustaining level") to distinguish business enterprise from a political enterprise. It is true that the producer (or transferer) of a good or service and the recipient both expect to profit from the transaction, or the transaction would not take place. But they anticipate profit in terms of their own individual fiscal, physical, and/or psychic calculi, which profit may be one stated only in part in financial terms. The point is that the concept of financial profit is much too narrow. In an affluent society in particular, much "profit" is of the psychically rewarding type. The business manager does not necessarily maximize financial gain alone, at least in the immediate, forseeable sense. *This is precisely where economics and business part company.* One analyst has observed: "My own belief is that the directors of such a well-run railroad as the Santa Fe try to run it well for the same reasons that the trustees of a great university try to run the university well." (Gardiner C. Means in "Collective Capitalism and Economic Theory," *Science*, vol. 126, no. 3268, August 16, 1957, p. 291.) In an oft-quoted article, O. A. Ohman has written: "The assumption of the 'economic man' and the automatic regulation of the enterprise system through financial incentives, which was once the cornerstone of managerial science, is no longer sound. We need to discover and utilize other appeals to get work done.... Money has lost much of its incentive value." ("Search for a Managerial Philosophy," *Harvard Business Review*, September–October 1957, pp. 44–45.)

a successful domestic businessman could expect to operate with the same effectiveness internationally. If "continuity" does not mean this, then it has no real meaning. My rebuttal is that as one moves across cultural-political frontiers, variables he may encounter can be of such a nature as to change the rules by which the system operates. For instance, the domestic marketing expert does not include within his calculus the nature of the social, political, and economic impacts of the product he is trying to market except insofar as they are legally determined. All concerned assume that the public is discerning enough to buy what is in its interest to buy. If it does not, then the public suffers. So what? But this picture changes dramatically if one moves into a culture in which the elite assume that popular short-run consumption pressure may run contrary to long-run national interest, that is, sustained economic growth at a catch-up rate under a sovereign government. Products not felt by the elite to support this long-run objective may be subject to severe restriction in their manufacture and sale, if not sooner, then later. Control, market, and assets may be lost by the firm insensitive to this new factor. The calculus for international marketing problems is thus not a simple extension of the domestic; entirely new variables enter into the picture, some of which may dominate the system. And, as a matter of fact, recent research would indicate that a good bit of the managerial theory developed out of the American experience may not be valid at all in reference to certain non-Western cultures.

This study is, in fact, an attempt to develop the calculus which, if used in selecting overseas projects, in structuring international enterprises, and in resolving operational problems, would enable business to reduce the area of conflict and, hence, become a more viable international concept. Although as a member of an essentially liberal society, I speak almost entirely of *private* business enterprise, public business enterprise would be subject to similar operational rules.

Outline of Study

The evidence of the past, which is explored in Chapter 1, underscores the enormous importance of Western enterprise in generating among non-Western peoples massive reaction to the West. (Western enterprise is the focus, because the modern business concept is essentially Western in origin.) This discussion is oriented to the political factor inasmuch as a society responds collectively via political action.

At first, Western enterprise acted through traditional political authorities — local chief, priest, headman, or sheikh — and thus strengthened them. But as investment deepened, the Westerners eventually undermined traditional authority to such an extent that Western political authority was pulled into the void — whether in the form of protectorate, extraterritorial concession, or direct colonial administration. The modernization of local political institutions thus tended to be blocked as Western enterprise and its parent governments assumed local political functions and won over the loyalty of many local nationals. As the two World Wars momentarily weakened the power umbrella shielding Western enterprise and as the Cold War made direct intervention no longer expedient, political authority shifted back to the host societies. A nationalistic fervor erupted, but the modern political institutions that would turn this fervor into constructive channels were notable by their absence, for the process of political modernization had been long contained by the exercise of political functions by Western enterprise and/or parent Western governments.

The historical dimensions of the problem having been thus established — which in a sense constitute the inputs into the modern international political system — Chapter 2 sifts private municipal and international law — that is, the outputs of the system — to find principles under which a common expectation of justice might develop as between Westerner and non-Westerner and thereby minimize conflict. Certain rules are suggested.

Chapter 3 refines these principles and rules by using the tools offered by economic and political theory to measure the impact of Western enterprise on non-Western societies. Although these measures cannot be reduced to anything like mathematical precision, they do constitute a basis on which a management may make an informed estimate of the impact of what it proposes to do overseas — and hence of the political risk inherent in that action. For in the end, all nonbusiness risks are translated into degrees of political pressures.

Finally, Chapters 4 and 5 explore the implications of the foregoing in terms of the individual Western firm. Answers are suggested to the general question: What innovations in company policy and structure are prerequisite for a profitable and reasonably secure existence in the international era? Chapter 6 summarizes the conclusions and speculates as to their significance.

My general thesis is that, just as the past behavior has filled a large reservoir of ill-will toward private Western enterprise in non-Western lands, a reverse flow might be possible in the future. Given greater wisdom, forbearance, farsightedness, and understanding, Western enterprise might conceivably create a favorable political response as it moves through the twilight of the national era into the international age. To do so, however, will take much hard-headed thought. It is not a self-evident truth that the concept of private business is really relevant and meaningfully related to the process of accelerated, catch-up development that will one day inevitably proceed in the non-Western world. Criteria, policies, and organization will have to be rethought and altered to fit into the radically different sociopolitical environment one can anticipate in the near future.

So, likewise, will many U. S. governmental policies — and those of other Western governments — have to be revised in order to enable private business to compete effectively with state business in many parts of the world. Although lying outside the scope of this present study, it should be recognized that Western public policy is an important variable in the background.

Weston, Massachusetts
November 1963

R.D.R.

Acknowledgments

So many persons have contributed to the concepts developed in this volume that it is difficult to single out individuals. However, at the risk of offending by omission, I must express special gratitude to Dean Howard Johnson and Professors Lucian Pye, Everett Hagen, Norman Padelford, Carroll Wilson, and Daniel Lerner, of the Massachusetts Institute of Technology; to Professors Stephen M. Schwebel, Bertrand Fox, A. J. Meyer, David D. McCelland and John B. Fox, of Harvard University; to Professor

John Fayerweather, of New York University; to Mr. Hamlin Robinson, of the Stanford Research Institute. At various phases of this study, which covered seven years, they provided intellectual stimulation or encouragement or both, without which this book would never have been written. In thus identifying them with this effort, they should in no way be held responsible for the shortcomings of the final product. Several of these men, I am sure, did not realize to what they were a party.

I owe a great debt to Professor Charles F. Stewart, of Columbia University, for his sympathetic and constructively critical reading of the manuscript.

I must also acknowledge the generous permission to reproduce bits and pieces of my earlier writings given by the *Boston University Business Review, University of Houston Business Review, Oregon Business Review, Journal of Marketing, Western Business Review, Business History Review*, and *Tradescope*.

Finally, I must thank collectively the many hundreds of international business practitioners who graciously permitted me to consume large chunks of their time in plumbing their experience and ideas. The same applies to the area specialists of the American Universities Field Staff, Inc.

R.D.R.

Contents

International

Business Policy

► ► ► ► **1**

The Historical Dimension

Merely by existing, the United States and the Western world as a whole bring to bear . . . a constant cultural pressure. But even though the idea of industrialization, expanded consumption, and political egalitarianism may pour forth equally for all . . . countries, what is absorbed varies widely from one to another. How and why and toward what ends each nation moves is conditioned by its own traditions and appreciations as well as by the historical course of its particular set of involvements with the industrially advanced nations.[1]

It is perhaps a truism that at different times and places Western business enterprise has exercised profound influence on the political cultures of Africa, Asia, and Latin America. However, the precise nature of that influence has not been well understood. Because political response is the collective reaction to any variable introduced into a society, it is upon the interaction between Western business enterprise and non-Western *political* cultures[2] that this chapter is focused.[3] Out of that interaction come the questions haunting the

[1] K. H. Silvert, "Political Change in Latin America," in *The United States and Latin America*, Herbert L. Matthews, ed. (New York: The American Assembly, Columbia University, 1959), p. 59.

[2] Political culture is defined as the manner in which a society is organized about, reacts to, and uses political authority. Political authority is equated with the power to make and enforce decisions relating to the integration and adaptation of a society in respect to either internal or external variables. (For further definitions refer to the explanatory Note at the end of this chapter.)

[3] This chapter is an adaptation of the author's article "Interrelationship of Business Enterprise and Political Development," *The Business History Review*, Vol. XXXVI, No. 3 (Autumn 1962).

thoughtful Western businessman of today: does he have a continuing role in Africa, Asia, and South America, where the bulk of the human race dwells? And if he does have a role, what is it? That these blunt questions are not soberly considered in the literature of Western business is due to our tradition of casually assuming the continuing validity of self-evident truths, truths which are neither self-evident nor necessarily true in other than a transient, culturally bound sense — if then.

Historical Patterns

The political consequences of Western business enterprise have varied enormously over the years. In recognition of that fact, the ensuing discussion has been divided into five great historical eras which, for convenience, have been labeled as the Commercial, the Exploitative, the Concessionary, the National, and the International. These terms are suggested as being generally descriptive of the nature of the dominant relationship existing between Western business and the non-Western world at different times during the past four centuries and of the forty or fifty years one can see ahead. Sometime after that final period, Western business, as a distinctive feature of the international landscape, may well disappear into a more general culture of world business.

In identifying these eras with specific time periods, one must necessarily admit to much overlap. What is being attempted is to develop the principal business characteristics of each era in terms of political implications. Obviously, it is impossible to treat all of the possible deviations from the norm.

The time sequence presented as being useful for purposes of analysis is:

The Commercial Era — from the age of the great explorers, about 1500, to well into the European industrial revolution, along about 1850.

The Exploitative Era — from about 1850 up to the years just prior to World War I.

The Concessionary Era — from the immediate pre-World War I period to the end of World War II.

The National Era — from World War II to about 1970.

The International Era — from about 1970 to sometime after the end of the century.

There is necessarily much blurring between succeeding eras, for in each the dominant relationship for the subsequent period is created. For example, in the present National Era a significant amount of Western business is already organized for life in the International Era. It is for this reason that one can predict with a fair degree of certainty what the next dominant form of relationship is likely to be.

One might also point out that when the structure of a business enterprise is too far out of phase with the appropriate pattern of relationship for the era in which it exists, the enterprise greatly increases its political risk. For instance, if the enterprise lags behind the development of the host political culture by assuming inappropriate political functions, the firm opens itself to charges of exploitation and political intervention. If it moves too far ahead by shedding political functions that the host society cannot perform, it inadequately protects itself. In both cases it is vulnerable.

The Commercial Era

The age of commercially motivated exploration opened the Commercial Era. It was an era characterized by individual entrepreneurs in search of personal fortune through the purchase of goods in distant lands, shipment to Europe, and then sale for large profits. The risk to both person and cargoes was great, and a high degree of personal motivation and of navigational skill were prerequisites for successful ventures.

The individuals involved tended to be military and naval adventurers, explorers, and missionaries, most of whom operated under the cloak of at least semiofficial sponsorship. For example:

> Columbus was made admiral, viceroy, and governor-general "in all those islands and mainlands which by his hand and industry" should be discovered. He was also promised [by Isabella of Castille] one tenth of all products which he might bring from the territory lying within his admiralty and was given permission to contribute at any time one eighth toward the equipment of westward-bound trading vessels and to retain a proportional share of the profits. . . .[4]

[4]Mary W. Williams, *The People and Politics of Latin America* (Boston: Ginn & Company, 1944), pp. 104–105.

Economic ambition played a major part in Columbus's desire to reach the Orient by sailing westward; and the hope of great riches from the undertaking was an important motive of even the pious Isabella.[5]

Initially, the commerce these early adventurers conducted was transient in nature, limited very largely to coastal areas. It could often be equated with legalized piracy and plunder. The capital of these entrepreneurs was floating, and could be withdrawn readily from an untenable position. Precious metals, spices, silk and slaves were the principal objects of trade. Permanent settlement was limited except in the Americas.

The political consequences of this form of "trade" on those exposed to it was undoubtedly fear and a closing of the ranks about traditional political authority, thereby stimulating the process of political socialization.[6]

When profits began to flow regularly from the new trade, given the nature of Western regimes at the time and their mercantilist convictions, it was natural that the European monarchs involved should require direct participation by the crown, desire a more permanent traffic, and attempt to establish a national monopoly so as to secure maximum returns. The organizational forms adopted by the European states varied somewhat, although in nearly all instances strictly private trade was severly limited. The Portuguese, as early as 1481, made the Guinea trade a monopoly of the ruling house, "oversight being vested in a government department."[7] Of the Spanish, it is reported:

> ... by 1495 Castilians were granted the right to go rather freely to the Indies for trade or other purposes, merely being required to depart and return by the port of Cadiz and to give to the Crown the use of one tenth of the space in their vessels and the same proportion of the profits made in the enterprise. During these early years no duty was charged on imports into Spain. Under these favorable terms voyaging to the Indies soon became so popular that Ferdinand and Isabelle saw that they could secure larger profits for themselves without crushing the movement; therefore, beginning in 1501, royal licenses imposing various new restrictions were required of all who wished to sail to the New World. The

[5]*Ibid.*, p. 164.

[6]Political socialization refers to the manner and degree to which the members of a society identify with a political culture.

[7]K. G. Davis, *The Royal African Company* (London: Longmans, Green & Company, Ltd. 1957), p. 18.

policy of strict control of trade and travel between Spain and the Indies, thus begun, continued for nearly three centuries with little abatement.[8]

Dutch commerce in southeast Asia was fostered, as a matter of policy, by the government.[9] Of the English companies, one scholar has reported:

> All of the chartered companies of the Restoration were in some measure identified with the royal power, and in some of them the connexion was drawn closer by the personal participation of the royal family: Charles II in the Royal Adventurers; Prince Rupert in the Hudson's Bay Company: the Duke of Monmouth in the Royal Fishery; and James, both as Duke of York and as King, in the East India and Royal African Companies.[10]

One of the exceptions to the general rule of governmental involvement was the development of private enterprise out of certain early missionary efforts, that in Hawaii perhaps being the outstanding example. This enterprise, quite unlike others of the era, had no Western base. It was compelled by circumstances to become localized very early in the sense of investment in local facilities, employment of local personnel, and development of autonomous locally based management. The degree of localization thus achieved perhaps explains in part why the Kingdom of Hawaii possessed such a relatively developed political culture by the end of the nineteenth century. Although perhaps somewhat relaxed in actual administration, the kingdom had been forced to develop a set of differentiated political institutions capable of coping with modern commerce.[11]

Characteristic of the era, however, were the great chartered companies established principally under English, French, and Dutch authority. Normally, these companies were granted broad powers of both a commercial and political nature.

> As its director, Sir Josial Child, once boasted, the India Company was a "sovereign state" itself. It declared war on the Mogul Empire; it had a fleet, an army and fortified settlements; it could coin money and make laws. Businessmen administered India in their own fashion, and a very lively fashion it was for a long time. . . .

[8]Williams, *op. cit.*, p. 165.

[9]G. C. Allen and Audrey G. Donnithorne, *Western Enterprise in Indonesia and Malaya* (London: George Allen & Unwin Ltd., 1957), p. 18.

[10]Davis, *op. cit.*, p. 103.

[11]Amusingly described by Samuel Clemens in *Roughing It* (Hartford, Conn.: American Publishing Company, 1872), pp. 477 ff.; see also James A. Michener, *Hawaii* (New York: Random House, Inc., 1959).

This business administration of India was not ended until Victoria's reign.[12]

As a result, the first continuing exposure of non-Western societies to Western business enterprise was to an undifferentiated institution. That is, all authority, commercial and political, resided in a single agent, who not infrequently doubled as the official local representative of the foreign power. Thus, the Levant Company in the Middle East, the British Royal African Company in Africa, the British East India Company in southeast Asia, and the Hudson's Bay Company in northwest America all performed consular functions for their sovereign as well as exercising local political power. An exception was the Virginia Company, chartered in 1606, for the settlement and exploitation of Virginia. In this case emphasis was on permanent settlement *by Europeans*, and the settlers soon came to be governed by a King's council, not by the Virginia Company.[13] The relatively sparse indigenous Indian population was simply brushed aside. The situation was similar in Spanish America, which "was looked upon as the private estate of the sovereign," thus preventing any recognition of right of occupancy by the Indians.[14]

Everett E. Hagen describes the pattern of Spanish conquest in Colombia by profit-seeking adventurers:

> Under the decrees of the king each conqueror was permitted to occupy an area of land and to take a number of Indians under his guardianship and require work from them, in return for which he was to assure their material welfare and to confer upon them the benefit of Christianity. In practice, and in spite of occasional rulings to the contrary from Spain, the lands became the property in fee simple of the individual Spanish families, and the Indians became slaves. . . .
>
> Spain's economic control of her colonies in the New World followed the usual mercantilist pattern. Trade was permitted only with the mother country, and on both sales to and purchases from the colony taxes were levied which greatly burdened the producers of the colony.
>
> Politically the dominance of the home government was complete.[15]

[12]Miriam Beard, *A History of Business* (Ann Arbor: University of Michigan Press, paperback ed., 1962), p. 430.

[13]N. S. B. Gras and Henrietta M. Larson, *Casebook in American Business History* (New York: Appleton-Century Crafts, 1939), p. 34.

[14]Williams, *op. cit.*, p. 193.

[15]Everett E. Hagen, *On the Theory of Social Change* (Homewood, Ill.: Dorsey Press, 1962), pp. 355–356.

The character of the great chartered companies is revealed in their charters. That of the Royal African Company specified that no subject of the crown other than the corporate members of the company was to visit West Africa except by leave of the company, which was authorized to seize ships and cargoes of all who infringed on the monopoly. The company was also empowered "to establish and govern forts, factories and plantations in Africa, to make war and peace with any heathen nation there, to raise troups, and to execute martial law." The charter was to run for 1,000 years and included 5,000 miles of coastline.[16] The Dutch East India Company was granted exclusive trading rights in the East Indies and permitted to make "alliances with native princes," to appoint governors, and to employ troops.[17]

In the beginning these companies confined themselves largely to trading and shipping, and their local efforts were designed primarily to promote and protect both. To accomplish this task, companies not infrequently acted to enforce local political authority. For example:

> In West Africa goods did not flow at all freely between the interior and the coast. The trading depots on the coast depended on the precarious and costly good will of the coastal chiefs, while the coastal tribes who had to be used as intermediaries in the trade with the interior were free to hold the European trade as ransom.[18]

Because of this dependence upon the coastal chiefs — and because of their geographical vulnerability — Western enterprise entered into protective alliances with those authorities who would cooperate, thereby strengthening the latters' position vis-a-vis interior political leaders. Thus it was that where the land mass was great and the physical environment, unfriendly to European comfort — such as tropical Africa — the coastal leaders tended to gain in relative political power. One can see the aftermath of this disparate political development in contemporary Africa (for example, in Ghana).

In southeast Asia the British and Dutch East India Companies initially used various forms of indirect rule. "The earliest period of British rule in India was dominated by the East India Company,

---

[16]Davis, *op. cit.*, p. 98.

[17]Allen and Donnithorne, *op. cit.*, p. 18.

[18]S. Daniel Neumark, "The Character and Potential of African Economies," in *The United States and Africa*, Walter Goldschmidt, ed. (New York: American Assembly, Columbia University, 1958), p. 94.

which was concerned not with changing Indian society, or even controlling it, but with making a profit,"[19] which is not to say that the seed of change was not unconsciously sown. One business historian has observed that the early activities of the East India Company "proved ruinous to the conquered people; the profiteering of the Company's servants who bought up rice in famine times, the terrible revenue laws, and the sanction of slavery, had a dire effect on the social fabric in a large part of India."[20] Nonetheless, the Western entrepreneur tended to occupy an "amalgant role" in that he operated within both his own and the foreign culture, but really attempted to change neither.[21]

Political scientist Lucian W. Pye has observed, in respect to southeast Asia, that the consequence of this indirect rule was "primarily limited to the sphere of the traditional elite."[22] Perhaps in a formal and an immediate sense this view is correct, but one suspects that as the subservient status of local political leaders became apparent to the indigenous population, their authority was undermined by a deep sense of dissatisfaction among the people as they sought out informal — and increasingly extralegal — political authority with which to identify. This process can be seen today in some peasant societies,

[19]Myron Weiner, "The Politics of South Asia," in *The Politics of Developing Areas*, G. A. Almond and J. S. Coleman, ed. (Princeton: Princeton University Press, 1960) p. 164.

[20]Beard, *op. cit.*, p. 430.

[21]Insofar as is known, Lucian W. Pye first used the term "amalgant" in this meaning in seminars given at the Massachusetts Institute of Technology in 1961. He used the word to differentiate one of six distinct roles linking the political center with the rest of the population. The six:

1. *Administrator*, one who holds the values of the elite and tries to effect change on the mass level.
2. *Agitator*, one who holds mass values and tries to upset the values of the elite.
3. *Amalgant*, one who is at home in both the elite and mass societies, and tries to change neither.
4. *Transmitter*, one who moves between the elite and mass and, without consciously trying to change either, acts as the man-of-the-people when with the elite and vice versa.
5. *Ideological propagandist*, one who attempts to combine the values of various groups in an ideological appeal.
6. *Political broker*, one who tries to link the interests and problems of one group with another.

[22]Lucian W. Pye, "The Politics of Southeast Asia," in Weiner, *op. cit.*, p. 84.

such as the Turkish, where the greater interest shown by the innovating, urban-centered, Western-oriented central government in the behaviour of local traditional political authorities (that is, the village headmen) has led to both greater support and control of these local leaders by the central government. In the process the role of village headman has become such an unsatisfying one that the traditional peasant elite has turned over the *legal* role of headman to lower status individuals. In a sense, the latter act as political buffers and scapegoats. Meanwhile, in many communities real political authority has remained with the traditional, but now extralegal, leaders. Where such a buffer system did not appear, the traditional elite lost its authority.[23] Hence, one can extrapolate a widespread dissatisfaction in southeast Asia with the role of the elite under indirect rule, both among the elite as well as elsewhere. It seems likely that many sons of the traditional elite, sensing the frustration of their elders, withdrew from the political roles traditionally theirs when they became of age, thereby breaking traditional obligations running from elite to folk. In turn, their sons or grandsons, sensing the unsatisfying "retreatist" roles of their forebears, tended to turn to political innovation, even to revolution in some instances.[24] But this is ahead of the chronological story.

As trade developed in the eighteenth and ninteenth centuries, the European pushed inland to sources of supply. It then became imperative that law and order be established along the lines of communica-

> The companies (*i.e.*, British and Dutch East India), anxious to ensure higher standards of law and order so as to protect the flow of trade, came to assume more and more quasi-governmental functions. In some cases this meant establishing ports which grew into commercial centers under direct company rule; in other cases it involved treaty arrangements with local rulers under which the companies indirectly took on many governmental functions. In all cases, however, the old patterns of authority were disrupted and the doors were open to extensive social change.[25]

[23]Described in Paul Stirling, *Social Structure of Turkish Peasant Communities* (unpublished Ph.D. dissertation, Oxford University, 1951), summarized in R. D. Robinson, "Social Structure of Turkish Peasant Communities" (New York: Institute of Current World Affairs, Jan. 1952).

[24]This social-psychological process is treated theoretically in Hagen, *op. cit.*, pp. 185 ff.

[25]Pye, *op. cit.*, p. 83.

tion. More direct rule began to appear, but only in limited areas. In time, the companies stood between the local ruler and their people:

> Although the ruling aristocracies often received greater revenues and more security under their treaties with the companies, in time they found that in their relations with their subjects they were being gradually ignored and replaced by Europeans who, however, sought in the main to conform largely to the traditional customs of the area.[26]

Perhaps more fundamental in inducing increasingly direct rule by Westerners was the withdrawal of the traditional elite from its now unsatisfying political role, a role which it could not occupy successfully in Western eyes because of the new skills required. And the Westerner, in conforming to traditional customs, was eventually to make many of those customs unappealing in the eyes of the surrounding populace. Decades later, as in revolutionary Turkey, for example, the reaction against many traditional customs was to be extreme, in part because they came to be associated with foreign domination.

Still, in most places Western enterprise continued to rely essentially upon traditional authority during the Commercial Era for the general maintenance of law and order even though erosion of traditional political authority had begun to set in to a greater or lesser degree for the reasons mentioned. The degree to which Western enterprise penetrated and upset the local political culture was probably a function of the size of the land mass, the importance of interior supply sources, European reaction to the climate, the alleged importance of the internal market (which determined the degree of exposure of the traditional culture), the level of local political development (such as size of political unit, degree of effective control), and the timing of Western interest. For example, in China and Japan Westerners never achieved the same degree of political penetration as they did in southeast Asia, the Middle East, Africa, and Latin America.[27]

Both China and Japan were able to erect barriers to foreign penetration before local political authority had become so undermined as to make a policy of exclusion or partial exclusion impossible. In both cases the Westerner faced relatively developed political systems in the sense that they were more differentiated, universalistic, affectively neutral, and achievement-oriented than those with which he had been confronted elsewhere outside of Europe, with the single

[26]*Ibid.*, p. 84.
[27]Allen and Donnithorne, *op. cit.*, p. 50.

exception of the Ottoman Empire.[28] Chinese, Japanese, and Ottoman leadership was capable of thinking in terms of national interest even if it were not always disposed to act in those terms. However, the similarity among the three stopped there.

It is said that in placing restrictions on foreign intercourse in 1717, China was moved "chiefly by a desire to preserve the national customs from contamination by the barbarian. The exclusion policy thus sprang from conservatism fortified by a consciousness of an immense superiority"[29] — and, one might add, protected by a vast land mass. The Ottoman Turkish case was somewhat different. There, foreign enterprise had been sealed off in extraterritorial conclaves and intercourse with the interior restricted. Initially, this situation had been felt to be a perfectly normal one in view of the non-Muslim character of the groups concerned. Islamic law, of course, could not properly apply to these people; hence, the law of the land could neither protect, judge, nor punish them. The Ottoman Turks, secure in their demonstrable military power vis-a-vis the West, did not fear Western enterprise; they disdained it. The Ottoman political culture was likewise protected by a large land mass, although considerably more accessible than China. It was also significant that the center of Chinese political authority lay in the interior; the center of Turkish authority, in the principal port city.

The Japanese government, on the other hand, was led to a policy of exclusion in the middle of the seventeenth century (1638) out of "fear of foreign aggression and the danger that foreign intercourse presented to the political regime."[30] Because of the relative unimportance of its raw materials, the apparent unattractiveness of the internal market, and the unflattering reputation of its people, Japan did not interest the Western businessman until comparatively late. By the time interest had developed (the mid-ninteenth century), the Japanese could already see the results of Western commercial penetration elsewhere in Asia and were thus encouraged to act vigorously to prevent a parallel development in Japan.

Financial interest by European monarchs in the expanding trade, plus the power of the interest groups identified with overseas trade

[28]For definitions of these terms, refer to the Explanatory Note at the end of this chapter.
[29]G. C. Allen and Audrey G. Donnithorne, *Western Enterprise in Far Eastern Economic Development* (New York: The Macmillan Company, 1954), p. 185.
[30]*Ibid.*, p. 185.

emerging in European trading capitals, forced greater and greater direct government involvement on behalf of the companies. As one writer observed, "To secure these essentials (that is, protection of assets, personnel, and trading rights), and also in many cases to forestall competition by other powers, governments were compelled, sometimes very reluctantly, to commit themselves further and further in support of trade."[31]

The combination of external political and military pressure and of internal demands for increased commerce (particularly in opium) finally forced China in 1842 to recognize the *right* of Western enterprise to operate in certain "treaty ports."[32] Western trading houses had their attractions for the Chinese; they were skilled in the techniques of foreign trade, possessed intimate knowledge of foreign markets, enjoyed customer confidence, and had at their disposal capital resources. By the same token, once admitted as a matter of right, the Westerners quickly acquired a near monopoly of China's foreign trade and the array of services supporting it — shipping, banking, insurance, and so forth.

It was not for another twenty years (1868) that Japan was compelled to open her doors to Western commerce. Meanwhile, a small well-contained Dutch enclave remained the sole legal trading channel with the West, as it had done for two-hundred years. Unquestionably, increased awareness by the Japanese of the threat of the superior technology brought into Asia by Western enterprise, including the gunboats that protected it, helped induce the rather abrupt commitment by Japan to a process of accelerated modernization by fiat. Fortunately for the Japanese, the social-psychological basis for technical and economic innovation was already present in Japanese society.[33] Meanwhile, Chinese political authority continued to resist the internalizing of the changes infecting the body social through the treaty ports. It was therefore true that the Westerner "had a more narrowly restricted role" in Japan's development than in China's.[34]

The Commercial Era really closed with the establishment of direct colonial rule in many parts of Asia, Africa, and Latin America and the recognition by China and Japan of the extraterritorial rights

[31]Neumark, *op. cit.*, p. 94.

[32]See Edith E. Ware, *Business and Politics in the Far East* (New Haven: Yale University Press, 1932), Chapter I.

[33]*See* Hagen, *op. cit.*, pp. 354 ff.

[34]Allen and Donnithorne, *Far Eastern Economic Development, op. cit.*, p. 96.

of Western enterprise. Within the Ottoman Empire the exemption from local legal processes, which had originally been in the nature of a disability forced upon Western enterprise by an all-powerful political authority, now assumed the flavor of a concession awarded by a weakened capitulating state. A foreign business house could establish itself in the country without the consent of the Ottoman government and could organize according to the laws of its own country. It was largely exempt from Ottoman taxation, and its foreign personnel enjoyed inviolability of a person and domicile and the jurisdiction of their own consular courts. Precisely because these political activities became a function of a foreign government, the pressure for local political development was reduced.

During the Commercial Era the political function embedded in Western enterprise remained largely undifferentiated from the commercial. By its example, Western business had thus not encouraged any greater specificity of function on the part of the local political culture. In many ways — outside of the Americas — the Westerners had initially strengthened traditional political authority by acting through it to maintain law and order, recruit labor, and gain compliance with agreements. However, by the end of the era the Westerners were beginning to undermine local authority in the coastal regions, even in the essentially noncolonial areas — China, Japan, and the Ottoman Empire. They did so by expanding the channels of external communication and by providing individuals a path of social mobility outside traditional routes. One might, by collaborating with the Western trader, accumulate wealth, influence, and power which would have been difficult to accomplish within the traditional system. He might be a tribal intermediary in coastal West Africa; a comprador or chief factotum in a Chinese port city; or, a dragoman in Constantinople or Smyrna. In all cases a local commercial class dependent upon the foreign trader — and to a certain extent protected by him — appeared in the coastal trading centers. Where the central political authority itself was located within the coastal area (as in the Ottoman Empire) the political center was peculiarly vulnerable. In the Ottoman Empire military misadventure and commercial and political intrigue had so weakened the central authority by the middle of the nineteenth century that it had become a virtual captive of Western enterprises and their governments. Japan was able to maintain its policy of exclusion for a few more years, but not China. In China the interior-located central authority had failed to continue effective

political control in the trading ports, where a substantial Chinese
trading class, alienated by the ultra-conservative posture of the Chinese government, had associated itself with Western enterprise. In
North and South America the lure of riches, the religious zeal of the
early merchant explorers, and the primitive nature of the indigenous
political culture, led to early settlement and direct rule under foreign
law.

The Exploitative Era

The pressures generated by the industrial revolution in Europe
for cheaper and more secure sources of raw materials changed the
nature of overseas European enterprise. Interest turned from the
exotic products, characterizing much of the Commercial Era, to industrial products — mineral ores and plantation crops. And as industry
developed in Europe, the external market in Asia and Latin America
became increasingly important. By the mid-eighteenth century Western business was no longer simply clinging to coastal positions; it was
moving inland. By the mid-nineteenth century large-scale permanent
investments had been made in mining, in land development, in interior
transport (principally railroads), in port facilities, and in processing
plants. Simultaneously, an increased number of European nationals
were drawn into the expansion. The investment was no longer a
floating one, and the settled European population overseas had become substantial.

Because of the more extensive European settlement in the Americas and the mercantilistically motivated policies pursued by the
absentee European overlords, revolution came early in the Western
Hemisphere. Here European mercantilism was in conflict with
European-American mercantilism. Where religious separatism was
overlaid on top of the economic-political conflict — that is, in North
America — nationalistic revolt errupted even before the end of the
eighteenth century. Where this and other American revolutionary
movements coincided with weakness at home in Europe, they sometimes succeeded in breaking the political ties. However, despite the
mestizo support of Bolivar and other revolutionaries in Latin America,
nowhere in the Americas did the indigenous population achieve political autonomy in the process. The natives were either relegated to
third-grade citizenship (peonage), as in South America, or reconsti-

tuted into interior colonies, as in North America (under the name of tribal reservations). Therefore, although local political rule was eventually established in the Americas, it was a rule by revolutionary groups dominated by those of European blood and culture and for the benefit of those of similar origin and culture. For this reason, many of the observations to follow do not apply to the Americas with the same force as they do to Asia, Africa, and the Middle East, although in Latin America revolution has been a continuing process as it penetrates to the Indian population. There, the European-Indian population ratio was much smaller than in North America, where in the end the Indian population could be all but ignored.

In Africa it was mining that pulled the colonial powers into the interior. Out of the total foreign capital invested in the continent from 1870 to the end of 1936, two thirds went to the "mineral territories."[35] Mining development requires heavy investment in interior transport, employment of a large labor force, and maintenance of internal law and order. In southeast Asia it was the development of both plantation agriculture and mining that created the necessity for colonial rule. In Latin America, because of the greater importance of the religious tie with Europe during this era, the picture was somewhat more complicated, but still the tenacity of colonial rule seems to have been very largely a function of the size of the permanent investment in interior mining and plantation development. (In North America successful political revolt had preceded the move by European enterprise — other than trading — into the interior. European-owned mining and plantation enterprises had not become a significant feature in the American colonies prior to 1776.)

The number of European nationals participating in these overseas ventures and the vital importance of their activity to European economies forced the home governments to become more directly involved. Governmental functions were taken over from the companies, and colonial administrations differentiated from the business enterprises established, although in the East Indies the Dutch government attempted commercial and economic development as a direct governmental function.[36]

In some instances, after a period of business enterprise, the home government converted the foreign companies to territories or companies. For

[35]Neumark, *op. cit.*, p. 96.
[36]Allen and Donnithorne, *Western Enterprise in Indonesia and Malaya, op. cit.*, pp. 23–24.

16   *International Business Policy*

example, Britain's Royal African Company, operating in equatorial West Africa, became His Majesty's mandate of Nigeria and the German Colonization Company became substantially the Hohenzollern empire in Africa.[37]

Extraterritorial concessions, some of which had been granted almost as acts of disdain by foreign governments, were now maintained by force if need be. In other cases, where important raw material sources were located, European governments attempted to justify and maintain protectorates. One of the more recent attempts along this line was Britain's efforts to erect a protectorate over Iran in 1919. National power and prestige thus became associated with secure access to important raw materials and, later, to sheer territorial domination quite apart from any enriching substance.

Men strongly embued with European Christian nationalism replaced the earlier adventurers and fortune seekers. Some of the companies were founded and perpetuated by government subsidy to serve in various capacities the nation or empire by which they were originated. Business for profit had given way to business for political gain. And the missionaries gave empire building a certain moral compulsion.

Initially, as has been noted, Western enterprise tended to preserve unchanged traditional political institutions so long as they remained functional to its purposes. However, during the middle years of the nineteenth century new methods of organization and production were introduced which led to a deeper penetration by Western enterprise. No longer were local skills adequate in either quality or quantity. Western technicians and skilled workers began to arrive. Where unskilled labor was inadequate either in quantity or incentive, Western enterprise imported it from slightly more developed or populated regions, or became involved in a training function, or both. Chinese and Japanese labor was brought to Hawaii; Indian, to southeast Asia; Levantine, to Turkey — thereby complicating the process of political socialization in each instance. (Meanwhile, domestic United States enterprise imported first African, and then Asiatic, labor.)

In Africa labor was concentrated in the sparsely populated mining areas and given rudimentary training. With investment in

[37]Charles M. Wilson, *Empire in Green and Gold* (New York: Holt, Rinehart and Winston, Inc., 1947), pp. 255–256.

settlement and training, concentration of labor became economically important, and the disintegration of the family and decay of tribal life began.[38] One scholar of African affairs has observed:

> The economic development over most of Africa in modern times can best be understood as the result of two migrations: (1) the migration of European traders, officials, settlers and entrepreneurs into Africa, carrying with them capital, equipment, skills, and governmental and economic organization; and (2) the migration of the African tribesmen out of their subsistence economy into the new money economy created by the Europeans.[39]

William Lever wrote in 1910:

> The fact is, the native has few wants, a little salt and a little cloth are his indispensables . . . Chief Womba at Leverville can be taken as an example. Twelve months ago he and his people were keen to bring fruit (which the company was buying). After 12 months or less of selling fruit, he is rich and lazy, has 10 wives, and his village is about 4 times the size it was, and he gathers little or no fruit.[40]

Outwardly, the traditional political leader was strengthened, but one could sense that it was a strength that became increasingly dependent upon the company. So long as he was subservient to its wishes, he was useful. When he became resistant, he could be cast aside, and the company could influence — if not dictate — the process of political recruitment (the manner and degree to which a society participates in legitimizing political authority). All of this was in part a function of the attempt to concentrate and stabilize labor in a routinized scheme of production.

In other cases, Western enterprise relied very heavily upon local ethnic minorities for specialized functions. For example, the Chettiars, a south Indian caste of bankers and moneylenders became in effect, "the channel by which Western banking resources were poured into . . . Asian business." Small traders, craftsmen, and independent miners obtained most of the credit they required from the Chettiars who, in turn, discounted the notes they received with Western banks.[41]

[38]Neumark, *op. cit.*, p. 100.

[39]Andrew M. Kamarck, "The African Economy and International Trade," in *The United States and Africa, op. cit.*, p. 127.

[40]Charles Wilson, *The History of Unilever* (London: Cassell & Co., Ltd., 1954), Vol. 1, p. 176.

[41]Allen and Donnithorne, *Western Enterprise in Indonesia and Malaya, op. cit.*, p. 205.

One of the results of Dutch East India Company activity in Java was the passing of domestic commercial activity into the hands of the Chinese. Meanwhile, the Javanese became a people of cultivators.[42]

In Malaya, Western banks conducted most of their business through Chinese compradores, whose duties consisted of guaranteeing Chinese customers, supervising the cash department, and advising on their recruitment of Chinese staff. They received most of their remuneration in the form of commissions on business introduced or guaranteed. Sometimes the job became hereditary.[43] European enterprise in the Ottoman Empire was associated closely with the Armenian, Greek, and Jewish communities, members of which provided Western enterprise with skilled labor, banking services, interpreters, and influence men. In Latin America the indigenous Indian populations provided only labor; the mestizos, the skills.

Commercial functions had long been relegated to outcast ethnic, religious minorities in a number of non-Western societies. Association with Western enterprise was not only materially rewarding for members of these socially frustrated groups, but it also added to their personal security. European enterprise of the Exploitative Era thus created and perpetuated well-defined roles for outcast minorities. At the same time, where it continued to exist, as an effective force, traditional political authority — now on the defensive — became even more conservative in resisting the incursion of economic incentive and technological change, the more so because these values became identified with low status groups.

Small, English-speaking minority enclaves of local nationals thus came to occupy the position of a potential cultural transmitter, the link between the outside world and the traditional culture. Yet, frequently they were neither identified with, nor really accepted, by either. These buffer groups thus tended to block the transmission of culture change and to minimize the exposure of the traditional political culture. Even where there existed a local commercial class that was racially and religiously indistinguishable from the larger society — as in China — still its members tended to be looked down upon by the rest of society.

In China foreign business came to be surrounded by a wealthy, English-speaking commercial group, members of which were ethnically identified with the larger society. Management of a leading English firm in Hong Kong, for example, admitted that it was entirely

[42]*Ibid.*, p. 20.
[43]*Ibid.*, pp. 205–206.

dependent on information supplied to it by its Chinese employees.[44] One suspects that these local nationals surrounding Western enterprise acted in an amalgant role in that they were at home in both worlds but made no attempt to change either. They did, however, represent an embryonic special-interest group destined to perform the politically significant function of gaining recognition for the social legitimacy of the business function, a function differentiated from the political. This recognition came about much more rapidly in those societies in which no buffer ethnic minority existed. In some instances — as in republican Turkey and Indonesia — the ethnic minority commercial groups were forcibly restrained and those identified with the ethnic majority encouraged to take over minority business activity. One could argue that the very success of the minority groups economically stimulated their replacement.

Also during the last part of the nineteenth century local interior markets began to grow to attractive size, in part because Western products came to be seized upon as symbols of status. It was found that the African's and Asian's desire for goods was as insatiable as that of people elsewhere — and far less satisfied.[45] Singer Sewing Machine salesmen and the peddlers of various consumer goods — thread, cutlery, weapons, patent medicines, and so forth — moved into the hinterlands. Law and order, the sanctity of commercial contract, and a sound currency became increasingly important, as did a cooperating merchant class.

By 1865 there were at least thirty, largely British-owned, trade and commission houses in Central America.[46] Many of these soon came to serve as local bankers as well as general merchants. They began by lending money for the exploitation of tropical products. In the normal course of foreclosing on bad debts, these coastal trading houses came to own large chunks of Central American real estate. In time, they became banking firms "for whom many an early Central American *presidente* or soldier-of-fortune dictator readily signed, frequently with an "x," practically any kind of English-written credit document that was set before him. Central America required credit."[47]

One of the chief preoccupations of Western enterprise of this era

[44]Allen and Donnithorne, *Western Enterprise in Far Eastern Development, op. cit.*, p. 48.
[45]Walter Goldschmidt, "Culture and Changing Values in Africa," in *The United States and Africa, op. cit.*, p. 182.
[46]Wilson, *Empire in Green and Gold, op. cit.*, p. 39.
[47]*Ibid.*

was the establishment of sound currencies with which to carry on its interior activities. Some companies themselves issued currency, as did the Colonial Sugar Refining Company in New South Wales in 1869. "In Indonesia and Malaya . . . there were no political restraints upon the introduction of [such] modern currency systems and financial institutions as the economic development of these countries at the hands of Westerners might seem to require."[48]

The record of Burma is perhaps characteristic of the era. Until the 1870's the colonial power — Britain — ruled indirectly through the hereditary chieftains. The opening of the Suez Canal in 1869 and the pressure for external markets generated by Britain's new industry (particularly textile) induced a deeper Western penetration. By 1886 Britain had extended its rule over all of Burma, an expansion accompanied by a distinct shift from the previous liberal policy to an emphasis on administrative "efficiency" in order to promote development — and a larger market. The result was a breakdown of village self-rule.[49] Among other things, the colonial bureaucracy began enforcing a system of law based on the Western idea of individual property ownership rather than Burmese customary law which recognized family possession. Further evidence of the breakdown of the traditional political system was a rapid growth in the crime rate. This disintegration was implicit in the introduction of a formal rule of law deemed necessary by the West for the conduct of business.[50]

China is a case in point.

> When Westerners took up residence in the ports, they wished to assure for themselves the amenities of life which their compatriots at home enjoyed. and at the same time their trading, manufacturing, and transport could not be conducted efficiently without services of the type normally provided in the West by municipal authorities or public corporations. The Chinese authorities were at first neither interested in, nor capable of introducing these public utilities.[51]

[48]E. R. Knox (ed.), *South Pacific Enterprise* (Sydney; Austl.: Angus & Robertson, 1956), p. 23.

[49]D. G. E. Hall, *Burma* (London: Hutchinson's University Library, 1956), p. 142.

[50]J. S. Furnivall, *Colonial Policy and Practice, A Comparative Study of Burma and Netherlands Indies* (Cambridge: Cambridge University Press, 1948), p. 135.

[51]Allen and Donnithorne, *Western Enterprise in Far Eastern Development, op. cit.*, p. 145.

Western trading houses in the treaty ports soon began to develop service utilities for themselves, from port facilities and shipyards to telegraph communications and power generation. Banking and insurance facilities are obvious prerequisites for the conduct of large-scale trade. Chinese institutions were not equal to servicing the new traffic, and foreigners filled the void.[52] Control of commercial finance and insurance is tantamount to control over shipping. For example, the unwillingness of the Western insurance companies to insure junks "persuaded the Chinese to ship their goods by foreign vessels."[53] And once foreign commerce becomes a foreign monopoly, a nation's foreign policy becomes captive, thereby blocking the development of this specialized political function.

The foreign-dominated financial institutions in China at times discharged responsibilities on behalf of the Chinese government "normally restricted to central or official banks." For many years "they supplied China with financial machinery necessary for coping with the financial problems associated with the modernizing of her economy."[54] Foreign banks supplied China with a significant portion of her currency, a right that "did not proceed from the Chinese Government, but from charters which [the banks] . . . had received from their home governments."[55] At times, upon request of Chinese authorities, they even held public revenues in order to prevent them from falling into the hands of "unauthorized political and military groups.[56] As the funds at their disposal increased and the pressure for new markets heightened, these institutions began to offer long-term industrial finance as well as short-term commercial credit.[57] Their penetration into the life of China increased apace. Foreign institutions, principally the Ottoman Bank, performed similar quasi-political functions within the Ottoman Empire and constituted the organizational vehicle for Western penetration, political and otherwise.

The growth of foreign domination was largely hidden from the bulk of Chinese society, limited as it was to certain coastal areas and out-of-sight control over finance and foreign trade. The same was

[52]*Ibid.*, p. 119.
[53]*Ibid.*, p. 120.
[54]*Ibid.*, p. 102.
[55]*Ibid.*, p. 112.
[56]*Ibid.*, p. 115.
[57]*Ibid.*, p. 114.

true of Ottoman Turkey. But so long as the status quo suited its interests, Western enterprise was a potent block in the path of political upheaval. In both China and the Ottoman Empire, Western enterprise demanded fiscal and administrative reform but blocked changes in the political culture which might have led to basic political reform, specifically, the expansion of the process of political socialization and recruitment. Western enterprise was a divisive political influence, and by assuming many quasi-political functions, it hindered the specialization of political function by local authorities.

Shortly after 1850 foreign mining interests began moving into the interior of China.

> The successful operation of a mining enterprise always depends upon the existence of efficient carriage to a market, and since China lacked an adequate railway and canal system, those responsible for sinking the mines had also, as a rule, to concern themselves with new means of transport. This extension of the physical area of operations increased the vulnerability of Western-owned undertaking.[58]

It also increased the interest of Western governments in expanding their areas of influence. In the early days plans for railway construction generated massive resistance by the Chinese authorities "not merely because railways were an obvious and ever-present demonstration of Western penetration, but because they offended against ancient beliefs and cherished traditions."[59] The Chinese struggled to keep the railways in Chinese hands, but they failed because of their need for capital and technical knowhow, plus political weakness. The railways were soon caught up in the struggle among the European powers for control of China and "came to form part of the diplomatic as much as the economic history of the period."[60]

A foreign power tends to exercise political authority over its railway zone, this device was used with signal effectiveness by Japan in its penetration into China. European penetration into Anatolian Turkey likewise accompanied railroad construction. Here the foreign owners actually collected taxes in the districts through which the lines passed.[61] Perhaps more than any other single aspect of Western

[58]Allen and Donnithorne, *Western Enterprise in Far Eastern Development*, p. 149.

[59]*Ibid.*, p. 134.

[60]*Ibid.*

[61]D. C. Blaisdell, *European Financial Control in the Ottoman Empire*, (New York: Columbia University Press, 1929), p. 128.

enterprise of this era, the construction of interior railway lines undermined traditional political authority, particularly that of a regional nature. Rail lines constituted dramatic and tangible evidence of Western superiority to the hitherto unexposed common people of the interior. (It is perhaps significant that in the contemporary National Era one of the first and most incessant demands voiced by the new governments has been the nationalization of their railways.)

In Japan it was very different. "The Japanese, though by no means willing to concede cultural superiority to the Westerners, seldom allowed prejudice or conservatism to deflect them from their study and evaluation of Western techniques."[62] They were able to contain Western enterprise, even after Japan was opened to international commerce in 1865, because the Japanese political authority had resolved to provide a large part of the ancillary services itself. Foreign experts were employed directly by the Japanese government. The government undertook to organize an adequate banking system, modern industry, and interior transport. This policy, and the ability of the Japanese to implement it, no doubt followed from the penetration of the Western technical and industrial concepts that occurred prior to 1865 and from the deep-seated changes in Japanese society of that earlier period.[63]

The bulk of the Japanese people never became disenchanted with their own political culture as a result of the activities of Western enterprise. Only those in certain coastal areas were exposed. In short, the Japanese "made up their minds to take over foreign ways of life not so much because they recognized the absolute merits of Western culture . . . as because the sooner they could display to the world a colourable imitation the sooner would the unequal treaties be revised."[64] And, the reason that they made up their minds to do so was because the social-psychological climate was appropriate. Significantly, the Japanese leaders granted neither communications nor mining rights to foreign interests, nor did they borrow from abroad.[65] The now captive Chinese and Ottomans had done all of these things in abundance.

[62]Allen and Donnithorne, *Western Enterprise in Far Eastern Economic Development, op. cit.*, p. 192.

[63]Described by Hagen, *op. cit.*, pp. 344 ff.

[64]E. H. Norman, *Japan's Emergence as a Modern State* (New York: Institute of Pacific Relations, 1940), p. 118.

[65]Allen and Donnithorne, *Western Enterprise in Far Eastern Development, op. cit.*, p. 224.

In Japan, where order was firmly maintained and where the Government was intent upon modernizing the country's institutions, the privileged status of the foreigners did not remain an essential condition for foreign enterprise, as for many years it did in China. Indeed by 1899 when the privileges were surrendered, they had probably become a handicap to foreign enterprise inasmuch as they tended to embitter relations between the Japanese and foreigners.[66]

In none of the three non-Western countries with semideveloped political systems as of this time — China, Japan and the Ottoman Empire — did Western enterprise deliberately undertake any program to encourage the internalizing of the political values and institutions which would have made the long-run climate more hospitable. No business-sponsored educational efforts are reported. Nor had Western business localized itself in any significant degree in the sense of developing *locally owned* ancillary services or by opening up managerial positions to local nationals. Foreigners remained in virtually all important posts even in China, Japan, and the Ottoman Empire. And everywhere, Western business had surrounded itself with intermediaries who effectively shielded it from direct relations with the indigenous culture.

The aim of much Western enterprise during this era was really political domination, not the successful conduct of business for profit, as had been true of the earlier era. The net impact was the shattering of old loyalties as traditional political authority was destroyed or seriously weakened by mine and plantation owners, by the vast interlocking interests of the agency houses, and by the obvious incursions of Western power into the countryside via railroad construction. At the same time, the process of political socialization was intensified in many regions in response to the penetration of foreign interests and by reason of improved communications. The presence of powerful Westerners tended to force members of the elite into close relationship with the common folk; local ethnic majority groups with important minorities; one religious community with another; one kinship group or tribe with another; and so forth. (One example of the effect of improved communication: in Ottoman Turkey the foreign post offices operating under extraterritorial jurisdiction actually functioned as distributing centers for revolutionary propaganda.) A search for new

[66]*Ibid.*, p. 195.

leadership began; traditional channels of political recruitment became unattractive as the system became identified with inferiority and/or subservience to the foreigner. Only Japan remained impregnable, and possibly precisely for the reason that Japan — of all the non-Western nations — eventually moved faster and further along the path of modernization. Its political culture could develop apace the technical and economic changes of the nineteenth and twentieth centuries. Elsewhere, a vast political seething became apparent in the non-Western world.

As many have observed, no role for the politician had been created in the new political milieu. Both Western enterprise and colonial administrators were, in support of the status quo, blocking a reorganization of the political recruitment process in order to conform to the changing political culture. Those few local nationals receiving higher education were "pumped into the civil service," thereby becoming "politically immobilized." While this may enrich the bureaucracy, "it leaves the game of politics and the task of political leadership to the less educated and the uninformed, and prevents the emergence of a discerning and critical public opinion outside officialdom."[67] Having effectively contained the ruling institutions of China and the Ottoman Empire and having set up colonial administrations and protectorates elsewhere, Western firms and their governments tried to prop up traditional political authorities and systems of political recruitment in the face of vastly intensified and altered patterns of political socialization. Western efforts to maintain traditional Ottoman authority, thereby preserving the position of Western enterprise in the face of rising Turkish nationalism, was a good case in point. Obviously, an explosive situation was in the making. This is not to say that the eventual revolts against Western authority and interests would not have occurred if the Westerners had acted differently. It is possible, though, that the revolutions would have been somewhat less violent and the ensuing era of chaos somewhat shorter if the Westerners had been more sensitive to the political needs of the subjugated areas, needs generated out of personality changes occurring among the surrounding populace partially as a result of the Westerners' presence.

[67]James S. Coleman, "The Character and Viability of African Political Systems," *The United States and Africa, op. cit.,* p. 43.

The Concessionary Era

A number of forces — in part generated by Western enterprise itself — had combined just prior to World War I to doom the colonial-extraterritorial system. The process of political socialization had broadened in some non-Western countries (for example, the association of hitherto conflicting local groups) to such an extent as to make effective political control difficult without heavy reliance upon some indigenous political regime at the very time that the latter's control was weakening. The association of foreign interests with traditional political authority tended to alienate the latter from its own political cultures and to block channels of political recruitment. At the same time, it was becoming more difficult to recruit Europeans for overseas employment. Coincidentally, political pressure was building up in Europe against the colonial idea, indeed against the whole concept of exploitative capitalism. Socialism was emerging as a politically significant force in Western capitals. Much of Latin America had revolted against foreign rule. Japan had succeeded in terminating (in 1899) the unequal treaties forced upon it after 1865. Finally, European power was being concentrated in Europe for World War I, which struggle culminated in a momentary diminution of effective Western power elsewhere.

The period which has been dubbed the Concessionary Era may be looked upon as essentially a transitional era, an era in which Western enterprise attempted to freeze its status in the face of a weakening power umbrella. Typically, it did so by means of the long-term concession contract granted either by friendly colonial administrators or nominally independent foreign political regimes. Africa was an example of the first type of grant; Central America, China, and Egypt, examples of the second. A deal with local authority might suffice to gain the concession, or the concession could be obtained by the threat of political-military intervention. In neither case was public opinion or national interest an important consideration on either side.

There is some indication that by the early 1900's some colonial authorities, notably the British, had become sensitive to the interests of the people whom they governed — or at least, to what the Westerner conceived these interests to be. In certain instances the British refused to grant long-term concessions to Western enterprise.

It was settled policy of the Colonial Office that the native population in West Africa under British rule should in general have secured to them rights to hold their ancestral soil without disturbance, to cultivate it as they would, and to do with its produce what they thought fit.[68]

Among others, William Lever attempted to secure long-term concessions in British West Africa for plantation development. He was refused. Shortly thereafter, in 1911, a Lever concession in the Congo was ratified by the Belgian Parliament. The company was authorized to build railroads, canals, telephone and telegraph lines, and other means of communications necessary for the development of palm oil production. It was further directed to improve the conditions of the people in the vicinity of its operations and to establish medical and education facilities which, insofar as the company's business permitted, were to be available — upon payment — to the general public. The natives were to be granted a minimum daily rate of pay, exclusive of rations, and the company was to encourage the circulation of money "the value and use of which were as yet imperfectly understood."[69] Thus, a strongly paternalistic relationship was envisioned. The concession was viewed as a vehicle for modernization and political consolidation under foreign authority.

These concession agreements were different from the earlier company charters in several important respects. *First*, they were granted by some local, differentiated political authority — colonial or nominally independent. *Second*, political authority was not to be exercised by the company in the name of the home government, and the award of political powers generally was somewhat more restricted than the complete carte blanche of the early charters. In some instances the company was simply required to reimburse the local political authority for the cost of the public services required by the enterprise, including the maintenance of law and order in remote areas. Thus, the company itself did not always undertake the functions of rule-making, rule-enforcement, and rule-adjudication. *Third*, now generally aware that their activities were cutting across lines of traditional political authority, companies tended to assume paternalistic postures. Unless they did so, it was apparent that they could expect serious trouble.

[68]Wilson, *History of Unilever, op. cit.*, p. 167.
[69]*Ibid.*, p. 172.

The Westerner's fear was now not that he was intervening too much in the foreign political culture, but that he was intervening too little. As the company bought out or otherwise weakened the political functions of the traditional leadership, those identified with the associated political culture expected the company to assume the same paternalistic responsibilities toward them as had the former leadership. Loyalties were not only broken, as in the preceding period; they were now transferred. But so were reciprocal obligations. Although reported of a later time period, the following comment relating to a Western enterprise in Ethiopia is revealing in this regard:

> The turnover rate among Ethiopian employees is now very low. This is in part owed to a transfer, now beginning to occur, of the traditional sense of loyalty from feudal patron to modern employer.[70]

In the more politically developed nations of the non-West — in China, Japan, the Ottoman Empire — the next era had already opened. Japan, had been the first to throw off the regime of extraterritorial rights (1899). Neither the Chinese nor the Ottomans were able to follow suit until after World War I. Their local political regimes were not sufficiently independent because of the massive hold that Western enterprise had been permitted to gain. Despite this strong hold, strong nationalistic movements within these nations had already developed to the extent that they precluded the granting of any additional privileges to Western enterprise, and there were incessant demands for the end of the extraterritorial regimes.

Typical of the Concessionary Era were the Lever concession in the Congo, the early oil concessions in the Arab Middle East, and the United Fruit Company's agreements with various Central American governments. Within the boundaries of the concession, each company tended to become all powerful and all providing. It became involved in housing, health and sanitation, finance, education, distribution of food and essential consumer goods, transport, and police protection.[71] When a local political authority attempted to constrain company activity, there was always the threat of foreign intervention on behalf of "international law" to enforce contractual rights. Most of the time the foreign enterprise could achieve its objectives "simply and directly

---

[70]Theodore Geiger, *The Case Study of TWA's Service to Ethiopia*, (Washington: National Planning Association, 1959), p. 69.

[71]See S. May and G. Plaza, *The Case Study of the United Fruit Company in Latin America* (Washington: National Planning Association, 1958).

by picaresque deals with the local caudillo."[72] In any case, the local government was frequently in no position to provide the services required by the foreign firm and was content to permit the incursion — for a price.

Because of their large local payrolls, some of these companies exercised massive influence on traditional institutions and values. This was particularly true in Africa and Latin America. Both areas were characterized by isolation (that is, sparse population and an exceedingly difficult terrain) and by self-sufficient social-political units, which meant that traditional political socialization was effective only within narrow geographical limits. In Africa there was the self-sufficient tribe; in Latin America, the self-sufficient hacienda. In both the commercial function of the town and the political function of the center were nominal. Therefore, large-scale Western enterprise meant the creation of new political authority, as people were concentrated in entirely new areas. The company provided virtually all of the services required in the new settlements, including the political output functions of rule-making, rule-enforcing, rule-adjudicating. Within their concession areas the companies were forced, albeit often reluctantly, into horizontal integration on a grand scale. Political and commercial functions became blurred in the process. When they realized the political leverage and financial profit such a spectrum of activity provided them, the companies frequently resisted subsequent intrusion on their domain. Their principal preoccupation was therefore with maintaining the status quo, in preserving political stability (that is, maintenance of the structure of political functions). Political change was thus contained.

The generalization might be made that the scope of political function assumed by Western enterprise was conditioned by the degree of specificity of function existing within the traditional political culture. That is, where effective, specialized political institutions existed, Western enterprise exercised only limited political functions. For instance, despite the size and scope of Western enterprise in China, it did not play as important a political role as it did in Africa. Western enterprise in Japan, where its political function was very restrained, was very different indeed.

After 1900 the system of compradores in China began to decay as

[72]*United States Business and Labor in Latin America* (University of Chicago Research Center on Economic Development and Cultural Change, Comm. on Foreign Relations, S. 86th Cong., 2d Sess., Jan. 1960), p. 50.

foreign enterprise assumed more direct control over its activities. More Chinese learned English, and more Westerners learned Chinese, which meant more direct communication between Western enterprise and Chinese society. In 1915 the British Chamber of Commerce in Shanghai opened a Chinese language school. In 1916 the Hong Kong General Chamber of Commerce did likewise. "During the inter-war period some Western firms required younger members of their staffs to attend classes in Chinese and paid bonuses to those who passed examination."[73] As this process proceeded, many foreign concession rights were given up in China. China's tariff autonomy was restored in 1928, and extraterritoriality was soon to be abolished (1943–1947).

Meanwhile, the United States had intervened directly in Central America on a number of occasions (Cuba in 1898, Dominican Republic in 1904 and 1912, Nicaragua in 1909, Panama in 1913, Mexico in 1913, and Haiti in 1916). In so doing, the United States had exhibited a twofold objective — "to restore order to the finances of the country involved and to build up and train military forces in each in order to maintain political stability."[74] One qualified scholar has written:

> The immediate results [of intervention] were beneficial, and . . . the long-range results were nil, or worse. We put political power in the hands of the military and made them invincible.[75]

The Concessionary Era was thus characterized by an effort by Western enterprise to consolidate its deteriorating position via long-term contract. In a sense, this tendency represented a retrograde movement in that it induced a further blurring between political and economic function. The Great Depression of the 1930's meant an even further reduction of European and American influence, and led to a greater employment of Asians, Africans, and Latin Americans in the effort to reduce the number of high-priced foreign supervisors and technicians. Local training began in earnest. The sheer numbers employed by Western enterprise had risen spectacularly during the post-World War I decade, but during the 1930's there was a cutback among unskilled labor and also in the public services rendered by the

[73]Allen and Donnithorne, *Western Enterprise in Far Eastern Economic Development, op. cit.*, p. 49.

[74]Herbert L. Matthews, "Diplomatic Relations," in *The United States and Latin America, op. cit.*, p. 148.

[75]*Ibid.*

companies. Paternalistic obligations were not being fulfilled, and those concerned began to form new loyalties.

Western enterprise, which during the preceding eras had in many areas effectively replaced local political authority, thereby blocking channels of political recruitment, was now failing in the paternalistic responsibilities that it had assumed. Indeed, given the social-psychological forces set in motion by this time (the 1930's), failure of this type of Western enterprise was possibly inevitable. Also, the visible signs of Western superiority were on the wane.

The influence of Western business can perhaps be likened to the legitimitizing of authority. "The average person tends to initiate deferential, approval-seeking behavior towards a person seen as more powerful than himself. . . . He is more likely to accept direct attempts to influence him from a person he defines as powerful."[76] Robert Presthus has pointed out that there are possibly four principal bases for the legitimization of authority:[77]

1. *Technical expertise*, which is particularly effective where the expertise is the same as that of subordinates, only greater.
2. *Formal role*, in which authority is structured to insure control by limiting information, centralizing initiative, restricting access to decision-making centers, and generally controlling the behavioral alternatives of members (reinforced by status symbols, rewards, and sanctions.)
3. *Rapport*, in which personal skill in manipulation and personal identity with generally held values are important.
4. *Generalized deference to authority* (fear, tradition, and so forth).

Western enterprise was faltering on all counts by the late 1930's. Its technical expertise was being shared by increasing numbers of local nationals. It was more and more difficult to structure authority in such a way as to assure foreign control simply through the retention of certain key managerial roles. Company managers overseas had never been called upon to be skillful in the manipulation of large numbers of non-Westerners; they had dealt only with the few, the traditional elite or a commercially minded minority. It was obvious that values dif-

[76]R. Lippitt, N. Polansky and S. Rosen, "The Dynamics of Power," *Human Relations*, Vol. 5, No. 1 (1952), pp. 44–50.

[77]Robert V. Presthus, "Authority in Organization," *Public Administration Review*, Vo. xx, No. 2 (Spring 1960).

fered as between Westerner and non-Westerner. And generalized deference to authority was decreasing as demonstrations of Western political and military power seemed less convincing. One observer expressed it this way:

> I am not an adult member of society so long as my tutor is present and active. When his services are no longer absolutely necessary I would like to discharge him rather than retain him around the locality on a pension, fussy, opinionated and critical.[78]

Another wrote:

> In an earlier generation . . . public relations [of Western enterprise in Latin America] was usually unnecessary since mass public opinion had little political significance. But a new social and political grouping emerged in Latin America and the pressure of social reform and nationalism forced an alteration in the practices of American firms.[79]

In other words, the very changes that Western enterprise itself had helped to set in motion in the non-Western world in terms of broadened political socialization, a search for new processes of political recruitment, and intensified articulation of political interest now turned to force a change in the structure of Western enterprise itself.

The long-run concessionary contract was thus primarily a holding device, an attempt to create stable political conditions in the face of obvious change. But the specter of nationalization and expropriation now held the center of the stage — in Latin America, in Turkey, in China, and elsewhere. Private international law was really developed by Western business in its attempt to hold onto vested property and contractual rights granted by personal, nationally irresponsible political authorities. It was now challenged by more broadly based, more differentiated, more responsible leadership.

A number of companies weathered the ensuing rise of violent nationalism profitably because they were already operating in the new era.

The National Era

With the outbreak of World War II the era of concessions was over, although some Western enterprise appeared strangely unaware

[78]J. S. Fforde, *An International Trade in Managerial Skills* (Oxford: Basil Blackwell, 1957), p. 23.

[79]*United States Business and Labor in Latin America, op. cit.*, p. 50.

of the changing political environment in Asia, Africa, and Latin America. They either were ignorant of it or refused to accept it. Those companies, continuing to operate in the postwar period under old-style concession agreements, were soon under political attack in many regions — the Anglo-Iranian Oil Company in Iran, the United Fruit Company in Guatemala, the oil companies in Indonesia, the Suez Canal Company in Egypt. In each case foreign military and political intervention was threatened on the heels of nationalistic moves to abrogate concessions, but without notable success even where actual intervention ensued.

Two new factors had entered the picture: nationally responsible political leaders and the Cold War. Countries such as Iran, Guatemala, Indonesia, and Egypt now had an alternative source of capital and technical skills toward which they could turn, and their bargaining power vis-a-vis Western enterprise was increased thereby. No longer could channels of expertise and capital be controlled by Western enterprise. Nor could local independence movements be contained

Also, in order to line up support for the Allied war effort, the Western powers had made specific promises to withdraw colonial rule, to abolish extraterritorial privileges, to create a representative world body. No longer could Western enterprise live under the protecting umbrella of Western power. Official intervention on its behalf was awkward and often against the larger political interests of the home governments.

World War II had the effect of vastly accelerating the process of transferring organizational authority to local nationals — in part by default, in part by deliberate training and transferral — a process that had begun during the Great Depression. During the war the supply of Western managers and technicians was further reduced. Local nationals had kept some foreign-owned enterprises going with little or no assistance from the owners. Also in the immediate postwar period many Westerners were reluctant to commit themselves to overseas business careers.

Europe also has been transformed and transformed in a way that has conspicuously lessened her capacity to export entrepreneurs and pioneers, although not, of course bureaucrats and economic advisors. Europeans are now "state-broken" (to use Schumpeter's term) and are therefore not to be stirred, as were their fathers, by the excitement of commercial adventures overseas, adventures which in any case their savings are becoming insufficient to finance. According to this view, the Asian rejection of European economic leadership appears to have coincided with the decline in the capacity of the former donors to supply it. On the other hand, it may be argued that the change of temper among Europeans has at least the merit of opening the way to a peaceful transition to self-government in those Asian territories which are determined to repudiate Western rule. This may be of real benefit to all parties.[80]

It should be added that in some underdeveloped countries local changes, combined with full employment in Europe and the United States, caused a steep rise in the cost of Western management. And increased foreign taxes, widened disparity in living standards between West and East, difficulties in remitting savings, and considerations of personal security, all combined to convince many Westerners that careers in Asia, Africa, and Latin America were somewhat less than attractive. Insofar as the European was concerned, particularly the British, material reward again became the dominant motive, for overseas enterprise was no longer backed by "the morals of . . . imperial expansion."[81] And the missionary voices were diluted and less compelling. But, with the rise of nationally responsible governments, it was no longer reasonable to hope for the big kill. The lure of the bonanza was gone.

Given these circumstances, Western enterprise of the immediate postwar era was compelled to localize itself if it were to survive the wave of nationalistic release that could be anticipated as the process of political socialization itensified still further, as channels of political recruitment became unblocked and were shifted, and as nationally responsible rule-making, rule-enforcing, and rule-adjudicating institutions were fashioned painfully from the disorder. It had to justify itself in terms of the interests of the host country, interests that were frequently only very inadequately defined by the new nationalistic leaders themselves.

Western enterprise stood in a precarious position because of its past association with foreign political interests and its exercise of political power within concession areas, which was now seen as an infringement of sovereignty. It was caught squarely between long-run non-Western, national interests (as one might objectively define the highly volatile short-run political interests voiced by the emerging nationalists) and the Cold War political policies of home governments.

[80]Allen and Donnithorne, *Western Enterprise in Indonesia and Malaya, op. cit.,* p. 285.

[81]Fforde, *op. cit.,* p. 137.

It is not surprising that in many areas those Western businessmen
sensitive to these pressures deliberately set apolitical courses and
went out of their way to disassociate themselves from political com-
mitments on either side. It became standard policy of at least some
American managements to avoid any relationship at all with United.
States embassies in the countries where they were doing business
Others, admittedly only a few, began to analyze all foreign projects
specifically from the point of view of their political vulnerability.
Projects representing too large a piece of a country's total economy
(such as the one steel mill), or a public service (such as transport and
communications), or ones in which the products were of political
significance (such as newsprint) were rejected for this reason and no
other.[82]

The character of the Western businessmen who did move abroad
in the postwar era was quite different from that of the predecessors.
By and large, they were professional managers representing large-scale
corporate enterprise. Many were concerned with manufacturing
ventures producing primarily for local overseas markets rather than
with extractive enterprises designed to feed home-based industry.
Many were interested only in specific, single-unit enterprises and
tried, insofar as possible, to steer clear of horizontal integration —
that is, involvement in activities not relating directly to their principal
activity. (The Arabian-American Oil Company, though an extractive
venture operating under a concession, was an example of such an
effort.) Probably most of these businessmen did not have, nor did
they often seek, the political protection of their own governments.
They were empire builders in the business sense, not the political.
Indeed, they not infrequently sought ways to insulate their foreign
activities from political pressures at home and from the operation of
their own national laws by setting up holding companies in third
countries and by moving into joint ventures with foreign nationals.
As the oil administrator in Saudi Arabia commented, the possible
operation of United States antitrust laws against the oil companies
participating in Aramco was not Arabia's concern and would not be
considered in Arabia's demands on Aramco.[83] Even the Canadians

[82]Richard D. Robinson, "W. R. Grace & Company — Foreign Investment"
(Harvard Graduate School of Business Administration, 1959, business case ICR-
167).
[83]Richard H. Nolte, "A Tale of Three Cities III (continued): Jedds and the
Oil Company" (New York: American Universities Field Staff, Inc., 1958), p. 13.

became irritated about the unwillingness of American-owned enterprise in Canada to sell to Communist China. The fact that the United States government forbade commercial relations with the Chinese did not interest the Canadians. The Cuban and Ceylonese governments undoubtedly felt within their rights to require foreign oil companies operating local refineries to process Soviet crudes, regardless of the United States policy on the subject. The fact that the United States government insisted on taxing foreign earnings of United States corporations so that the total tax paid approached the normal 52-percent rate on corporate earnings irritated those governments which were trying to attract greater investment by means of tax incentives.

In some cases the newcomers entered into relatively short-term contracts with the host government in the attempt to stabilize certain legal conditions (that is, taxes, ownership, remittance of earnings, exchange rates, labor regulations, customs and visa requirements, and the threat of expropriation), but these differed from the concessions of the previous era in that they related to specific enterprises and to a limited number of carefully defined subjects. They bestowed virtually no political authority. Indeed, at the insistence of some governments, principally the Latin American, Western enterprise was compelled to sign away its right to appeal to its own government for diplomatic intervention in case of conflict. This insistence was a measure of the awareness on the part of these governments of the political content of past enterprise. Also, these new contracts were typically limited to ten or twenty years, not the fifty or one-hundred years characteristic of the earlier period. Some governments — such as the Indonesian, Japanese, and Indian — explicitly refused to guarantee foreign property and contractual rights for longer periods.

By the early 1950's there was a growing awareness by Western management that concessions or contractual relations could be severed effectively by a government if the enterprise did not support national economic and political interests. And, cautiously, private international law began to recognize this principle. A number of legal authorities, even in the West, argued that if the general welfare were served by the expropriation of foreign property rights, even though unaccompanied by adequate compensation, the government had the right to act.[84] In several instances where land or basic resources or utilities were nationalized, the foreign government was obviously in no

[84]See Chapter 2, pp. 50-54.

position to pay adequate, effective, and prompt compensation as the time-honored formula required. The new political leaders dared not hesitate to effect popular reforms — whether it was the nationalization of oil in Iran, land in Cuba, or the Suez Canal in Egypt — simply because they could not pay the foreign interests, whose claims were based anyway on rights given by discredited political authorities and often under duress.

Even some of the old-timers, rather belatedly, began changing the nature of their relationship with foreign governments. It was reported, for example, that:

[Following 1954], . . . the [United Fruit] company . . . developed a new approach with respect to its relations to Latin American national governments. In general this might be described as a "partnership" relationship, as reflected by the statement of one of the national presidents who said: "We feel that we are now in partnership with the United Fruit Company." Ecuador is the one country [as of 1958] in which the United Fruit Company is operating without a general contract agreement with the central government. This not only reflects United Fruit's confidence in the political stability and good faith of Ecuador in dealing with foreign capital but demonstrates that it is possible to build up such confidence on both sides through a record of mutually beneficial relationships maintained over a period of years. . . . It is possible that the future will see a general evolution toward the abolition of special contracts between foreign-owned corporations and sovereign governments, except where specific permits are required by law for a public-utility type of operation.[85]

Some realized that general concession contracts were important only where local law was inadequate to cope with the problems generated by modern enterprise. Where local law was adequate (*i.e.*, sufficiently differentiated and specific) and the rule-enforcing and rule-adjudicating processes were sufficiently developed in the sense of performing in an universalistic and affectively neutral manner, the rationale for special contracts was illusive to say the least. (See Explanatory Note at end of chapter.)

In the United Fruit Company case it is curious that Ecuador was found to be the most "dependable" of the countries in which the firm was operating. One outstanding authority on Latin American political culture rated at least two other states within the company's range

[85]May and Plaza, *op. cit.*, p. 216.

of interests as substantially more developed than Ecuador, which he identified as possessing an elite that was "moving violently toward nationalistic aspirations, but with sluggish response in the body social."[86] "Dependable" in the commercial, business context makes sense in relation to a politically stagnant state or one in which the level of political development, as has been defined here, has reached the point where one may feel fairly confident that further *violent* changes in the *legal* basis of the state are unlikely. It is with the continuity of law that business is primarily concerned, not with the continuity of political regimes.

It is the relative newcomers to international business — the manufacturers — that by and large appear most sensitive to the new political environment. Many of the old-timers, clinging to traditional relationships, have made their positions within the new political environment exceedingly vulnerable. In 1959 junior members of the United Fruit management, for example, confidentially predicted serious trouble in several Latin American enterprises unless their company moved quickly to restructure its relationship with local governments, specifically, to end the regime of special contracts and to get out of the ownership of farmland, which they held to be highly vulnerable to political pressures.[87] It has been observed that the newer United States entrants in international business have, by and large, been more successful in operating within the new political environment, possibly because (1) the decision-makers in these internationally inexperienced firms have not been "old foreign hands" with a now obsolete expertise to protect and (2) they had no past to live down.

Summary

Each historical era has provided somewhat different motivations for Western enterprise in Asia, Africa, and Latin America — from personal fortune seeking, to empire building, to protecting one's own, to market development. Meanwhile, the relationship of the enterprise to the political structure shifted from an unequal negotiation with, or sheer imposition of company wishes by force upon, the local sovereign — *i.e.*, company sovereignty — to colonial rule and extraterritoriality,

[86]Silvert, *op. cit.*, p. 216.
[87]Personal interviews.

to politically tinted concession agreements, to the nationalization or localization of economic activity. These two variables — motivation and political environment — produced varying effects upon overseas political cultures, which effects depended in large measure upon accessibility (location, land mass, and climate), of the foreign culture, the attractiveness of its internal market (population size, density, and relevant characteristics), and the level of indigenous political development (degree of political socialization and of effective, differentiated political function).

During the early Commercial Era only rarely did the profit-motivated, trade-oriented Western company pry far into the interior. Outside of the Americas, it relied generally upon local authority, whether it was exercised by a tribal chieftain or Arab sheik, to keep commerce moving to the coast. The Westerner had little capital and few settlements ashore that required direct and sustained protection. Gradually, however, direct company rule appeared as Westerners penetrated more deeply and found themselves challenged by the local political culture. As trade grew, Western sovereigns came to take a more active interest in their overseas trading communities. When the industrial revolution in Europe multiplied the demand for raw materials, Western enterprise plunged into the interior to develop mines, plantations, and internal transport. With it went direct, colonial rule or extraterritorial jurisdiction. The protection of permanent investment in the interior, of the growing numbers of European settlers, and of the extended lines of overland communications became important. Political authority — *i.e.*, the political output functions — were now assumed directly by the Westerner, in part by his governments, but to a significant extent directly by Western enterprise itself, particularly in the mining and plantation areas. In so doing, channels of political recruitment were severed and evolutionary change in shifting those channels, blocked. Western enterprise rarely tolerated political radicals and revolutionaries. Indeed, one suspects that some potential innovators tended to gravitate to the more materially rewarding and achievement-based careers associated with Western enterprise, initially as intermediaries between that enterprise and the traditional political culture, but later, they came to resist both. Admittedly, evidence is too sketchy to prove this hypothesis, but individual cases can be found.

The very presence of the Westerner and the new political ideas of nation and government which he brought with him eventually began to cause a broadening and intensifying of the political socialization process. Improved communications, heightened physical mobility of people caught up in economic enterprise (that is, concentration and urbanization), and eventual hostility to the Western incursion, all served to accelerate this process. But when independence came, there was no generally recognized way in which the recruitment function could proceed and new, nationally responsible political power could be legitimitized without a violent power struggle. This specialized political function that would have made a more orderly change possible had not been able to evolve under foreign political and economic domination — or at the very least, containment. What had been encouraged were extralegal political institutions which had tasted no real responsibility for the public welfare. Western enterprise had become the victim of developments it itself had helped set in motion.

Western enterprise generally had enjoyed a privileged status under Western rule, which position it attempted to retain, via long-term concession agreements, in the two interwar decades. This was the period of emerging nationalism during which Western political power was gradually withdrawn. Virtually all extraterritorial regimes were abolished, and traditional forms of political colonialism were clearly in their last few years.

Although preceded by earlier developments in specific regions, Asiatic and African nationalism really became an irresistible force only during and immediately following World War II, thereby coinciding in time with (1) the growing inability on the part of Western enterprise to staff its overseas ventures with Europeans to the same degree as before and (2) the appearance of an alternative source of capital and skills that the Cold War situation implied. The process of localization, begun during the Great Depression and characterizing the new national era following World War II, accelerated the transmission of managerial and technical skills, the employment of local nationals in managerial positions, and the formation of international joint ventures.

In the 1960's, after nearly twenty years, Western enterprise has thrown off much of the political stigma formerly attached to it. Many of the new nationalistic governments of Asia, Africa, and Latin America are explicitly seeking private Western capital, though on their own terms. Scores of foreign investment laws have been enacted by these governments defining the conditions and incentives offered to foreigners. The term "investment" as used here includes investment in the transmission of skills (via management, license, or technical assistance contract) as well as finance. Financial investment is desired, but only where local resources are inadequate. It is increasingly recognized that the real significance of Western enterprise lies in the skills that it is in a position to transmit — and to transmit with relative effectiveness because of the day-to-day *working* relationship that exists between Western and local nationals employed within a relatively stable organizational context.

It is quite clear that, for a variety of reasons, economic development has become inseparable from the process of political development. Indeed, economic development is often presented explicitly as the rationale for political development. As evidence of the high political content of economic development, many of the new governments have moved directly into the field of production, often in partnership with private interests, both local and foreign. It is equally obvious that "economic development in the fullest sense is a process entailing the concurrent growth of superior technical and managerial skills."[88] A people may acquire such skills spontaneously by internal social processes, by learning them from others, or by employing others to exercise the skills for them. In any case, the desire for innovation must precede such efforts. Having helped stimulate the social-psychological process generating dissatisfaction with the traditional and creating demand for change, Western enterprise is faced with mounting pressure to transmit the skills to ease the resulting frustration gap between the demand and the reality.

Out of these pressures on Western business enterprise, three disturbing questions emerge:

1. Does private international law recognize the new political-economic environment in resolving conflict between Western enterprise and non-Western states? If not, how might it?
2. Can the economic and political interests of the newly emerging independent societies of the non-West be sufficiently defined so as to give substance to new legal concepts and provide operational guides for Western enterprise?
3. Are the implications of the foregoing in terms of the policies and organization of the Western firm necessarily such as to limit the business role?

[88]Fforde, *op. cit.*, p. 1.

EXPLANATORY NOTE

Implicit in this chapter is a model of political modernization, a process which the incursion of Western business enterprise has affected in many ways — sometimes accelerating it, sometimes retarding it, sometimes seriously unbalancing it (such as the simultaneous acceleration of political socialization and the blocking of political recruitment). To make explicit what has been implicit, the following definitions are offered.

The term *political* refers to the influencing, manipulating, or control of groups (often national in size, but not necessarily) in order to advance group national interests — in other words, the struggle for power in the broad Morganthau sense.[89] The totality of coherent political activity represents a political culture, which is more precisely defined as the manner in which a society is organized about, reacts to, and uses political authority. Political authority, in turn, is equated with the power to make and enforce decisions relating to the integration and adaptation of a society in respect to either internal or external variables.[90] As very succinctly spelled out by Gabriel Almond, and simplified and somewhat modified here, a political culture may be analyzed in terms of eight differentiated political functions:

Input Functions

1. *Political socialization* — the manner and degree to which the members of a society identify with a political culture.

2. *Political recruitment* — the manner and degree to which a society participates in legitimizing the exercise of political authority.

3. *Articulation of interest* — the manner and degree to which a population makes known its demands for the exercise of political authority.

4. *Aggregation of interest* — the manner and degree to which interests relating to political authority are aggregated.

5. *Communication of interest* — the manner and degree to which political interests are communicated to the political authority.

[89]See Hans Morganthau, *Politics Among Nations* (New York: Alfred A. Knopf, 1950), Chapter I, and Quincy Wright, *The Study of International Relations* (New York: Appleton-Century-Crofts, 1955), Chapter 13.

[90]This typology of political culture and political change is adapted from Gabriel A. Almond, "A Functional Approach to Comparative Politics," in *The Politics of Developing Areas* (Princeton: Princeton University Press, 1960), pp. 3–64.

6. *Rule-making* — the manner in which decisions are made by the political authority and the degree of their inclusiveness (*i.e.*, geographical, social, temporal, content.)

7. *Rule-enforcement* — the manner in which political decisions are enforced and the degree to which enforcement is achieved.

8. *Rule-adjudication* — the manner in which conflicts among rules and between rules and enforcement are resolved, and the degree to which judgments are enforced.

The development of a political culture from primitive to modern may be traced in terms of these eight functions. The idealized modern political culture is presumed to be one in which all political functions are (1) affectively neutral, that is, are governed by expected results, not by immediate impulses or emotion); (2) individual-oriented (tend to value the individual rather than the collectivity); (3) universalistic (affect all members of the political culture similarly); (4) specific (are differentiated, not diffuse); and (5) achievement-oriented (treat persons or objects on the basis of ability to accomplish a given end, not on the basis of qualities unrelated to this ability).

For example, one of the earliest moves toward the modern is perhaps the differentiation of the political culture itself from the religious. Generally, a somewhat later development is the relating of the dominant political culture to all individuals within a given geographical area — that is, the establishment of a universal political authority admitting of no racial or religious bars. Following such expansion and intensification of the political socialization process may be a movement to extend the political culture impartially to all citizens and to define political roles on the basis of ability rather than various ascriptive norms. Often accompanying these developments is a broadening of the process of political recruitment, which tends to generate a different manner and intensity of interest articulation. Another characteristic of political development is the formation of specialized interest-aggregating and communicating functions and of differentiated rule-enforcing and rule-adjudicating agencies — that is, differentiated from the rule-making. At some point during this whole process a differentiation of the economic or business culture from the political will usually appear. There is possibly a tendency for the two to remain largely undifferentiated until the business culture becomes so highly specialized and professionalized as to adopt substantially different values and roles from those associated with the political. Business then tends to be blocked from the performance of any significant political function other than aggregating and communicating its own interests.

Quite apart from the manner or style in which these various political functions operate, but likewise relevant to the level of political development, is the degree to which they are effective. That is, as political modernization proceeds, the process of political socialization tends to deepen, political recruitment to broaden, interest articulation to increase, interest aggregation to intensify, interest communication to diversify, and the political output functions to expand. The *degree* to which a political function operates may thus be quite distinct from its *manner*. For example, one may conceive of a political culture in which political socialization results in a high degree of identification with the political authority by all those within the society, but the manner in which that identification is expressed may be highly affective. An example might be a nomadic tribe.

▶▶▶▶ 2
The Legal Dimension

Law seldom justifies a violent change in the status quo.[1]

One finds that the historical record of Western enterprise in the non-Western world is a very mixed one. Occasionally, an enterprise was functional in the sense of aiding and abetting the political development of a people. Very frequently, however, it became anachronistic and dysfunctional because of a disinclination to structure itself to accord with the political circumstances of its environment. Indeed, much Western enterprise was perhaps politically dysfunctional from the start in that its initial entry was possible only by reason of conquest and superior power. One can present as evidence in support of this thesis the massive residue of ill-will toward Western business in large areas of the world.

Western business, and the parent political states, have responded to this hostility and subsequent attack by erecting a theory of private international law seeking to justify and perpetuate the status quo vis-*a*-vis foreign-owned assets. Except in extreme cases, the national interest of the host country even yet is not a relevant legal fact when conflict arises. So long as private international law thus recognizes the validity and relevance of only one interest — that of the private property owner — it is foredoomed to failure. To survive as a significant force in non-Western development, Western business must restructure its international relationships and seek legitimacy under a legal theory quite different from that current among Western tribunals, a fact that the international legal literature of the West virtually ignores. The purpose of this chapter is to review the present status of law in this regard and to suggest how it might be reframed so as to provide a viable vehicle on which all might turn for the equitable

[1]A. W. Ford, *The Anglo-Iranian Oil Dispute of 1951–52* (Berkeley: University of California Press, 1954), p. 29.

45

resolution of conflicting interests within the area of international business.

It is quite obvious that there is widespread and sometimes vocal reluctance on the part of many Asian, African, and Latin American states to submit to international adjudication, whether by international tribunal or arbitration, their differences with the Western industrial powers in respect to injury to aliens. Implicit in this reluctance is doubtless a feeling that international law, as presently formulated, inadequately recognizes national interest within the context of accelerating political and economic change. Evolutionary processes are being telescoped in time, and there seems to be widespread suspicion that traditional international law has not evolved to pace this accelerated social evolution.

Views on Foreign Investment and International Law

The Havana Charter of 1948, signed by fifty-four national delegations, included several reservations in respect to foreign investment in that Article 12 specified that a member of the International Trade Organization would have the right:

(i) To take any appropriate safeguards necessary to ensure that foreign investment is not used as a basis for interference in its international affairs or national policies;

(ii) To determine whether and to what extent and upon what terms it will allow future foreign investment;

(iii) To prescribe and give effect in just terms to requirements as to the ownership of existing and future investments;

(iv) To prescribe and give effect to other reasonable requirements with respect to existing and future investments.[2]

As explained in a subsequent United States government report, these clauses were in a sense a compromise of two positions: *one*, represented by many of the underdeveloped countries, insisted that a state might expropriate alien properties for public use with something less than full, prompt, and effective compensation; and *the other*, represented by the Western capital (the exporting states), demanded enforcement of traditional rules in regard to compensation.[3]

[2]U.N. Conf. on Trade and Employment, *Havana Charter*, 12 (1948).
[3]Subcomm., House Comm. on Foreign Affairs, 80th Cong., 2d Sess., *The International Trade Organization* 54–55 (Subcomm. Print 1948).

United States Position   The Foreign Aid Act of June 1962 made the United States position quite explicit. It required the President to suspend aid to any nation daring to expropriate United States property without adequate, just, and prompt payment or to withhold payment of legitimate debt to United States businessmen.[4] This article reinforced a provision of the Sugar Act passed shortly before which required the Chief Executive to suspend sugar imports from any nation failing to compensate for the taking of United States-owned property, to terminate discriminatory taxes or "restrictive maintenance or operational conditions not imposed or enforced with respect to property of a like nature owned or operated by one of its own nationals" or nationals of another country.[5] Yet, the United States felt quite within its right to enforce the Buy American Act, and the subsequent Presidential Executive Order of December 17, 1954, which directed that United States governmental agencies purchasing materials for public use procure such products from domestic sources unless (a) these products were not available domestically, (b) the responsible agency head determined that domestic purchase would not be in the public interest, or (c) the responsible agency head determined that the cost of the domestic product was unreasonable. An unreasonable cost was considered anything exceeding a foreign bid by 6 percent, or by 10 percent if duties and certain other costs were excluded from the foreign price. Prior to that time, a 25-percent differential had been permitted.[6] This was a clear case of disciminatory legislation.

In the United Nations   After twenty nine sessions of debate the United Nations General Assembly adopted the following resolution in December 1952:

The General Assembly,
Bearing in mind the need for encouraging the underdeveloped countries in the proper use and exploitation of their natural wealth and resources.
Considering that the economic development of the underdeveloped countries is one of the fundamental requisites for the strengthening of universal peace,

Remembering that the right of peoples freely to use and exploit their natural wealth and resources is inherent in their sovereignty and in ac-

[4]Pub. L. 87–565, Part III, Ch. I, Sec. 618(2) (c).
[5]Pub. L. 87–535, Sec. 15(c).
[6]Memorandum dated Feb. 16, 1955, printed and circulated by the Westinghouse Electric Corporation, p. 1.

cordance with the Purposes and Principles of the Charter of the United Nations,

1. *Recommends* that all Member States, in the exercise of their right freely to use and exploit their natural wealth and resources whenever deemed desirable by them for their own purposes and economic development, to have due regard, consistently with their sovereignty, to the need for maintaining the flow of capital in condition of security, mutual confidence and economic co-operation among nations;

2. *Further recommends* all Member States to refrain from acts, direct or indirect, designed to impede the exercise of the sovereignty of any State over its natural resources.[7]

Apparently some spokesmen for Western business took this statement to mean that governments of capital-scarce countries thereby had the right to take what foreigners had invested in their countries "with little regard to contracts or just compensation."[8] Indeed, within a year the Guatemalan government quoted the resolution to justify the taking of certain lands owned by the United Fruit Company, against payment of Guatemalan government bonds.[9] The Soviet foreign minister likewise referred to the resolution during the 1956 London Conference in justifying Egypt's seizure of the Suez Canal against a promise of compensation.[10]

Meanwhile, in 1955, the Third Committee of the United Nations General Assembly had adopted a resolution that included the following paragraph:

The peoples may, for their own ends, freely dispose of their natural wealth and resources without prejudice to any obligations arising out of international economic cooperation, based upon the principle of mutual benefit, and international law. In no case may a people be deprived of its own means of subsistence.[11]

While the United States, the United Kingdom, and the Netherlands opposed such a declaration of economic self-determination, the

[7]U.N. Gen. Ass. Off. Rec. 7th Sess. Res. 626, Supp. No. 20, at 18 (A/2311) (1952).

[8]H. M. Fleming, *States, Contracts and Progress* (New York: Oceana, 1960, p. 60.

[9]Aide-memoire delivered by the ambassador of Guatemala to the U.S. Department of State, June 26, 1953.

[10]*The Suez Canal Problem* (Washington: U.S. State Department, 1956), Publ. No. 6392, p. 98.

[11]U.N. Doc. A/C.3/ L.489 (1955).

Asian-African-Arab bloc pressed in favor of it. The United States wished to be assured that the language did not intend to impair legal rights of individuals or authorize expropriation without adequate, prompt, and effective compensation.[12]

In the spring of 1960 the United Nations Economic and Social Council instructed the Secretariat to study measures to facilitate the adjustment of disputes related to private investments. Mexico, Argentina, and Venezuela during subsequent debates in the General Assembly contended that international arbitration of such disputes conferred special advantages on foreign investors and was unacceptable. The Soviet bloc opposed any system that would protect investments. However, a number of underdeveloped countries — including Pakistan, Indonesia, Saudi Arabia, Guinea, and Malaya — endorsed some means of protection. The Indian delegate believed legislation offering guarantees against expropriation and nonconvertibility should be provided by the capital-exporting countries. The upshot was a resolution sponsored by Indonesia and Pakistan instructing the Secretary-General to study and report on the feasibility of establishing national and international insurance systems to protect investors from noncommercial risks.[13]

Fleming comments on the running argument in the United Nations:

> The trend of debate in the United Nations has tended to show a "class division" between those favorable to the rights of foreign investors, and those opposed. A hard core of Western nations, both small and large, have voted consistently in favor of fair treatment; a hard core of Soviet satellites have voted just as consistently against any rights for foreign capital; and many other nations, including those of Latin America, Asia and Africa, have voted neutral or unfavorably toward foreign capital.[14]

There can be little doubt that a substantial difference of opinion exists, although to assume that what the West wants may be equated *ipso facto* with "fair" rather begs the question. Rather than simply condemning those who differ with the Western view, one should examine *why* these differences exist. Do these differences represent a

[12]J. N. Hyde, "Permanent Sovereignty over Natural Wealth and Resources," *American Journal of International Law*, Vol. 50 (1956), p. 856.

[13]U.S. Council of the International Chamber of Commerce, "Economic Issues at the Fifteenth General Assembly of the United Nations," *Notes on International Economic Issues*, Vol. 57 (Jan. 27, 1961), p. 2.

[14]Fleming, *op. cit.*, pp. 60–61.

genuine clash of interests and legitimate fears? Can they be reconciled? (Naturally, it is the underdeveloped countries outside the Soviet bloc to which the discussion is pointed.)

In Legal Literature   The conflict between the developed and underdeveloped nations has been the subject of much analysis and discussion by legal writers. Kenneth S. Carlson observes:

> The wide-scale postwar nationalization of property in Great Britain and Europe caused certain views to be expressed which had first appeared in connection with the Hungarian-Rumanian land dispute. . . . These were to the effect that fundamental changes in the political system or economic structure of a state justify interference on a large scale with private property and may justify partial compensation to aliens.[15]

What Carlson described as a European phenomenon has become one of world-wide significance as new, nationally responsible and independent political regimes of revolutionary character in Asia, Latin America, and Africa seek to extend their nationality over their own resources and basic enterprises.

A. P. Fachiri has pointed up the conflict as one of principle.

> Foreigners establish themselves in a given European country upon the faith of a known system of law and civilization, and it does not lie with that country, even if it is recently erected into an independent state, to alter that system to their detriment and then to say: this is legislation of general application; neither you nor your Government are entitled to complain or interfere.
>
> On the other hand, it is indisputable that full scope is allowed under international law to the internal organization of the state for the purpose of securing its progress and well-being — or what the competent authorities regard as such — and that foreign states are not in general entitled to intervene even if the measures taken are prejudicial to their subjects.[16]

Behind this conflict in principle stands the undisputed fact that international law as presently articulated is of Western manufacture. A. S. Miller states:

> The system of public international law as it is known today is largely a product of Western thought and Western values. It is the legal counter-

---

[15]K. S. Carlson, "Concession Agreements and Nationalization," *American Journal of International Law*, Vol. 52 (1958), pp. 274–275. The Hungarian-Rumanian land dispute referred to occurred following World War I.

[16]A. P. Fachiri, "Expropriation and International Law," *British Yearbook of International Law*, Vol. 6 (1925), p. 170.

part of the classical theory of international trade in so far as it related to economic matters.[17]

And J. H. W. Verzijil has written:

> Now there is one truth that is not open to denial or even to doubt, namely that the actual body of international law, as it stands today, is not only the product of conscious activity of the European mind, but has also drawn its vital essence from a common source of European beliefs, and in both of these aspects it is mainly of Western European origin.[18]

The point is that so long as Westerners (that is, Europeans and North Americans) were investing in disorganized, largely static, nationally unconscious societies led by regimes totally irresponsible to their own national interests, (that is, the economic well-being of their people under a modernizing and sovereign political regime), it was perhaps reasonable to apply and enforce Western legal principles. In most nonWestern areas local legal and political institutions were inadequate to articulate and act in the national interest. Very frequently, they could not even enforce their own law, and the traditional law of many was wholly inappropriate to modern economic enterprise. If the latter were to exist at all, an adequate legal environment had to be created by Western enterprise and their parent governments.

In his dispute with Mexico over the seizure of certain agricultural lands owned by American nationals, the American Secretary of State made this point:

> The statement in your Government's note to the effect that foreigners who voluntarily move to a country not their own assume, along with the advantages which they may seek to enjoy, the risks to which they may be exposed and are not entitled to better treatment than nationals of the country, presupposes the maintenance of law and order consistent with principles of international law; that is to say, when aliens are admitted into a country the country is obligated to accord them that degree of protection of life and property consistent with standards of justice recognized by the law of nations.[19]

Bearing in mind the comment by Miller and Verzijil, the reader is urged to reread the above statement with the word "Western" in-

[17]A. S. Miller, "Foreign Trade and the 'Security State': A Study in Conflicting National Policies," *Journal of Public Law*, Vol. 7 (1958), pp. 46–47.

[18]J. H. W. Verzijil, "Western Influence on the Foundations of International Law," *International Relations*, Vol. 1 (1955), p. 137.

[19]Note from the Secretary of State to the Mexican ambassador in Washington, August 22, 1938, *U.S. Foreign Relations*, Vol. 5 (1938), p. 685.

serted before the phrase "international law" in line six and before "law of nations" in the last line. The West can no longer claim to represent the majority of the civilized community of nations, nor does its practice constitute "the law of nations." When one now speaks of the "principles of law recognized by civilized nations," he refers just as much to Mexico, Brazil, Egypt, Turkey, and Indonesia as to France, the United Kingdom, and the United States.

Some writers have felt the conflict to be so fundamental as to be irresolvable. W. Friedman has written:

> The controversy between the states that maintain an international minimum standard for aliens, even if this means preferred treatment over nationals, and those states that do not go beyond the acknowledgement of equality between nationals and aliens, is unlikely ever to be resolved. The first group will generally consist of the capital-exporting states, interested in the protection of their foreign investments and the commercial activities of their citizens abroad. The latter will consist of the capital-importing states in a relatively primitive stage of economic development.[20]

One might also observe that there have been a number of instances of Western discrimination against aliens (particularly non-Western), including prohibitions in respect to land ownership, employment, government contracting, and ownership of utilities. A significant part of the early European investment in the United States was confiscated without compensation.[21] Perhaps the difference is that the capital-exporting countries have been in a position to prevent significant alien penetration, so great has been the disparity in the character of political leadership and institutions and in the degree of effective national power as between the capital exporters and capital importers.

It has been observed by Thomas Huang that:

> There is a genuine need for reasonable profits, good will, and protection against outright economic spoliation for states rich in natural resources but lacking in capital to exploit them. On the other hand, an investor who invests capital in foreign states in major concessions should also be protected against measures amounting to intransigent nationalism or zenophobia. Due to the disparity of the legal and "real" status of the

---

[20]W. Friedman, "Some Impacts of Social Organization on International Law," *American Journal of International Law*, Vol. 50 (1956), p. 503.

[21]Reference is to the default of state and private securities in the 1830's. See L. H. Jenks, *The Migration of British Capital to 1875* (New York: Knopf, 1938), pp. 99 ff.

parties to a concession agreement, the continuing relationship over a long period of time, and the mutual interest in the prosperity of the parties in the "joint venture," there are imponderables which no legal virtuosity can guard against. A concession agreement transcends the bounds of mere legal rights and legal obligations. The balance between theoretical *de jure* power and *de facto* financial power requires clearly established equitable principles for the guidance of the parties before they plunge into the venture.[22]

He goes on to assert the belief that "progressive development and codification of international law" should take care of this gap in the present legal order of the world community, so that there can be established a stable legal regime for the economic development of economically underdeveloped countries based upon the "general principles of law recognized by civilized nations."[23] Here, Huang is obviously not equating "civilized nations" with those of Western Europe and North America but with the entire world community of organized, recognized nations. Hence, "the general principles of law" to which he refers are not necessarily the present, Western-inspired rules of law, but a system of commonly recognized equity which would constitute the implied conditions for any contract or agreement entered into by nationals of two or more states.

S. L. Brierly points out a further complicating factor:

> When a State claims, as it is often reasonable that it should claim, something which is not the legal right, something even which it knows it can have only by alteration of the legal position, it is useless to suggest that it submit the determination of the claim to legal decision. It knows beforehand that the answer of the law will be adverse, and that answer is precisely what it claims to have altered.[24]

Perhaps, Alejandro Alvarez was saying the same thing when he contended that "classical international law" was based on an individualistic philosophy and was static. In its place he urged a new legal concept, one that was dynamic and founded on the idea of the social interdependence of all nations. Its aim should be the promotion of the general interest and the furthering of international solidarity, not the mere nourishing of individualism. The new international law was

[22]Thomas T. F. Huang, "Some International and Legal Aspects of the Suez Canal Question," *American Journal of International Law*, Vol. 51 (1957), p. 296.
[23]*Ibid.*
[24]J. L. Brierly, "The Judicial Settlement of International Disputes," *Journal of the British Institute of International Affairs*, Vol. 4 (Jan. 1925), p. 237.

seen by Alvarez as not something strictly juridical. "All aspects, political, legal, social, economic, psychological must be considered. In fact, there are no strictly legal issues. It approaches nearer to the notion of equity, without being merged in it."[25]

Justification for Injury to Aliens

In the various draft conventions regarding international responsibility of states for injuries to aliens, there are included no provisions clearly defining an alien's responsibility for injury to a state. Almost without exception, both awards and commentaries carry the implicit assumption that what is in the interest of the wealthy state, or the capital exporter, is likewise in the interest of the general community of nations. Even the titles of various draft conventions are revealing:

> *International Code of Treatment for Foreign Investments* (International Chamber of Commerce, 1949)
>
> *International Convention for the Mutual Protection of Private Property Rights in Foreign Countries* (Society to Advance the Protection of Foreign Investments, Cologne, 1957)
>
> *Convention on the International Responsibility of States for Injuries to Aliens* (Harvard, 1960)

A complementary convention on the "International Responsibility of Aliens for Injuries to States" might be appropriate. Surely one of the major difficulties blocking general acceptance of these injury-to-aliens conventions is precisely the lack of adequate definition of injuries to states by aliens and the remedies flowing therefrom.

The Harvard draft convention simply defines "sufficient justification" for injury to an alien as including:

> (1). The imposition of punishment for commission of a crime for which such punishment has been provided by law,
>
> (2). The actual necessity for maintaining public order, health and morality in accordance with laws enacted for that purpose ... (except when measures taken against the injured alien clearly depart from the law of the respondent state or unreasonably depart from the principles of justice and maintenance of order generally recognized by municipal legal systems),
>
> (3). The valid exercise of belligerent or neutral rights or duties under international law or a treaty,

[25]As described by W. Samore, "The New International Law of Alejandro Alvarez," *American Journal of International Law*, Vol. 52 (1958), p. 41.

(4). The contributory fault of the injured alien, or his voluntary participation in activities involving an unreasonable risk of injury,

(5). Particular circumstances . . . generally recognized by municipal legal systems as constituting such justification.

Even if such a justification were established, all the injured state can do is to take property without compensation, and there is even doubt on that point, as will be noted. There is no rule whereby a state can claim damages over and above the seized property. Responsibility and remedy seems to be very largely in one direction. As D. P. O'Connell has so succinctly observed, "A right is the logical correlation of a duty; the one cannot exist without the other . . . *Right* requires performance by another; duty requires performance by its possessor."[26]

The author has not been able to find any reference to an international award in which a tribunal has set aside contractual obligations on the grounds that the alien interest was operating in such a manner as to be injurious to the economic or political interests of the host country. Nor has any award been located in which a tribunal has found a concession or contract to have been negotiated under duress by a foreign power, thereby invalidating the obligations of the victimized contracting state. And yet, the history of Western enterprise in Latin America, Africa, and Asia, provides many examples in which concessions or other contractual relations were extracted under undoubted duress. The Iranian government could certainly have raised the issue in its conflict with the Anglo-Iranian Oil Company.

Indeed, a search of the literature reveals no systematic analysis of international law from the point of view of the economic, social, and political interests of those states attempting to accelerate their development at a catch-up pace. What is the law when vested foreign interests, or aliens enjoying acquired rights, clearly impede that development? There seems to be none. In short, a necessary precondition for effective international law is lacking — specifically, common expectation of justice as between the capital-exporting and capital-importing nations.

A common rebuttal to a Western demand for prompt, effective and adequate compensation for the taking of property or valuable

[26]D. P. O'Connell, *The Law of State Succession* (New York: Cambridge University Press, 1956), p. 741.

rights acquired through contract is inability to pay on the part of the non-Western state, at least inability to pay *prompt* compensation. Payment in long-term government bonds or via some self-liquidating arrangement, such as in the case of Iranian oil, has become common. Although Western governments often feel politically compelled to accept such *ad hoc* arrangements, the reservation is almost invariably expressed that deferred payment is not in accord with generally recognized principles of international law. (In fact, deferred payment is not equal to the value of present payment unless interest is added.) However, where foreign ownership of a given resource or industry is substantial, it is frequently true that prompt, effective, and adequate compensation by the nationalizing state is clearly impossible — with or without interest. In other words, application of the traditional rule would effectively block many reforms felt by the underdeveloped countries to be necessary for their development. One wonders what attitude in the United States would be if a substantial share of railroads, farm lands, mineral resources, and public utilities were owned by foreign interests and the wealth were insufficient to offer immediate and adequate compensation. One suspects that this rule of Western-inspired international law is at least, in part, a function of greater Western wealth.

It has been held that "the straitened circumstances of the nationalizing state do not by themselves afford any basis for the international validation of its act" in that "a state may not rely on its own law with a view to evading its international obligations."[27] But what if the "straitened circumstances" have in part been brought on by the alien property owner and/or his government? Surely Justice Holmes' famous observation — "In general, it is not plain that a man's misfortunes or necessities will justify shifting the damages to his neighbors shoulders"[28] — is no longer of universal validity in this age of the *welfare state*, of *mutual security*, and of *international assistance*. In fact, the moral responsibility for shifting many damages wrought by misfortune or necessity from the weaker to the stronger is recognized. Social welfare programs supported in large measure by graduated income taxes rest squarely on this principle.

A 1952 United Nations resolution urged "the governments of Member States, in working out their fiscal policies, to give active

[27]Carlson, *op. cit.*, p. 275.
[28]Pennsylvania Coal Co. v. Mahon, 260 U.S. 393, 414 (1922).

consideration to making funds available for projects of agrarian reform" and invited "the institutions making international loans to give sympathetic consideration to loan applications from underdeveloped countries for development projects which are designed to implement their programmes of agrarian reform."[29] To date, it appears that no international financial institution has been willing to entertain loan applications to finance the taking of foreign properties, even in the case of agrarian reform or of nationalizing basic national resources.

Therefore, for a newly established, *nationally responsible* political regime there may be no road open by which it may acquire ownership of its own resources without contravening traditional rules of international law. Even if proof of past or present injury by the alien interest could be established, there is no reason to believe that international tribunals would consider such injury as cause for setting aside the rule requiring prompt, effective and adequate compensation.

Relevant Doctrines

Despite the lack of clear precedent in regard to uncompensated (or partially compensated) taking of alien property or acquired rights in cases heard before international tribunals, there has been some discussion of the issue by various writers. Likewise, certain developments within Western municipal law are relevant.

The criticism may be made that the ensuing discussion is based too much on that of the legal writers and not sufficiently on cases. The reason for the examination of Western law is to pin down those concepts developed within the context of that law that are relevant to a formulation of legal principles which *should* govern relations between states of unequal economic and political power and social development. Traditional international law has obviously failed to provide viable principles under which a common expectation of justice could emerge. What is being sought is a new statement of international law which might give rise to a common expectation of justice as between the powerful and the weak nations. In so doing, a number of international and municipal law doctrines are examined for clues as to the

[29]U.N. Gen. Ass. Off. Rec. 7th Sess. Res. 625, Supp. No. 20 at 18 (A/2361) (1952).

terms in which international law must be stated if a real international community is to emerge.

Public Interest   One of the more puzzling and perplexing issues is the weight given to considerations of "public interest" in resolving conflicts involving contracts or understandings entered into by a public entity and private persons, whether of an international character or purely domestic.

There are two important international arbitral awards in which the matter of public interest was of central concern. The first, *Czechoslovakia v. Radio Corporation of America*,[30] related to a traffic agreement concluded between the parties for the establishment and operation of a direct commercial telegraphic circuit between Czechoslovakia and the United States. It provided that each should transmit exclusively over the circuit every available message within its control destined to or for transit through the country of the other, unless routed otherwise by the sender. Somewhat later, claiming that the number of messages transmitted from the United States to its territory was insufficient, Czechoslovakia moved to establish a second service via Mackay Radio for telegrams marked by the sender "via Mackay Radio." Czechoslovakia argued that in so doing it was trying to increase business and was thereby acting in its national economic interests. The award, rendered at the Hague in 1932, held that the agreement established an irrevocable co-partnership between the two parties for the ten-year period specified in the agreement. It was held further:

> By an agreement in virtue of which two or several persons agree in pooling their efforts alone, or together, with other properties, for the purpose of mutual profit, a community for mutual profit is formed. . . . No member is allowed to entrust the cooperation to a third party, or to admit anybody into the community, or to engage in a business which is injurious to the community.[31]

The tribunal disagreed with the argument that the state could not allow itself to be bound by the tendency of commercial undertakings, namely, the maximization of profit, and was exclusively directed by the consideration of commercial advantages for its citizens.

> Even if the agreement should be considered a public law agreement, the State cannot repudiate the obligation which it contains without showing

[30]*American Journal of International Law*, Vol. 30 (1936), p. 523.
[31]*Ibid.*, pp. 528, 534.

that public interests of vital importance would suffer if the agreement should be upheld under the rules of civil law.[32]

The tribunal found no "public interests of vital importance." There had been no complaints from a technical point of view and the single circuit could adequately handle the traffic. The tribunal observed further:

> When a public institution enters into an agreement with a private person or a private company, it must be assumed that the government has intended by this agreement to benefit its citizens. But that this expectation sometimes proves to fail in not giving the country as large a profit as was expected, cannot be considered sufficient reason for releasing that public institution from its obligations as signatory of said agreement.[33]

The broad implication of the award is that a government which enters into a contract with a private party in a profit-seeking enterprise does so as a commercial partner. It may not breach the contract even though at a later date the agreement operates against national economic interests unless they be "vital." Nor may the government participate in any other enterprise whose interests might conflict with the first.

The award in the second of these cases, *Radio Corporation of America v. China*,[34] was handed down at the Hague in 1935. The Chinese government and the Radio Corporation of America (RCA) had agreed to operate a direct radio telegraphic circuit for commercial communications between China and the United States. Subsequently, the Chinese government concluded a similar agreement with Mackey Radio & Telegraph Company, which agreement was protested by RCA as a violation of its earlier agreement. RCA cited the Czechoslovakian case as precedent. China argued that it had cooperated successfully and profitably with RCA and had thereby fulfilled its obligations.

> As a public service, it was and is the Chinese Government's duty to give the public the opportunity to avail itself of other special facilities, and the RCA contract leaves such liberty with regard to the establishment of other circuits.[35]

[32]*Ibid.*, p. 538.
[33]*Ibid.*, p. 534.
[34]*American Journal of International Law*, Vol. 30 (1936), p. 535.
[35]*Ibid.*, p. 538.

The Chinese contended that the Czechoslovakian case was not entirely analogous. Furthermore, the decision there had been incorrect. "The existence of a relation of partnership could not be admitted; and China's right was reserved." In the earlier case it had been specified that Czechoslovakia "shall transmit exclusively over the said circuit every message within its control." In the Chinese case there was no reference to exclusiveness.[36]

The tribunal found that:

> The Parties cannot be held, in making the agreement to have acted with the intention to start a common enterprise with the object of making profits together (the *animus contrahendae societatis*), which is essential to the contract of partnership. This can certainly not be assumed to have been the attitude of the Chinese Government. In making useful provision for the working of a radio-telegraphic circuit between its territory and another country, the government envisages the establishment of a public service, in order to promote the interests of its people, to encourage their international communications (business relations and personal relations) and to make them enjoy the advantages of modern scientific development in this field. It makes no difference that the government will desire to make such a service pay, cover the expenses and, if possible, yield surplus advantages. The Radio Corporation on their part will of course look upon the enterprise as a business interest. But in dealing with a government, they will be fully aware that the other part is acting from a more general point of view.[37]

The implication here is that a condition to be read into any agreement between a private interest and a government (except as it runs afoul some explicit provision) is that the agreement shall continue to operate in the highest public interest. A government, unless it specifically binds itself within a joint venture, cannot be held to have entered into a commercial partnership for the sole purpose of seeking profit. The burden of proof to establish the contrary is on the private party, and in this case RCA failed to show that it "had made financial sacrifices or investments of such a nature and such an importance that the object of its dealing with China should thereby have been practically and reasonably exclusive."[38] The tribunal declared:

> As a sovereign government, on principle, is free in its action for the public interest as it sees it, it cannot be presumed to have accepted such restric-

[36]*Ibid.*, p. 546.
[37]*Ibid.*, p. 542.
[38]*Ibid.*, p. 541.

tion of its freedom of action, unless the acceptance of such restriction can be ascertained distinctly and beyond reasonable doubt. . . . Contracts affecting the public interest are to be construed liberally in favor of the public.[39]

In the Czechoslovakian case the tribunal went far beyond the exclusive clause, which the Czechs may have been forced to accept in order to get any telegraphic circuits at all at that particular time, by holding that the government had in effect entered into a commercial partnership and, hence, could not enter into potentially conflicting agreements with third parties. In reading the award, one is forced to conclude that the decision would have been the same even in the absence of the exclusive clause. Therefore, no clear rule emerges from these two awards, for they conflict.

In reference to domestic Western practice, J. D. B. Mitchell has written:

> There is a tendency to assert that the motive of economy, of the restriction of public expenditure, can never justify the interference by the state with its own contract. In an age when state investments and public works may be used as instruments of public policy, it would seem that that assertion cannot be accepted in all cases.[40]

In 1945 the United States Supreme Court held that a state had the authority to "safeguard the vital interests of its people" though this might involve modifying or abrogating existing contracts. The majority invoked the growing recognition of public needs as a reason for preventing "the perversion of the [contract] clause" into "an instrument to throttle the capacity of the State to protect their fundamental interests."[41] In commenting on this case, Henry Rottschaefer concludes, "The theory that there is implied in every contract a term reserving to the state their sovereign powers to protect those interests is not only expressed but applied."[42]

In more general terms, Rottschaefer writers:

> The grant of a legal monopoly or other special privileges, the possession of a monopoly in fact, the existence of excessive competition among consumers and that the commodity or services belonged to the class of

[39]*Ibid.*, p. 540.
[40]J. D. B. Mitchell, *The Contracts of Public Authorities* (London: London School of Economics, 1934), p. 233.
[41]East New York Savings Bank V. Hahn, 326 U.S. 230, (1945).
[42]H. Rottschaefer, *The Constitution and Socio-Economic* Change (Ann Arbor: University of Michigan, 1948), p. 195.

necessities, were all involved to support the conclusion that a particular business had become affected with a public interest.[43]

In a 1934 case the Supreme Court held that "the statement that one has dedicated his property to a public use" was "merely another way of saying that if one embarks in a business which public interest demands shall be regulated, he must know regulations will ensue." An enterprise affected with public interest "can in the nature of things, mean no more than that an industry which, for adequate reasons, is subject to control for the public good."[44] It would be reasonable to conclude that if the public good demanded the breech of an exclusive franchise, the government would be justified in so doing.

S. Williston states:

> Grants of franchise and contracts or agreements affecting the public interest are to be construed liberally in favor of the public . . . the rules favoring the public is based on a different reason from ordinary rules of interpretation. There is no reason to suppose that the parties in fact intended to favor the public, and when the court so assumes, it does so because it is in their interest to so assume.[45]

And again:

> . . . no state will enforce a bargain, though valid when made and where performable, if the enforcement of the particular right claimed to arise therefrom is contrary to a strong public policy of the forum.[46]

Mitchell concludes in reference to contracts entered into by a government:

> No government can be taken to be possessed of such foresight that one can safely say that its contracts may not in the future work serious harm to the State if rigidly enforced. Some restriction upon the scope of the constitutional limitation designed for the protection of contractual rights is therefore necessary.[47]

Such implied conditions in public contracts are not limited to United States practice. In France, "in administrative contract, the

[43]*Ibid.*, p. 157.

[44]Nebbia v. New York, 291 U.S. 502 (1934).

[45]S. Williston, *A Treatise on the Law of Contracts* (New York: Baker, Voorhis & Co., 1936), pp. 1799–1800.

[46]*Ibid.*, p. 5094.

[47]Mitchell, *op. cit.*, p. 84.

administration always retains control over the subject matter of the contract despite its terms, at any rate so far as that contract is justified by the public interest."[48] The test of an administrative contract lies in (1) the nature of the parties, (2) its relationship to public service, (3) the intent of the parties in entering into contract, (4) the conferring on the contractor of some of the privileges of administration. The administration has the power to adapt administrative contracts to the changing needs of the public service. "Thus, concessions giving a monopoly of street lighting by gas were converted, in effect, to concessions of street lighting by the most up-to-date methods and therefore, by electricity."[49]

Although apparently subject to some modification, it has been observed in Great Britain that "the most important, since capable of the widest application, of the modern rules is that formulated in *The Amphritite* [case], namely that it [the Crown] cannot by contract hamper its freedom of action in matters which concern the welfare of the state."[50]

It seems quite clearly established in Western practice that public contracts may be terminated or altered unilaterally by the public authority on the grounds that the public interest so demands. Also, it is recognized that the public interest may intrude itself into purely private contracts — for example, in the matter of price controls. In the latter, it could be claimed that an acquired right is thereby destroyed without compensation.

The whole subject of the renegotiation and termination of United States defense contracts is likewise relevant to the discussion. In a wartime situation, or during a major defense effort, uncontrolled competition does not provide the government protection against excessive profit making by contractors. "The profits of Government contractors cannot be unrestricted; they must be held to a level acceptable by the public."[51] The original idea of the 1942 Renegotiation Act[52] was one of voluntary repricing in the light of experience, conducted during the life of the contract. The refund of excessive profits

[48]*Ibid.*, p. 182.
[49]*Ibid.*, p. 186.
[50]Rederiaktiebolaget Amphritite v. The King, 3 K.B. 500 (1921).
[51]R. Braucher, "The Renegotiation Act of 1951," *Harvard Law Review* Vol.66 (1952), pp. 270–271.
[52]65 Stat 7, 1951, 50 U.S.C. App. Sec. 1211–1233, Supp. (1952).

was compulsory. If the amount could not be determined by agreement, the determination was to be made unilaterally by the government.[53]

The 1951 Renegotiation Act[54] applies to the contracting of all public agencies designated by the President as "exercising functions having a direct and immediate connection with national defense."[55] Whether a renegotiation clause is inserted in a contract or not is irrelevant. Under the 1951 act, in the determination of what portion of profits is excessive, these factors are considered: efficiency, reasonableness of costs and profits, source of capital (practice seems to treat government financing as tending to limit the contractor's contribution only to management), extent of risk assumed, contribution to the defense effort ("inventive and development contribution and cooperation with the Government and other contractors in supplying technical assistance"), and the character of the business (that is, source and nature of materials, extent of subcontracting, complexity of manufacturing technique, rate of turnover).[56] President Eisenhower stated the official policy thus:

> As a nation, we recognize that so long as defense expenditures represent more than half of the national budget, we must do everything in our power to see to it that the maximum return is received for each dollar spent. On the other hand, we must also be careful not to interfere unwisely with the traditional commercial relationship between the Government and its suppliers.[56]

Apart from the taking of excess profits, although quite legal at the time of their accumulation, the government also has the power to terminate public contracts at its pleasure. That a government officer authorized to enter into contracts for the government may suspend, in the public interest, the work under contract and enter into a binding agreement for the compensation to be paid for the partial performance was established as early as 1876[58] and is assumed to be still applicable.

The contractor views the inclusion of a termination article in a military contract as a real, though contingent hazard. His primary need is to

[53]Braucher, *op cit.*
[54]65 Stat 7, 1951, 50 U.S.C. App. Sec. 1211–1233, Supp. (1952).
[55]Braucher, *op. cit.*, p. 380.
[56]*Ibid.*
[57]H. W. Fensterstock, "The Rationale of Renegotiation," *Federal Bar Journal*, Vol. 16 (1956), p. 101.
[58]United States v. Corliss Steam-Engine Co., 91 U.S. 321 (1876).

have, in advance of contracting, a reasonable basis for estimating the consequences to him of the Government's continuing option to terminate a contract at its pleasure. ... Risk will be minimized not only by assurance that the amount finally received upon settlement will fairly compensate the contractor for his partial performance, but also in anticipation of expenditures and final settlement, prompt and orderly plant clearance, adequate interim financing, and clear delineation of the rights of subcontractors.[59]

The law contemplates a voluntary termination agreement, but if none is forthcoming, the contracting officer may "unilaterally determine in accordance with a formula the amount due." The formula allows as profit for a fixed-price contractor an arbitrary percentage of cost and for a cost-plus-fixed fee contractor, a portion of the fixed fee based on the extent of performance.[60] It should be noted that the government does not undertake to compensate the contractor for future earnings lost by reason of the unilateral termination of contract. Because of the tendency of the United States government to limit defense contracts to domestic suppliers, no case has apparently arisen in which an alien supplier has sued for full recovery on the basis of unilateral breech of contract. In such an event, would an international body look behind the determination of excess profits by the United States government to enforce such an award, thereby giving aliens more favorable treatment than its own nationals?

The principle that a public contract, even though not containing specific provisions permitting such, may be altered or terminated in the public interest is a well-established Western practice. Mitchell points out that although the "law permits a governmental agency to fulfill the fundamental purposes for which it was created, even though so doing may involve interference with vested contractual right which an individual may have against that agency," it is also true that:

The principle of governmental effectiveness only operates, and is only intended to operate in cases where otherwise the disadvantages to the community would be considerable; it is not for example intended to enable a governmental body to escape the consequences of a contract which turns out to be disadvantageous in the ordinary sense. The preeminence of the principle of public service is not absolute and there is implicit in it an acceptance of private rights.[61]

[59] R. Wienshienk and F. Feldman, "The Current Challenge of Military Contract Termination," *Harvard Law Review*, Vol. 66 (1952), pp. 51–52.
[60] *Ibid.*
[61] Mitchell, *op. cit.*, p. 17.

On the other hand, apparently the federal courts will not look behind a declaration by responsible state authorities that a contract has been altered or terminated by the state on the grounds of public interest. Chief Justice Taney declared in 1853:

> It can never be maintained in any tribunal in this country that the people of a state, in the exercise of the powers of sovereignty, can be restrained within narrower limits than those fixed by the Constitution of the United States, upon the ground that they made contracts injurious or ruinous to themselves. The principle that they are the best judges of what is for their own interest, is the foundation of our political institutions.[62]

Arguing by domestic Western analogy, one might reasonably contend that there can be no such thing as a wrongful taking of alien property by a government so long as the constitutional authorities declare the taking to be in the vital interest of the nation. By definition, if such authorities feel the expropriating to be in the national interest, it is. If this is so, no government is obligated to do more than to compensate the contractor or concessionaire for *actual cost* of the investment made up to the time of the take-over, which amount may be substantially less than the market value of the property, that is, expected future earnings discounted to the present.

Rebus sic Stantibus   There is another line of reasoning which would release a state from international obligations under certain circumstances. The point of departure is the presumption in contracts and treaties that things will remain in the same condition as they were at the date of agreement, *rebus sic stantibus*, that is, that the agreement can be performed in the same circumstances as existed on its date.[63] A. Owen points out that the general test a United States court uses in implying conditions into a contract is one of "reasonableness." First, is the condition to be implied so obvious that it goes without saying? Second, is the implied condition certain, free of all speculation? Third, is the implied condition necessary?[64] One test: "If somebody had raised the question when they [the parties] were originally making the bargain, what would they both have said about it?"[65]

Queen Elizabeth, in a dispute with the Netherlands in 1595,

[62]Ohio Life Insurance Co. v. Debolt, 16 Howard 428 (1853).

[63]A. Owen, "Implied Terms in Contract," *Law Journal*, Vol. 102 (1952), p. 300.

[64]*Ibid.*

[65]O'Grady v. M. Saper, Ltd., 3 *All England Law Reports* 527 (1940).

"took the view . . . on the opinions of jurists and statesmen, that every convention, although sworn, must be understood to hold only while things remain in the same state. . . ."[66] The doctrine of "frustration of contracts" developed by English courts during the past half-century is analogous to the doctrine of *rebus sic stantibus* as defined by some within the context of international law.[67] The doctrine in German law "is a rule for determining the real wills of the parties to the contract and is unrelated to such ideas as a right of self-preservation, necessity, impossibility of performance, and injury to the interests of the parties."[68] Also relevant, if not exactly analogous, is the French theory of *imprévision*, which embodies a rule by which a party having a contract with the government may gain a revision of the contract so as to reduce a burden produced by entirely unforeseen changes of circumstances, although the change of circumstances does not create a situation of *force majeur*. The French courts have not, however, applied this theory to contracts between private persons.[69]

In a California case,[70] a public contract was set aside by reason of an unanticipated rise in cost. In the decision, the court cited *Williston on Contracts,*

. . .the general rule is that an increased expense does not excuse the performance of a contract. However, when an increase in cost which could not have been foreseen by the parties becomes so excessive that performance is totally impracticable, many courts take the liberal view that the promisor is excused on the ground of impossibility.[71]

There is a difference of opinion among the authorities as to whether the principle of *rebus sic stantibus* is a recognized rule of international law or not, but the majority of them seem to admit that "as a principle at least of international morals and public policy it is well established."[72] T. Y. Huang observes that "most early writers

[66]R. Zouche, *An Exposition of Fecial Law and Procedure, or of Law Between Nations and Questions Concerning the Same* (1650), quoted by C. Hill, in "The Doctrine of *Rebus Sic Stantibus* in International Law," *University of Missouri Studies*, Vol. 9 (July 1934), pp. 46-47.

[67]C. Hill, *ibid.*, p. 18.

[68]*Ibid.*

[69]*Ibid.*, p. 19.

[70]City of Vernon v. Los Angeles, 45 Cal. 2d 710, 290 p. 2d 841 (1955); comment in *U.C.L.A. Law Review*, Vol. 4 (1956), p. 122.

[71]Williston, *op. cit.*, p. 1936.

[72]J. W. Garner, "The Doctrine in Rebus Sic Stantibus and the Termination of Treaties," *American Journal of International Law*, Vol. 21 (1927), p. 511.

recognized the fact that all treaties are necessarily concluded under the tacit condition of *rebus sic stantibus*," and he appends a long list of authorities to support this position.[73] Wharton interpreted the rule to embrace "all cases in which the reason for a treaty has failed, or there has been a change of circumstances as to make its performance impracticable except at an unreasonable sacrifice."[74] Chesney Hill has written that the following is the only definition of the rule recognized as "customary international law":

> A treaty of perpetual or indefinite duration which contains no provision for revision or denunciation lapses, in the sense that stipulations which remain to be performed cease to bind the parties to the treaty, when it is recognized by the parties to the treaty or by competent international authority that there has been an essential change in those circumstances which existed at the time of the conclusion of the treaty, and whose continuance without essential change formed a condition of the obligatory force of the treaty according to the intention of the parties.[75]

Hill adds that the doctrine of *rebus sic stantibus* has not been defined either by international tribunal nor treaty and there is no definition upon which there is general agreement by the writers. He advances the following juridical basis in explaining why a change of circumstances might legally alter treaty obligations:

1. The change, if foreseen, would have altered the original intentions of the parties.
2. Fulfillment after the change is injurious to a fundamental right of one of the parties.
3. The change frustrates the objects of the treaty.
4. The change makes the fulfillment of the treaty impossible.
5. The change may adversely affect the interests of a party whose interests the treaty was meant to promote.
6. Certain changes of circumstances by their very nature affect the obligations of a treaty.[76]

He then goes on to list the limitations of the doctrine:

1. Its application is limited to perpetual treaties.
2. The state must invoke the change within a reasonable time.

[73]T. Y. Huang, *The Doctrine of Rebus Sic Stantibus in International Law* (Shanghai: Comacrib Press, 1935), p. 17.
[74]Quoted in Garner, *op. cit.*, p. 512.
[75]Hill, *op. cit.*, p. 83.
[76]*Ibid.*, p. 8.

3. The state cannot itself be responsible for the change that it is invoking.
4. Only executory provisions of the treaty may be terminated.
5. Termination may arise only from mutual agreement or by decision of some competent international authority.
6. The doctrine relates to termination and not revision.[77]

Hill tells us that "fundamental right" of a state may be defined in terms of its existence, self-preservation, independence, and development, although he admits that some writers strenuously deny any fundamental right of development.[78] which is tantamount to saying that one has the right to life but not to growth. Brierly lists five fundamental rights: self-preservation, independence, equality, respect, and intercourse.[79] Implicit in all five is, surely, the right of growth or development. Various writers have equated "impossibility" with "physical impossibility, moral impossibility, impossibility except at unreasonable sacrifice."[80] Those who hold that a "treaty deserves its obligatory force solely from the fact that it promotes the interests of the State" hold that it may lose that obligatory nature when the "equilibrium of the interest of the parties is disrupted by change of circumstances."[81]

Other writers have declared that a state may repudiate a treaty whose performance conflicts with the rights and welfare of its people. "All treaties are null which in any way oppose the development of the free activity of a nation or which hinders the development of its industry or commerce."[82] Others have stated that "if ample notice be given beforehand and the demand is refused, the dissatisfied party, under necessity of being released from the unbearable obligations, and in the absence of an international court, may be justified in declaring its release from the obligations by unilateral action."[83]

There have been a number of instances in which the doctrine of *rebus sic stantibus* has been applied unilaterally by states abrogating agreements, such as:

1. *Termination of capitulations by Turkey in 1914–1923.* The

[77]*Ibid.*, pp. 77 ff.
[78]*Ibid.*, p. 10.
[79]J. L. Brierly, *The Law of Nations* (New York: Oxford University Press, 1960), p. 50.
[80]Hill, *op. cit.*, pp. 11–12.
[81]*Ibid.*, p. 12.
[82]Garner, *op. cit.*, p. 512.
[83]Huang, note 73 *supra*, pp. 33–34.

right to invoke the doctrine was generally denied by the Western powers.

2. *Franco-British dispute in Morocco (1922).*
3. *Termination of extraterritoriality in China between 1926 and 1930.* In the dispute with China on the issue, Belgium, in condemning the unilateral termination, insisted that there was a principle of law which obliged a party to a treaty to negotiate for the revision of that treaty when the essential circumstances relevant to the treaty had been modified.
4. *Termination of consular jurisdiction in Persia (1927–1928).*
5. *Free Zones dispute between France and Switzerland between 1928 and 1932.* France relied upon the doctrine to terminate the treaties of 1815 and 1816 which had created certain rights for the benefit of Switzerland.[84]

Perhaps of the greatest interest in this regard was the Russian indemnities case of 1912 which went before the Hague Arbitration Tribunal. Turkey had claimed that she had no obligation to pay interest damages to Russia for nonpayment of indemnities. The award, handed down in November 1912, included the following:

> The exception of *force majeure*, cited as of the first importance, may be maintained in public international law as well as in private law; international law must adapt itself to political necessities. The Imperial Russian Government expressly admits that the obligation of a State to fulfill treaties may give way "if the very existence of the State should be in danger, if the observance of international duty is . . . self-destruction."[85]

One can equate *force majeure* here with *rebus sic stantibus*, for conditions changed so as to endanger the existence of one of the parties. The tribunal went on to refuse the exception of *force majeure* because it concluded that the payment or the securing of a loan for the payment of the relatively small sum due the Russians would not "imperil the existence of the Ottoman Empire or seriously compromise its international or external situation."[86] But given the precarious position of the Turks at this time, and subsequent events, this finding was open to serious question in fact.

It seems quite clearly recognized that states do reserve the right

[84]Summarized from Hill, *op. cit.*, pp. 46 ff.
[85]Quoted in Hill, *op. cit.*, pp. 23–24.
[86]*Ibid.*

to renounce international obligations which, by reason of change of circumstances, run contrary either to the original intent or become injurious to the national interest. Presumably the same rule would apply with equal, if not greater, force in the case of contracts entered into by governments with private aliens. One might add that one of the more important changes of circumstances occurring in the 1950's and 1960's is the coming to power of nationally responsible political regimes for the first time in a number of states — that is, regimes which, for the first time are at least attempting to act in the national interest and are not a captive of some Western power. (This problem is dealt with in more detail in the discussion of state succession below.)

A relevant development within American contract law has been noted by a number of authors, including A. S. Miller, who comments:

> Contract has shown a tendency to become more and more standardized, even "compulsory." A new term — contracts of adhesion — has entered the American legal lexicon. It may now be fairly said that larger and larger segments of the national economic life and larger and larger portions of the national resources are controlled through the medium of contracts awarded and entered into after "negotiation" between parties of unequal bargaining power. This means, among other things, that one of the parties is able to force acceptance of his own terms in the transaction. The transaction, accordingly, creates not a contractual relationship (in the historical sense of consensual agreement), but one based on power. . . .
> The weaker party, with a need for goods or services, cannot go to another source. Either he is faced with a monopoly (as in a public utility), or he finds that all competitors use substantially the same clauses and do business in substantially the same way. The act of submission in the relationship of power finds little recognition in contract law, which is still based on notions of equality of bargaining position.[87]

It is suggested that the analogy between this domestic problem and that of an underdeveloped country negotiating a concession agreement with a large international corporation may be very close. At the time of negotiation the country may have no alternative but to accept the conditions laid down. Later, as the country obtains some leverage over the alien corporation because of its local investment in fixed equipment, one can anticipate a unilateral change in the terms of the

[87]A. S. Miller, "Government Contract and Social Control: A Preliminary Inquiry," *Virginia Law Review*, Vol. 41 (1955), p. 31.

concession, a change perhaps more extreme than what would have been demanded initially in a more equal situation, for there now exists a certain punitive motive — that is, a desire to recoup for past "exploitation." Frederick Kessler has pointed out:

> In dealing with standardized contracts, courts have to determine what the weaker contracting party could legitimately expect by way of services according to the enterpriser's "calling," and to what extent the stronger party disappointed reasonable expectations based on the typical life situation.[88]

Unfortunately, this principle seems to have no recognition in international law, or at least the underdeveloped countries do not have sufficient confidence in the practice of international law to induce them to submit their disputes to such a test.

In recognition of such risks many governments no longer are willing to negotiate long-term agreements for ninety-nine-years, or even for fifty years. For example, the Indonesian law on foreign investment apparently provides that the government may guarantee to foreign industrial enterprise freedom from expropriation or nationalization for a period of not more than twenty years and for foreign-owned plantations a period of not more than thirty years.[89] The Indian government, in agreements with certain companies, has likewise limited its guarantee of nonexpropriation to twenty or thirty years. The Japanese government rarely gives permission for a Japanese firm to enter into a licensing agreement with a foreign firm for longer than five years. Underlying such limited guarantees or agreements is the thesis that an alien has the right to a return on an investment for a specified time only, after which time the property may be nationalized, particularly if the alien provides no continuing service not procurable locally. One suspects that the silence of international law on these points has had the effect of shortening the time of international concessions or other forms of agreements. Increasing competition for concessions or other forms of agreements is the other part of the explanation. In the 1930's, other than the Standard Oil Company of New Jersey, there were no politically acceptable alternatives in Saudi Arab eyes for development of Saudi oil under conces-

[88]Frederick Kessler, "Contracts of Adhesion — Some Thoughts about Freedom of Contract," *Columbia Law Review*, Vol. 43 (1943), p. 637.

[89]"Draft Bill on Foreign Investment," Djakarta, June 27, 1957, mimeo., an official translation, Art. 13. *See also Foreign Commerce Weekly* (Oct. 1958).

sion. The choice was British Petroleum or Standard.[90] Saudi Arabia had to take what it could get. The same was true of the Iranian concession in the early days of the oil development there. Today, with the Japanese, Italians, Russians, plus various European and American interests all competing, the situation is very different.

Karl Llewellyn has written:

> When one is . . . tempted to assume legal contract or even factual promises as an utterly essential feature of our economy [*i.e.*, the United States], it challenges attention that so much of current financing proceeds on flexible and revocable "understandings" as to line and conditions of credit. And such flexibility is a marked trend in marketing of goods as well, wherever long-range buyer-seller *relations* come to seem more important than exact definitions of the risks to be shifted by the particular dicker in terms of quantity, quality, or price. Output and requirement contracts, maximum and minimum contracts, contracts with quality, quantity and kinds to be specified from month to month, and sliding scale price arrangements — these are symptomatic of an economy stabilizing itself along new lines.[91]

For nations in rapid transition from primitive to industrial, the need for flexible economic relations is even greater. What may be in the national interest one year, may not be so five years hence. As in the domestic situation, business associates must ultimately rely upon mutuality of interests, regardless of what specific terms may be written into a contract. In a rapidly evolving society the parties to an agreement may find it impossible to foresee important changes in circumstances even a few months off.

One writer states:

> *Pact sunt servanda* — contracts should be performed — is perhaps the most basic premise of Anglo-American contract law. But when, subsequent to the formation of a contract, an event occurs or a pre-existing fact is discovered which makes performance impossible or substantially more burdensome than anticipated, the promisor may sometimes be discharged from his duty to perform.[92]

[90]Old Ibn Saud, the feudal king of Saudi Arabia, apparently chose the American company because the Americans lived further away, and because they seemed interested only in oil and "were not likely to interfere in Saudi Arabia's internal affairs. The British, he implied, always mixed politics with their oil." (Harold H. Martin, "The Oil of the Arab World," *Saturday Evening Post* (Feb. 17, 1962, p. 51.)

[91]K. N. Llewellyn, "What Price Contract? — an Essay in Perspectives," *Yale Law Review*, Vol. 40 (1931), p. 727.

[92]"The Fetish of Impossibility in the Law of Contracts," *Columbia Law Review*, Vol. 53 (1953), p. 94.

The doctrine of uncontemplated turn of events may apply in situations where, "although the contract is not strictly frustrated, the ensuing turn of events is so completely outside the contemplation of the parties that the Court is satisfied that the Parties, as reasonable people, cannot have intended that the contract should apply to the new situation."[93] In such a case a United States court may qualify the terms of the contract.

One might suggest that in a number of international cases there may well have been an uncontemplated turn of events. Otherwise, why have so many governments, having granted concessions of special conditions to foreign corporations on an apparently friendly basis, turned about and condemned these same corporations?[94] What condition had changed? Can *all* of these altered positions simply be laid to the rapacity of foreign regimes? One doubts it. And yet in few cases heard before international tribunals have the tribunals deliberately sought and objectively analyzed the reasons underlying this change in attitude.

State Sovereignty   Almost indistinguishable from certain aspects of the doctrines of public interest and *rebus sic stantibus* is that of state sovereignty.

"The United States has specifically rejected the theory that the state, when engaging in commercial activities, forfeits its sovereign position."[95] But there is considerable confusion. W. Friedman asserts:

> The traditional doctrine is that governments entering into international commercial transactions and, in particular, governments seeking foreign loans, can never be deemed to have submitted to a law other than their own, because to hold otherwise would derogate from their sovereignty.[96]

Chief Justice Taney in the *Ohio Life Insurance Company* case held:

> The powers of sovereignty confided to the legislative body of a state are undoubtedly a trust committed to them to be executed to the best of their

[93]H.K.T. "Contract: Uncontemplated Turn of Events," *Law Journal*, Vol. 100 (1950), p, 677.

[94]Examples: the Mexican oil concessions, Turkish utility concessions, Brazilian telephone concessions. A specific case brought to arbitration was the "Martini Case," *American Journal of International Law*, Vol. 25 (1931), p. 554.

[95]W. Friedman, "Some Aspects of Social Organization on International Law," *American Journal of International Law*, Vol. 50, (1956), p. 478.

[96]*Ibid.*, p. 482.

judgment for the public good; and no one Legislature can, by its own act, disarm their successors of any of the powers or rights of sovereignty confided by the people to the legislative body, unless they are authorized to do so by the constitution under which they are elected. They cannot, therefore, by contract, deprive a future legislature of the power of imposing any tax it may deem necessary for the public service — or of exercising any other act of sovereignty confided by the legislative body, unless the power to make such a contract is conferred upon them by the constitution of the State.[97]

Certainly the same principle must apply in the realm of international law. No state can be held liable under a contractual obligation unless that obligation is legally binding upon it under its own laws. To hold otherwise would subvert the very principle of popular sovereignty.

Brierly seems to find an inherent conflict between the concept of state sovereignty and international order.[98] There can be no order among sovereign states (that is, universally respected rules or relations); all can act as they wish, and they do. But he speaks not at all of the force of reciprocity, in personal law as well as in international. Surely man does not obey law simply to create "order" as Brierly implies.[99] Neither do nations. One can think of a number of "orders" that might be far less preferable to an individual or to a nation than "chaos." At least, "chaos" holds some hope of ultimate change within it. Man obeys law — that is, submits to an order — because he wishes others to obey the same law, and he realizes that if he refuses to do so, he cannot reasonably expect others to obey. The same might be said of states or nations, whether federated or independent. A rule of law will be observed by Nation X only so long as it is important to Nation X that others obey the same rule. By "Nation X" is meant the articulated consensus within that society over an appreciable period of time. National sovereignty will be limited exactly to the extent and in the manner that Nation X feels that it is in its interest for the sovereignty of other nations to be limited. This is the "order" of which Brierly writes, although apparently without realizing it. The willingness of the individual to limit his personal sovereignty rests upon precisely the same basis. There is nothing metaphysical, mysterious, or idealistic about it.

A nation breaks accepted rules in the knowledge that reciprocity

[97]Ohio Life Insurance Co. v. Debolt, 16 Howard 431-(1853).
[98]Brierly, *op. cit.*, pp. 46–47.
[99]*Ibid.*, p. 57.

can be expected. The Cuban government undoubtedly felt that the nationalization of United States-owned property in Cuba was more important to its well-being than the possible elimination from the United States market of Cuban sugar. Order is enforced by reciprocity. If one party feels that the anticipated reciprocal action is an inadequate deterrent, it is likely that there is a basic inequality — if not inequity — in the original status quo which that state seeks to alter, even if in so doing it runs counter to generally accepted rules of international law (just as society itself is probably responsible for a large share of crimes committed by individuals). Better law enforcement and clearer codification of law are perhaps not the most effective methods by which order may be restored, but rather correction of the basic inequities. Brierly talks not at all of the need to correct international inequities, whether sanctified by contract and treaty or not.

In international law, national sovereignty may be equated with the power of the state to alter any obligation or commitment that runs counter to vital national interests. A state cannot be bound to any agreement that proves injurious to itself. It follows that the state cannot permit itself to be the unwilling defendant in any action, the unfavorable outcome of which will injure vital national interests. The whole issue hangs on what constitutes vital national interests, which is precisely what the authorities avoid discussing in any specific terms. This vagueness, the author submits, is an important reason why many of the non-Western states, whose interests are very different from the more developed states of the West, cannot permit themselves to be judged under Western-inspired international law. And yet, as has been shown, within Western municipal law there is a great deal of precedent on which basic national interest might be defined in more precise terms.

State Succession   The general rule is that successor states are required to recognize treaties and concessionary contracts entered into by defunct states.[100] Various qualifications, however, have been entertained, both in practice and in authoritative writings.

Following the cession of Cuba and the Philippine Islands by Spain to the United States in 1898, the United States took the position that "a concession must not only be related or attached to the territory ceded, but also granted for its exclusive benefit."[101] The United States Attorney General advised that "the concession granted

[101]O'Connell, *op. cit.*, p. 115.
[100]Huang, note 22 *supra*, p. 295.

to the Manila Railway Company to build a railway in the Philippines had been inspired by Spanish imperialistic motives." Therefore, the United States was not bound to recognize the concession. "The most that could be said was that there was an obligation of equity imposed on the United States to compensate the concessionaires for the advantages which would accrue to the new administration from the laying of the railway."[102] The British reacted negatively to this view:

> There is no warrant for the contention . . . that the obligations undertaken by Spain in relation to the companies in question are divisible into those for the general benefit of Spain and those exclusively for local benefit. To admit such a contention would leave it open, in all cases of conquest and cession, to the succeeding Government to repudiate the obligations of their predecessors on alleged grounds of motive, which, even if they could be proved to have existed, cannot affect the right of property secured by individuals or Companies as a consideration for executing works of local improvement. . . . Such a consideration is, in our opinion, contrary to recognized principles of international law.[103]

D. P. O'Connell declares:

> A successor State cannot be compelled to carry on with an arrangement made by its predecessors which are either contrary to the public interests or obstructive of the realization of its own idea of social development. . . . The expropriation of a concession, however, is only justified when accompanied by a recognition of the equities of capital and labour, and to appropriate to itself the benefits accuring therefrom, is unjustifiably to enrich itself. The concessionaire's equitable interest is an acquired right constituted by his activity, and international law imposes on the successor state a correlative duty to make restitution to the extent of its enrichment.[104]

But the extent of the enrichment may be substantially less than either cost price or anticipated earnings discounted to the present, for enrichment should be judged not in profit and loss terms but in terms of net contribution to national product or welfare. Note the phrase, "advantages which would accrue to the new administration" in the previously quoted United States opinion concerning the Manila Railway Company.

[102]*Ibid.*

[103]Opinion of Nov. 30, 1900, *Foreign Office Confidential Papers*, Vol. 7516, no. 44, appendix no. 71, quoted in O'Connell, *op. cit.*, p. 113.

[104]O'Connell, *op. cit.*, pp. 130–132.

O'Connell goes on to say:

> In order that the rule of international law with respect to compensation
> shall be operative, certain conditions must be fulfilled. The concession
> must have been regularly and *bona fide* obtained, with a proper observ-
> ance of legal forms, and it must not be conditional either on continued
> survival of the predecessor State, or upon any other factor, which cannot
> be fulfilled. The law of predecessor State is the criterion for determining
> these matters. As there is no question of an obligation to continue the
> terms of the concession, it is immaterial that the concession is contrary to
> the public interest of the successor State, or in violation of its treaty
> obligations.[105]

He concludes that state practice generally favors the principle that
all "personal treaties" lapse upon annexation. By personal treaties,
he refers to political treaties (those relating to alliance, neutrality,
amity, or pacific settlement), economic agreements (those concerned
with subsidies, commerce, tariff, and preference), administrative
agreements (those involving matters of post and telegraph, drug
control, protection of women and children, aerial and nautical naviga-
tion), and judicial treaties (those relating to extradition or enforcement of foreign judgments).[106] He does draw a distinction apparently
between annexation and the establishment of a new regime by
extralegal measures, such as revolution. However, here again, the
explicit statements frequently uttered by such regimes to the effect
that they will honor obligations surely carry the implication at least
that they might feel no compulsion to honor those obligations if
deemed contrary to their interests. (It should be recalled that one
of the sources of international law is national practice.) That many
revolutionary regimes have honored the obligations of the ousted
governments because it appeared in the interest of the new regime to
do so does not establish a general, automatic obligation on the part
of successor regimes.

When the United States pressed the case of one of its citizens,
Robert E. Brown, against Great Britain on the grounds that he had
suffered a denial of justice by the predecessor state, the South
African Republic, the United States admitted that there was no
general ability in international law for the torts of a defunct state.
But, as Brierly points out, the Anglo-American Pecuniary Claims

[105] *Ibid.*, p. 134.
[106] *Ibid.*, pp. 15–17.

Tribunal which heard the argument went further, and "held that a state acquiring territory by conquest is under no obligation to take affirmative steps to right a wrong that may have been committed by its predecessors."[107] Brierly concludes, "The law on this point is reasonably clear."[108]

Why then is not the law relative to the reverse situation not equally clear, namely, that a successor state is not obligated to perform on an agreement entered into by the predecessor state that it feels commits an injury against the new state? That a state was founded by the extralegal overthrow of the predecessor regime by a domestic group makes the argument even stronger, for it may be presumed that a revolutionary regime represents national interest more adequately than an annexing power. Nor does revolution constitute an international wrong as does annexation by force. If a revolutionary regime feels that even at the risk of reciprocal action and international censure it must terminate an obligation of the predecessor regime, then the presumption must surely be that that obligation runs contrary to what the new regime feels to be important national interests. Some of the Middle Eastern oil concession agreements are cases in point. Sheik Abdullah H. Tariki, a former general director of petroleum and mineral affairs in Saudi Arabia, observed, "These contracts were made when the Arab countries were too poor and ignorant to know the value of what they were selling . . . . No concession is any good if the people are dissatisfied with it."[109] Implicit in this statement are new national political regimes sensitive to popular dissatisfaction.

Coercion

Where one party is under the domination of another, or by virtue of the relation between them is justified in assuming that the other party will not act in a manner inconsistent with his welfare, a transaction induced by unfair persuasion of the latter, is induced by undue influence and is voidable.[110]

Undue persuasion, even without the element of fear, is enough to

[107]The Robert E. Brown Claim, *British Yearbook of International Law*, 1924, p. 210.

[108]Brierly, *Law of Nations, op. cit.*, p. 149.

[109]Martin, *op. cit.*, p. 52.

[110]*Restatement of the Law of Contracts* (St. Paul: American Law Institute Publishers, 1932), Vol. 2, p. 954.

constitute undue influence within the meaning of this rule. Relationships that ordinarily fall within such a rule include parent-child, guardian-ward, husband-wife. The test is whether or not words of persuasion have undue weight. If the dominated party is in no position to oppose, even if he so desired, then the element of fear or force need not be established.

> Where duress by one person compels another to perform physical acts manifesting apparent assent to a transaction, the transaction does not affect his contractual relations if the party under compulsion
> (a) does not know or have reason to know the nature of the transaction to which he apparently manifests assent, or
> (b) is a mere mechanical inducement without directing will in performing the acts apparently indicating assent.[111]

The analogy of both rules to a colonial administration acting for a subject people is an obvious one. An equally compelling analogy is that of a state that dominates the political institutions of another, such as in the case of a Soviet satellite. In neither case can the dominated society said to be bound by obligations undertaken on its behalf by the dominant authority.

Also relevant to the discussion is the comment by Justice Felix Frankfurter included in his dissent in the *Bethlehem Steel* case.

> Is there any principle which is more familiar or more firmly embedded in the history of Anglo-American law than the basic doctrine that the courts will not permit themselves to be used as instruments of inequity and injustice? Does any principle in our law have more universal application than the doctrine that courts will not enforce transactions in which the relative positions of the parties are such that one has unconsciously taken advantage of the necessities of the other. . . . The courts generally refuse to lend themselves to the enforcement of a "bargain" in which one party has unjustly taken advantage of the economic necessities of the other.[112]

Frankfurter's opinion may not have been convincing in this particular instance because it was no less than the United States government itself that he saw as the party subject to duress. Nonetheless, few would quarrel with the general burden of his dictum. In this case the United States had argued that in contracting with the Bethlehem Steel Corporation the government had been acting under duress in that it had to have ships and no alternative sources were present.

[111]*Ibid.*, p. 950.
[112]United States v. Bethlehem Steel Corp., 315 U.S. 289, 326 (1942).

It was thus compelled to accept Bethlehem's conditions. The government argued that the circumstances were analagous to those under which courts of admiralty had held contracts to the unenforceable. In particular, it pointed to the principle that courts of admiralty "will not tolerate the doctrine that a salvor can take advantage of his situation to avail himself of the calamities of others to drive a bargain, nor will they permit the performance of a public duty to be turned into a traffic of profit."[113] The Supreme Court held that "the captain of a ship in distress on the high seas who is completely at the mercy of his salvor cannot be likened to a sovereign power dealing with an individual contractor."[114]

The court may have been perfectly correct in a case involving the most powerful government in the world, but the same finding might not have been appropriate in the case of a relatively weak government.

Many of the concessions and foreign properties that have been the subject of international legal conflict have been negotiated either with colonial governments or nationally irresponsible regimes clearly dominated by a foreign power, or with weak regimes that saw no alternative but to acquiesce. Consider a hypothetical example of a small, underdeveloped state possessed of some valuable resource but which possesses neither the capital nor the skills to develop this resource. What if a large foreign corporation offers to develop the resource, but only on terms unduly advantageous to itself, such as embodied in some of the early oil concessions? The corporation may be the only firm interested in the project, or — more likely — by arrangement with others it may make certain that no competing offers are made. Later, after the original concession is entered into, other foreign groups come forward with very much more attractive offers. Is the state obliged to suffer under the terms of the original statement? International law is quiet on this point. It would seem that domestic Western law is far more equitable than that applied in the international area.

O'Connell writes:

> The ordinary principle that a new State does not inherit the treaties of its predecessor does not, it would seem, apply to the case of the emergence to full sovereignty of a semi-sovereign or self-governing community. Where treaties are contracted for such a community by its suzerain, protector or

[113]*Ibid.*, p. 304.
[114]*Ibid.*, p. 305.

constitutional superior acting as its agent, such treaties are properly personal to the autonomous or semi-autonomous region, and there is no reason why they should not continue to bind it after the agents' disappearance.[115]

In other words, a colonial power may enter into all sorts of treaties and concessionary agreements for its own benefit on behalf of the colonial society and, upon its withdrawal, expect international tribunals to enforce those obligations upon the newly independent state. It seems that, by analogy with domestic law as enforced in the United States, such a state could unilaterally void any obligations so formed that it felt to be contrary to its interests. And in so doing it could not be held liable for compensation. Surely the only equitable rule would be that a colonial administration or its instrumentalities enter into such obligations at their peril, namely, at the risk of later unilateral abrogation without compensation. If such a rule existed, colonial powers might be more constrained to give greater consideration to the long-run interests of the society which they were binding in obligation.

According to Thomas Huang:

> An outstanding characteristic of the concession is that the grant is not made under legal compulsion, but at the absolute discretion of the conceding state. If this element of discretion is lacking, then in the strict sense, the grant is not a concession. That political pressure and indirect means have been exerted to secure the grant does not necessarily invalidate the concession if the laws of the conceding state have been complied with.[116]

But "political pressure and indirect means" applied by a powerful state to ring a concession out of a weaker state might also constitute duress if it could be shown that either the weaker state could not have refused or that a refusal would have jeopardized that state in some material way. If there were any hint of jeopardy, then the conceding state did not in fact possess "absolute discretion." Presumably, a treaty or concession entered into by a weaker state under these conditions would be void from the start, and a breech of its conditions by the weaker state could not possibly make it liable under international law. If it were otherwise, then international law is nothing more than the law of the jungle.

[115]O'Connell, *op. cit.*, p. 43.
[116]Huang, note 22 *supra*, p. 292.

Unjust Enrichment The principal rebuttal to accepting any justification for a taking without compensation (other than in the exercise of the police power) has been the invoking of the principle of *enrichissement sans cause*, which is held to be one of the general principles of law recognized by civilized nations.[117] In general, what is meant is that "one man's property should not be improved at the expense of another."[118] Kessler, in commenting upon the application of the principle in domestic United States law, observes:

> An owner may not obtain the construction of a building in 1947 at 1945 prices if the delay is not the contractor's fault. And the lessee of a coal field has, upon its depletion, been excused from paying a fixed minimum royalty to the extent that such payment would exceed the total per ton royalty on the amount of coal that could feasibly be mined.[119]

And O'Connell writes:

> The juridical justification for the obligation to pay compensation is to be found in the concept of unjustified enrichment, which lies at the basis of the doctrine of acquired rights. . . . The title holder is not indemnified because the State has committed some tortious act, nor because it has broken a legal relationship existing between him and itself.[120]

"Compensation is paid simply as an equitable alleviation of the enormous economic sacrifice demanded on behalf of the community."[121]

It is generally recognized that municipal law may afford nationals less than full compensation "because in such a case, each individual affected, as a member of the same community, is enriched at the same time, by the sacrifice of others. . . . This explains the diminishing scale of compensation as the circle of individuals affected widens."[122] In the Anglo-Iranian Oil Company case, dismissed by the International Court of Justice on jurisdictional grounds, a dissenting opinion was entered in which it was said that an invocation of the interests of the nationalizing state would not justify internationally a

[117]Carlson, 5 *op. cit.*, p. 265.
[118]"The Fetish of Impossibility in the Law of Contracts," *Columbia Law Review*, Vol. 53 (1953), pp. 89-100.
[119]*Ibid.*, p. 100.
[120]O'Connell, *op. cit.*, pp. 103-104.
[121]Georges S. F. C. Kaeckenbeech, *British Yearbook of International Law*, Vol. 12 (1935), p. 16.
[122]B. Cheng, "Expropriation in International Law," *The Solicitor*, Vol. 21 (1954), p. 100.

payment less than full compensation to a foreigner who was "by the very fact of nationalization, . . . cast from the national community in whose favour nationalization . . . (had) been carried out."[123]

Upon reading the literature, one might well conclude that inadequate stress is placed the words "unjustified" or "without cause," in the phrase *enrichissement sans cause*. The implication is that enrichment for cause is justified. What cause? One searches in vain for an authoritative statement. Therefore, it would seem pointless for nationalizing states to argue that there was justified cause before international tribunals, as some have suggested they are honor-bound to do if their political leaders are sincere in the charges they have frequently made in public utterances against Western enterprise.

For example, in canceling the concession of the Standard Oil Company of Bolivia,[124] the Bolivian government charged that the company had provoked a war in order to acquire a location for a pipeline in the Chaco. In commenting on the case, J. L. Kunz casually dismisses this charge as nonsense.[125] But was it? Perhaps so, but it seems that the whole case could have hung on this issue. The apparent absence of a serious international investigation of the charge only leads one to the belief that even if a strong presumption could have been established against the company in this regard, the obligation of the Bolivian government under international law for prompt, effective, and adequate compensation would not have been affected. In the Anglo-Iranian Oil case at least one thoroughly competent observer has charged that the British company had been unjustly enriching itself for years at the expense of the Iranian government through sales to the British government at reduced prices, arrears in royalty payments, the withholding of royalties for damages for which the Iranian government was not responsible, and the taxation of profits by the British government before division with the Iranian government.[126] Why, then, did not the Iranian government argue that the taking was justified, enrichment with cause? It is obvious: there was no reason at all to anticipate that any inter-

[123]*International Court of Justice Reports (1952)*, p. 162.

[124]"Executive Decree of 13 March 1937," 1 *Annuario Administrativo de 1937* (Bolivia) 519 (1937); translation in *U.S. Foreign Relations*, Vol. 5 (1937), p. 277.

[125]J. L. Kunz, "The Mexican Expropriations," *New York University Law Quarterly Review*, Vol. 17 (1940), p. 372.

[126]Max Thornburg, "The Anglo-Iranian Oil Trouble," Case ICR 217 (1959), Harvard Graduate School of Business Administration.

national tribunal would hear such evidence. Otherwise, why are the writers so silent on what constitutes cause for an uncompensated taking?

Police Power   The preceding discussion leads into a consideration of the police power, which is one of the unquestioned powers of any sovereign state. For example, what if a firm specifically refuses to abide by municipal law or decree — as did the United States oil companies in Cuba and British oil companies in Ceylon when directed to accept Soviet crude for refining and distribution? That one disagrees politically with the municipal law is irrelevant to the legal argument in a situation in which national sovereignty is recongized.[127] Other cases in point are Ghana's decision (April 1961) to annul foreign-owned concessions if found "prejudicial to the public safety or interest"[128] and the seizure by a Brazilian state of a subsidy of the International Telephone and Telegraph Corporation on the grounds that the latter was providing inadequate service.[129] The point is that even if prejudice to the "public safety or interest" or refusal to provide adequate service were established to everyone's satisfaction, these facts would still be irrelevant to international law as it stands. For instance, the Foreign Aid and Sugar Acts, already cited, which threaten to terminate United States aid and commerce if debts to United States businessmen are not recognized, make no distinction between a taking that arises out of acts prejudicial to public safety or interest and a taking that does not.

In 1872 the United States Supreme Court in the *Slaughter House* cases[130] gave the name "police power" — which it stated to be "incapable of very exact definition or limitation" — to the general principle stated in a passage of Kent's *Commentaries on American Law* to the effect that "every person ought to use his property as not to injure his neighbors, and that private interests must be made subservient to the general interests of the Community."[131]

---

[127]Jeanne Kuebler, *Protection of Investment in Backward Countries* (Washington: Editorial Research Record Reports, Vol. II, No. 2, July 11, 1962), pp. 504–505.

[128]*Ibid.*, p. 506.

[129]*Ibid.*, p. 501.

[130]John W. Wallace (ed.), *Cases Argued and Adjudged in the Supreme Court of the United States* (Washington: W. H. & O. H Morrison, 1873), p. 36.

[131]J. Kent, *Commentaries on American Law* (Boston: Little, Brown and Company, 1873), Vol. 3, p. 340.

Mitchell comments:

> The cases seem to suggest that, at any rate so far as it operates on the contracts of public authorities, the ambit of the power as being inalienable, or as overriding contractual rights is somewhat narrower than is suggested by the phrase "public welfare." The narrower bounds, although imperfectly defined, appear to be limited to regulations necessary for the protection of public health, public safety, and public morals.[132]

In the earlier American cases a broader definition had been advanced, such as when Justice Stephen J. Field in an 1884 opinion[133] emphasized the economic aspects of the welfare of the community in speaking of the police power. He described it as the power "to prescribe regulations to promote the health, peace, morals, education and good order of the people and to legislate so as to increase the industries of the State, develop its resources and add to its wealth and prosperity." It would seem that as a State becomes richer, the definition of the police power tends to become narrower. In a subsistence society any act limiting or lessening the resources available to that society could reasonably lead to an intervention of the state through its police power. There is no margin for misuse. As a state becomes wealthier, such a use of the police power perhaps becomes more difficult to justify.

Kunz points out that it is within the sovereign right of any government to expropriate (to take and use with compensation) property as a sanction for the violation of criminal law, to regulate or even destroy it in the interest of public welfare. International law recognizes the distinction known in American common law between taking in exercise of eminent domain, which requires compensation, and the exercise of the police power, which does not. But where property is in fact taken and title transferred to others, expropriation is deemed to have taken place. Kunz concludes:

> That is why cases cannot be quoted, as some writers do, as precedents for expropriation without compensation where the exercise of the police power affected private property rights of aliens without compensation.[134]

For example, in the case of the emancipation of slaves, where title to property was abolished, the title was not transferred. Nor was title transferred when liquor was destroyed under the Prohibition

[132]Mitchell, *op. cit.*, p. 97.
[133]Barbar v. Connolly, 113 U.S. 27 (1884).
[134]Kunz, *op. cit.*, p. 350.

Amendment. But surely this distinction is not always valid. What of the seizure of contraband drugs and arms? Are the goods always destroyed?

In commenting upon the Mexican expropriation of foreign oil properties, Kunz refers to the labor dispute in which the companies refused to abide by a government edict as a pretext deliberately engineered by the Mexicans.[135] Was it? In a public statement Emery N. Cleaves, vice president of the Celanese Corporation of America, said of the Mexican record:

> As far as the dispossesed oil companies [in Mexico] are concerned, I believe the present managements readily admit that their predecessors made a mistake from which they learned a valuable lesson. Moreover, six companies were not expropriated, being willing to accept the government offer, and today are still operating on terms more favorable than is now possible in the Middle East.[136]

If the Mexican government position was so impossible, why did six foreign oil companies continue to operate? It seems odd that almost never do international legal writers or tribunals give more than passing thought to the charges lodged by foreign governments against the Western companies being expropriated. At least as defined in some of the earlier American cases, the use of the police power might be justified. One would like to have some of these cases argued on that basis. However, as international law is presently formulated, it is doubtful that the arguments would be heard.

In the initial phases of some of these conflicts the foreign state did not threaten to confiscate but merely attempted to force a foreign company to operate in a different fashion. If the United Fruit Company had acceded to the Guatemalan demands to release abandoned banana land for cultivation in other crops, would the Guatemalan government have attempted to expropriate them? One does not know. A publication of the National Planning Association admits that the holding of abandoned banana land out of cultivation by the United Fruit Company has caused unnecessary hardship to the Guatemalan economy.[137] But the United States Department

[135]*Ibid.*

[136]E. N. Cleaves, "Economic Climate for Manufacturing in Mexico," address delivered to the Conference on Business and Industrial Opportunities in Mexico, Michigan State University, Feb. 2, 1957.

[137]S. May and G. Plaza, *The Case Study of the United Fruit Company in Latin America* (Washington: National Planning Association, 1958), p. 104.

of State declared at the time of the threatened seizure:

> The Government of the United States . . . sees no shred of justification in
> agrarian legislation sanctioning the seizure of property of American
> citizens in Guatemala contrary to international norms.[138]

And, the company took the position that all of the lands were necessary to its continued existence. Why did the United States government not investigate the charges more seriously and objectively
before quoting international law to the Guatemalan government?
The implication is that such charges were considered to be irrelevant,
even if they could have been established.

The use of the police power in the Guatemalan and Mexican
cases, as in other situations, has led to threatened or actual expropriation. If a foreign owner refuses to accede to the police power of a
foreign state, what recourse is there but for the state to expropriate?
But in determining the compensation due the foreign owners, will an
international tribunal recognize the economic injury caused by the
manner in which the alien has operated his property? There is no
reason to believe so, for there is no precedent. Therefore, the distinction which Kunz draws between the exercise of eminent domain
and of police power is not quite as clear-cut as he makes out.

Summary   After examining the various doctrines which might
conceivably be invoked to protect the national interests of a state
injured by aliens, it seems quite obvious that as presently defined
there is little reason for an injured state to expect the application by
international bodies or foreign governments of any of these doctrines
in such a manner as to protect its interests. The central problem
originates in the fact that what constitutes *national or public interest*,
and significant injury thereto, has been only vaguely and inadequately
defined. Oddly, domestic contract law as practiced in certain Western
countries seems to have gone very much further than international
law in recognizing the supremacy of national interest and reading
such recognition into contracts as an implied condition.

> In 1595, Queen Elizabeth declared that a man is more strongly bound to
> his country than to a private promise and that princes are not bound by
> their contracts when the contract results in public injury.[139]

[138]Aide-memoire by U.S. Department of State, Aug. 29, 1953, *Department of
State Bulletin*, Vol. 29 (1953), p. 357.

[139]Zouche, in Hill, *op. cit.*, pp. 46–47.

The doctrine of *rebus sic stantibus* is likewise too obscure to be relied upon by an allegedly injured state. From the point of view of national interest, when is performance under a contract or treaty unreasonably burdensome? The authorities are silent. No tests in economic, social, or political terms are even suggested. Yet, for a society undergoing accelerated development, flexibility in legal relation is even more essential than for the more mature, less dramatically changing societies of the developed nations. Circumstances are constantly arising that could not have been foreseen but which, if they had, would have altered the nature of the original agreement.

Until there is substantially more agreement on what constitutes national interest, it is surely unreasonable to expect nations — particularly the underdeveloped — to limit their individual sovereignties to the extent of submitting to international tribunals the sovereign right to alter or terminate international agreements or contracts deemed by the state to run counter to vital national interests. And the rules relating to the obligations of successor states, as presently defined, are unduly favorable to the more stable political regimes of the West. Almost by definition, vital national interests as recognized by a revolutionary regime — or a newly independent regime — are very different from those recognized by the ousted ruling group or colonial power. When one introduces the *doctrine of coercion* into the discussion, it becomes clear that equity demands that any agreement entered into by nations of greatly unequal power should be subjected to certain tests before being enforced by any international body.

In examining the *doctrine of unjust enrichment*, one finds that the doctrine operates very largely in one direction. It would be perfectly logical, and plausible, for a state to show that a foreign interest had unjustly enriched itself at the expense of its economy or human resources. There is no reason, however, to believe that international tribunals would even recognize such justification for a taking with partial or no compensation — let alone listen to and consider, the evidence. If this judgment is not correct, then all that can be said is that there is a strange absence of cases of this type in view of the very checkered history of Western enterprise in Africa, Latin America, and Asia.

Finally, the *doctrine of the police power* as it appears in international law has been restricted to a very narrow range. A direct and immediate relation to public health, safety, and morals must be established. There must be no hint that the invocation of the police power was a pretext for an uncompensated transfer of title. On the other hand, as suggested in earlier American cases, a broader application of the police power may be justifiable within a near-subsistence or economically weak state where an optimum use and distribution of resources may be fully as urgent as the control of, say, a disease.

The Nature of Injuries to States

J. L. Brierly observes:

> The conduct of a state does not fall under international law merely because it may affect the interests of other states; this may be true and yet the matter in question may fall within what is called the "domestic jurisdiction" of a single state. For example, legislation restricting immigration is not a matter which affects the interests only of the countries of immigration; it creates serious difficulties for countries which have a surplus of population, and where economic life has come to depend on emigration facilities . . . practically the whole sphere of international economic relations, except where mutual concessions have been arranged by treaty, belongs to domestic jurisdiction.[140]

Tariffs, raw materials, markets — "matters which often underlie the rivalries of modern states and provide the causes, if not the occasions, of their disputes"[141] — lie almost entirely beyond international law. Brierly goes on to say that international law can never become really effective until it can include at least some of the matters now lying within the realm of domestic jurisdiction. He concludes:

> . . . for so long as it has to be admitted that one state may have its reasonable interests injuriously affected by the unreasonable action of another, and yet have no legal basis for complaint, it is likely that the injured state, if it is strong enough, will seek by other means the redress that the law can afford it.[142]

And if a state is not strong enough? It may seek to indemnify itself for injury by moving against vested foreign interests within its jurisdiction. In the post-World War II years, because of the unsteady

[140]Brierly, *Law of Nations, op. cit.*, p. 75.
[141]*Ibid.*
[142]*Ibid.*

power balance between the Soviet Union and the United States, the weaker states have been able to seek such self-indemnification without too much fear of physical retaliation by the more powerful interested states. The failure of the Anglo-French-Israeli attack on Egypt to accomplish any constructive purpose probably writes the end to the forceful intervention on behalf of Western capital, at least so long as the present power balance remains. The West also has, of course, the weapons of withheld economic and military assistance and closed markets. Such retaliation for moves against Western business interests, which some United States congressmen have occasionally demanded, is of doubtful value. In many areas such threats result merely in an expansion of Soviet activity. The withholding of financing for the Aswan Dam is a good example. Indeed, some of the underdeveloped nations — as, for example, Turkey — show signs of being somewhat uneasy about the degree to which they have committed themselves to the Western cause, thereby undermining their own freedom of action in case of conflict of interest with the West.

It seems much has been done to encourage this system of international blackmail by failing to construct a system of international law which would adequately recognize and protect the interests of the rapidly evolving, weaker states. Naturally, the Soviet bloc wishes to prolong the period of international anarchy as long as possible. One suspects that the Soviet effort may be very largely effective until it is recognized (1) that a genuine conflict of legal principle exists, (2) that Western-derived international law no longer necessarily represents the "general principles of law recognized by civilized nations," (3) that the emergence of nationally responsible political regimes in many of the non-Western nations necessitates a restructuring of commercial and business relationships regardless of formal legal obligations, (4) that the situation is so complex and shifting that principles of equity rather than a code of law would perhaps be more appropriate, and (5) that a system of equity must necessarily encompass all dimensions, from political and economic interests to psychological reactions, the overriding criteria being "the general interest." The problem then becomes one of defining "the general interest."

Origin To define "the general interest," it is necessary to examine the originating instrumentalities of relevant injuries to states. The following classification is offered as useful:

A — A colonial administration or protecting power.

B — A dominating state, or its instrumentalities (including private groups of nationals).

C — An indigenous, but nationally irresponsible regime.

D — The operation of domestic law of a foreign state, generally more powerful in terms of effective reciprocity.

E — The persistence of contract provisions after a change of circumstances unforeseeable by a reasonable man at the time of agreement.

Whether a given international obligation is binding on a foreign state or not should be determined in part by testing the validity of its origin. Although one cnnot exhaust all of the permutations and combinations, several tests for validity suggest themselves:

In respect to A *and* B

Was the agreement — or the laws under which it was made — freely ratified by an independent, sovereign body of indigenous origin?

Could the dominated state have refused agreement?

If it had refused, could it reasonably have expected material injury in any way?

Did the dominating nation — or its instrumentalities — deliberately limit, at the time of agreement, the alternatives from which the dominated state might have chosen?

In respect to A, B, *and* C

Was the agreement of such a nature that a reasonably intelligent man would have seen that it would operate contrary to the interests of the society in which it was to be performed or on whose behalf it was presumably to be performed?

In respect to D

Was the injury by the foreign state intended?

Would the abolition of the offending domestic law cause a greater relative injury to the enacting state than to the injured state?

Could the initially injured state have brought about comparable injury to the other state by domestic legislation?

In respect to E

> If both parties had known at the time of agreement of the foreseen circumstances, how would they have reacted?

> Does the change of circumstance materially alter the relationship of the parties?

> Does the change of circumstance burden one party with significant injury or risk of injury not contemplated at the time of agreement?

In general, injury to a state may arise in event the state is inarticulate, represented by an irresponsible regime, is relatively weak in effective political or military power, or is economically unable to threaten complete reciprocity in event domestic legislation by another country runs contrary to its interest. All four conditions characterize the recent past of many of the newer states of Latin America, Africa, and Asia, and may still hold to varying degrees.

The underlying principle implicit in these comments is that *the instrumentality or national of a relatively powerful state, in entering into an agreement with a relatively weak state, must expect — in event of subsequent challenge — to carry the burden of proof in establishing that the agreement is not contrary to vital interests of the weaker state.* Western firms with long and successful records in non-Western areas have acted precisely on this premise. Management has deliberately considered company policy and practice from the point of view of the long-run interests of the non-Western society.[143] Whether those interests happened to be articulated or enforced by the contemporary colonial administration, or by the irresponsible, self-seeking local elite, was irrelevant. In the long run, security of assets and market position rested upon genuine mutuality of interest. As unforeseen circumstances arose, agreements were altered — often at the initiative of the Western management itself. Unfortunately, far too few firms operated — (and are operating) — in this manner — that is, in their own, enlightened, self-interest, or, looking at the other side of the coin, in the long-run interest of the host state.

Definition Injury may be usefully catalogued into injury originating abroad (in Country or Countries *A*) and that originating

[143]For example, see R. D. Robinson, *Cases in International Business* (New York: Holt, Rinehart and Winston, Inc., 1962), pp. 55, 100.

within the injured state (Country *B*). Possible injury to a state may be found in:

Injuries originating abroad (within A)

1. Tariffs or exchange restrictions enacted by A that impede the marketing of *B*'s products.
2. Discrimination by *A* in respect to *B*'s entry into an important national market.
3. Refusal by *A* to sell to *B* needed goods and services on reasonable terms.
4. Enforcement of immigration quotas by *A* against nationals of *B*.
5. Refusal by *A* to permit the employment by *B* of the skilled nationals of *A*.
6. Refusal by *A* to deliver economic and military assistance that had been promised and in anticipation of which *B* has committed its own resources or given some variety of irrevocable political or military commitment.
7. An international agreement by Countries *A*, or nationals thereof, to fix prices or other terms of trade materially affecting *B* — without *B*'s consent.
8. The withholding or taxation by *A* of foreign earnings derived from operations within *B* and which are the property of *B* or of its nationals, without *B*'s consent.
9. The sale of goods, that are competitive with those of *B*, by *A* within *B* or within third countries at prices below cost.
10. The arming by *A* of a state hostile to *B*, or the grant of other aid and support, thereby causing *B* to commit a greater share of its resources to defense than would otherwise have been necessary.

Injuries originating within the injured state (within B):

1. The capitalization, within an enterprise owned by *A* or its nationals in the territory of *B*, of resources that have their origin in *A* but which were available within *B* at equal or lower cost.
2. As adequate local capital becomes available, the refusal to permit local ownership at a fair price (that is, anticipated future earnings discounted to present value).
3. The unnecessary use or wastage of *B*'s scarce resources by instrumentalities of *A* working within *B*.

4. The export of raw materials or partly finished goods from B by instrumentalities of A that could be further processed within B without substantially reducing the competitive position of those goods.

5. Refusal of an A-owned enterprise in B to supply the local market in a reasonable and equitable manner.

6. Refusal of an A-owned enterprise in B to export into third markets if such be reasonable and profitable.

7. Unreasonable restraint, by an instrumentality of A within B, upon B's nationals in respect to participation in the proceeds flowing from a contract.

8. The import, by an A-owned enterprise in B, of goods and materials, the local development of which is economically and commercially feasible (if the foreign exchange used for the import is scarce).

9. Injury caused by A-owned enterprise in B to locally owned enterprise in B.

10. In the absence of a further contribution by instrumentalities of A of goods or services not available within B, the repatriation of profits from B to A by those instrumentalities after the investment plus a reasonable profit has been recouped (if the relevant foreign exchange is in scarce supply).

11. The enforcement of the terms of an agreement entered into initially by an instrumentality of A (acting as either a monopolist or monopsonist in relation to services of products of B, a weaker state) when other competent groups appear and offer significantly better terms from the point of view of B.

12. Ownership by A's nationals or instrumentalities of properties or rights within B of such a basic and important character that ownership by aliens infringes upon the independence and sovereignty of B. (A suggested test: would A tolerate ownership by B's nationals of similar properties and rights within A and which constitute the same importance relative to the gross national products of A and B?)

13. The refusal by instrumentalities of A, active within the territory of B, to accede to any laws or regulations laid down by the legally constituted authorities of B, whether an action before an international body is contemplated by A or not.

14. Undue influence upon the local government, or active support or participation in opposition political groups or movements.

15. Acts of violence against, or the transgression of, the legal rights of local nationals.
16. The use of the contract or enterprise controlled by *A* nationals by the government of *A* as a political or economic lever against *B*.

Such injuries as those suggested above may constitute important impediments to national economic and political growth, as a few Western economists and others have begun to recognize.[144] Some of these injuries lend themselves to fairly accurate calculation.

Suggested Rule The following general rules might be a useful guide, although further clarification — which perhaps can only be established through practice and precedent — is obviously needed.

Rule 1

Real or juridical persons who enter into international contracts that are clearly contrary to important national interests of the state or states in which a material part of the contract is to be performed do so at their own risk. The contract is null and void from the start, and no obligations on the part of the injured state arise, and hence there is no question of compensation.

Rule 2

Contractors who perform on international contracts, even though the contract be legal and binding within the meaning of Rule 1, may forfeit all of their contractual rights if their performance is conducted in such a manner as to be contrary to the national interests of such state or states. The obligation of the latter to pay adequate, prompt and effective compensations in event of a taking terminates upon such a finding, though an obligation to pay some form of partial compensation may be invoked under international law.

Rule 3

In event the government of an alien contractor (Government *A*) causes injury to the contracting state (*B*), and the contractor's property or rights are seized by *B* in retaliation, the contractor has an international claim against *B* for prompt, effective, and adequate compensation as soon as *A* compensates *B* for the original injury.

[144]For example, see G. Myrdal, *An International Economy* (New York: Harper & Row, Publishers, 1956); M. D. Bryce, *Industrial Development, A Guide for Accelerating Economic Growth* (New York: McGraw-Hill Book Company, 1960), especially chapters 2 and 10; and R. D. Robinson, "Conflicting Interests in International Business Investment," *Boston University Business Review*, Vol. 7 (Spring 1960), p. 3.

These general rules should be interpreted very specifically by international tribunals.

There seems to be no equitable reason why the value of property
or rights acquired by an alien and which are taken by a public interest
should be compensated except in the medium of exchange in which the
investment was actually made. For example, compensation paid for
assets acquired by an alien through the process of plowing back local
earnings surely need not be in anything other than local currency.
W. C. Gorden has so appropriately observed:

> If the growth [*i.e.*, of foreign investment] occurs as the result of rein-
> vesting earnings, capital gains and losses, a gift of property, or as a result
> of the change of the country of residence of the owner of a piece of prop-
> erty, it is not so clear that the creditor country has provided anything
> worth having so far as the debtor is concerned. The foreign investment
> has contributed nothing to justify the repayment burden which is sub-
> sequently felt by the debtor country.[145]

Gorden was speaking of the eventual repatriation of earnings. How
much more the repayment burden if one is speaking of compensation.
The rule, in a sense the logical implication of those already outlined,
might be along the following line:

Rule 4
    Payment of compensation by Government B for property or rights
    of a citizen or legal entity of Country A taken by Government B may be
    made in the currency in which the investment was made.

Institutional Implications

Inherent in this argument is the assumption that some competent
judicial body exists. Such, of course, has not been true. The only
agencies operating in this area are the International Court of Justice,
mixed claims commissions, national claims commissions, and arbitral
tribunals. The *International Court of Justice* hears only conflicts
between states; its forum is not available to private persons unless
their cause be espoused by their respective states. Because of the
pre-eminence of political interests, states are generally reluctant to

[145]W. C. Gorden, "International Investments: Process and Motive," in P. D.
Zook, *Economic Development and International Trade*, (Dallas: Southern Methodist
University Press, 1959), p. 61.

do so. Furthermore, many states, including the United States, have refused to accept compulsory jurisdiction. *Mixed claims commissions* are established by separate treaty when events generate many claims by the nationals of one state against another state, or its nationals. A mixed claims commission, composed of nationals of the two states at issue, is limited in time and area of jurisdiction by the treaty that created it. In addition, the commissioners are more likely to be advocates of national interests than of law. A *national claims commission* may be a permanent or semipermanent body to allocate funds collected by the parent government on behalf of its nationals from a foreign government. Funds so collected are allocated to national claimants by the national claims commission on the basis of the value affixed to the injury suffered. Inasmuch as the intergovernment settlement is frequently of a political nature and represents some variety of compromise, each claimant may receive proportionately less than he feels justified. In the actual negotiations only representatives of the two governments meet. In this atmosphere, principles of legal equity are rarely relevant. *Arbitral tribunals* are appointed as authorized in the contract or agreement alleged to have been breached to hear and decide a particular issue. Arbitration is also specified in a number of international agreements, such as the General Agreement on Tariffs and Trade. Although by far the most popular means of settling international dispute among private persons or firms of different nationalities, the arbitration process encounters many difficulties. Chief among these are (1) the lack of uniformity of the law applied, (2) the lack of adequate reporting, (3) the problems of enforceability (in federal states such as the United States), and (4) the time and expense.[146]

Strongly urged by a number of students of the problem is the creation of a special system of tribunals to hear private international cases. These tribunals would be permanent and require no government espousal of causes. Member governments, by treaty, would obligate themselves to enforce judgments.[147]

[146]For a discussion of these institutions, see Martin Domke (ed.), *International Trade Arbitration* (New York: American Arbitration Association, 1958) and Richard B. Lillich, *International Claims: Their Adjudication by National Commissions* (Binghamton: N.Y. Syracuse University Press, 1962).

[147]For two such suggestions, see Louis B. Sohn in Domke, *op. cit.*, pp. 63–76, and Richard D. Robinson, *Private Foreign Investment* (Washington: Hearings before the Subcomm. on Foreign Trade Policy of the Comm. on Ways and Means, H. R., 85th Cong., 2d Sess. Dec. 1–5, 1958), p. 554.

3
Economic And Political
Dimensions

The many conflicts inherent in the social, economic, and political disparity between the wealthier mechanized states of the West and the poorer, nonmechanized states of the non-West makes one suspect that a general community of interest will arise within international business only to the extent that international bodies and Western governments — and business itself — observe the rules of equity of the type suggested at the conclusion of Chapter 2. To make these rules operational, however, an important question left dangling must be answered: How may the national interest be defined? If the concept cannot be defined, the suggested rules collapse. By "definition," the author means the description of a method of analysis sufficiently objective and tangible to create a strong possibility that different persons will be led to similar conclusions under similar circumstances. If they are not so led, the generalizations of Chapters 1 and 2 are meaningless.

In Chapter 3 an attempt will be made to define the national interest in as precise terms as possible. By utilizing the tools of modern economic and political theory one can whittle down the national interest concept to tangible size. The question to be answered is: How may the impact of a business investment on a non-Western society be estimated in terms of the host nation's long-run interests? These interests may not be articulated, nor even sensed, by the political elite *of the moment*. Eventually, to be sure, they will be, and in a very explicit sort of way. National interest in these non-Western states may be equated with sustained material improvement at a catch-up rate under a modernizing, sovereign national government.

Four components are present — economic growth, political modernization, sovereignty, and national unity. For purposes of the following discussion, it will be assumed that given the international environment of the mid-1960's, sovereignty and national unity are prerequisites for political modernization. That is, anything easing the exercise of national sovereignty or the consolidation of national unity is assumed to contribute to political modernization. The implicit assumption that national sovereignty and national unity are necessary preconditions for political modernization may be effectively challenged if one speaks of past or future eras — that is, of any other than the present "national era." In this era, with the contemporary international environment, a good case in support of this underlying assumption can be made. In any event, national interest is almost universally defined now to include national sovereignty and national unity. The interesting variables of the present, then, are economic growth and political modernization. Eventually, as suggested in the final chapter, these processes may create conditions (new values) that compel changes in those factors held constant; that is, national sovereignty may give way to a supranational sovereignty and national unity, or to cross-national functional unity.

The problem splinters into two closely related parts: (1) How can one estimate the effect of a Western business enterprise on the long-run economic growth rate of the host society? (2) How can one estimate the enterprise's effect on the modernization of a sovereign national government? The two queries are related because it is unlikely that growth in the physical well-being of a people can long proceed without parallel development of political functions. The reverse is equally unlikely. Hence, when national growth is spoken of, it refers to both economic growth[1] and political modernization.[2] The author cannot envision the two apart.

The reason for attempting at least a semirigorous analysis of what a firm proposes to do in an underdeveloped country within the context of the national interests of that country lies in the near certainty that the host government will analyze the project in similar terms — if not at first, then later. The Western businessman must be prepared to defend the utility of his local enterprise — and his relationship with it — in terms of sustained economic growth and political modernization. If he cannot, he compounds his risks to the point of jeopardizing

[1]Sustained increase in real, per-capita, national product.
[2]Sustained increase in the degree to which political functions are affectively neutral, collectively oriented, universalistic, specific, and achievement-oriented. (See Chapter 1, pp. 43.)

his entire business relationship. The fact that he may get away with such disregard for the time being is beside the point. In the long run he is helping to dig the grave of the free enterprise concept, whatever his immediate profits might be. Social responsibility is inherent in the concept of freedom — whether it be freedom of speech or of enterprise.

Impact on Economic Growth

It has been said that "the nation has become not merely a political system, but also an incentive for economic growth."[3] Western enterprise has been an important factor in generating that economic incentive through the social-psychological and economic processes described in Chapters 1 and 2 — an incentive which is really founded on an induced belief in the possibility and desirability of constant material improvement. But, one suspects, because of the unbalanced economies Western businessmen have helped to create in those countries where mining and plantation crops have been important, and because of their efforts to maintain 100-percent ownership and control of their foreign ventures, Western business generally has failed to provide a really viable basis for sustained national growth in the non-Western nations. Local resources were developed and used in producing for foreign customers. Management and control was kept in foreign hands. Local ownership was barred. A minimum of the value added was retained by the host economy. The calculus used for investment decisions — which involved local resources (land, labor, and so forth) as well as foreign — maximized the benefits to the foreign economies, not those accruing to the local (except as these interests might accidentally coincide). Where investment was concentrated in a few minerals or crops, the probability of overlap was less than would have been true in the case of more diversified enterprise.

In relation to southeast Asia Lucien Pye notes:

> It is significant that the pattern of Western economic activities in Southeast Asia has been one in which the merchant and trader were followed by those involved in the extractive enterprises — in mining, oil, and plantation crops — but this did not lead to a higher stage of industrial production. By creating dual economies in most of the Southeast Asian soci-

[3]Karl von Vorys, "Some Political Incentives for Economic Development in India, Pakistan, Burma and Ceylon," *The Western Political Quarterly*, Vol. xi, No. 4 (Dec. 1959), p. 1064.

eties, this pattern of Westernized economic activity gave the peoples of the region a sense of the possibility of a higher standard of living, but it did not provide an adequate basis for an expanding economy that might have improved the lot of everyone in the region.[4]

By economic growth, of course, is meant sustained increase in the goods and services produced by a population measured on a per-capita basis. Therefore, the first measure of the impact on economic growth suggesting itself is the direct effect the operation of a Western enterprise has on the per-capita national income of the host society, that is, the *national income effect*. The experience of many underdeveloped countries has pinpointed foreign exchange strangulation as a serious (probably chronic) deterrent to sustained rapid growth. Consequently, the *balance of payments effect* is a second important measure, a measure really concerned with a nation's external economic balance in a structural sense, a factor partially determining a nation's ability to sustain growth. Inasmuch as increase in directly productive investment requires a higher level of social overhead investment, often only available from public sources, the *public revenue effect* is a third measure. This measure involves internal economic balance and is likewise a measure of one of the factors affecting a nation's growth capability.

All three concepts provide only relatively short-run measures, for growth is sustained in the long run by the allocation of resources to ever more productive use (*i.e.*, to uses increasing productive capacity) and by continuous innovation, the latter relationship being convincingly demonstrated by Everett Hagen.[5] The fourth measure, then, has to do with the *growth-generating effect*, which leads into the political area.

At the outset, it is necessary to underscore one important difficulty in using any of these measures in specific situations. *The measures are relative, not absolute.* That is, although a given project may be judged to have a positive effect on per-capita national product, yet the commitment of scarce resources to that project may be judged contrary to national interest because some other project would make a larger contribution. This is precisely where so many studies relating

[4]Lucian Pye in G. A. Almond and J. S. Coleman (eds.), *The Politics of the Developing Areas* (Princeton: Princeton University Press, 1960), p. 105.

[5]Everett E. Hagen, *On the Theory of Social Change* (Homewood, Ill.: Dorsey Press, 1962).

to the effects of foreign investment fall down.[6] The mere proof that a given project is of benefit is inadequate so long as any scarce factors are involved, unless it can be demonstrated that these factors are not likely to contribute more to growth if employed in other uses. This observation is equally relevant to the discussion of the balance of payments effect, the public revenue effect, and growth-generating effect.

It should also be borne in mind that for virtually every project in which Western enterprise may be involved something of value will be destroyed or expended. *One cannot simply add up the benefits*, as many writers have done, and thereby derive the measure of impact.

Furthermore, any quantitative statement of the national income, balance of payments, or public revenue effect of a given enterprise necessarily assumes a price system, for one works in money terms — given the need to aggregate. If these effects are used to determine the "desirability" of a given enterprise from the point of view of economic growth, (1) factor prices must be assumed to represent the relative contributions per unit of the various factors and products to the growth process, and (2) these relative contributions must be assumed to reflect the relative availabilities of these factors and products. There are several reasons why current prices may not reflect these relationships even approximately: (1) market organization may be so poorly developed as to affect supply-price and demand-price elasticities (that is, simply by improving market organization, elasticities may be changed); (2) the factor market may be deliberately controlled; (3) demand may be determined by factors other than long-term growth considerations (that is, prices cannot be assumed to represent marginal utility in terms of growth);[7] (4) price relationships may change over time in an unanticipated way, perhaps because of the projected enterprise itself, general economic growth, or structural change. (In

---

[6]For example, S. May and G. Plaza, *The Case Study of The United Fruit Company in Latin America* (Washington: National Planning Association, 1958); as well as other NPA case studies.

[7]In an emerging society — one emerging into the era of economic incentive and mass consumption — the *personal* marginal utility of immediate consumption may be set by the individual consumer almost without reference to *sustained growth* in consumption, which fact is reflected in the price structures. Therefore, current prices do not cause an allocation of goods and services of the sort to maximize growth, or even to approach that state of affairs.

an underdeveloped country, where economic predictions are likely to be unsophisticated and the market poorly organized — including the futures' market — current prices are much less likely to be set in anticipation of future changes in relationship than in a more developed society.) Therefore, in measuring the impact of a given project, assumptions about present and future prices should be made explicit.

Some economists have observed that the contribution to economic growth of individual projects cannot be measured meaningfully,[8] so interdependent is a national economy. In terms of precise quantification this claim is undoubtedly correct. But it is likewise true that the development of precise measures for an *entire* development program is an unrewarding objective, even if one postulated perfect knowledge about the intentions of all state agencies and private entrepreneurs. National growth is not an *impersonal economic* process. It is, first, a *human* process generated out of the battle waged endlessly in man's personality between desire and innovation, on the one hand, and lassitude and traditionalism, on the other. How will individuals react to given economic opportunities? Surely not in any predetermined manner, one guesses. Second, the growth process can be measured only in part by economic concepts, for *political* modernization is an important component, a component lending itself even less well to quantification. Therefore, one should be forewarned not to lean too heavily on economic measures alone. In the final analysis, a judgment based on knowledge and experience must govern, not mathematical formulas. More simply, economic growth is not the only goal.

It is the author's view that measures of contribution to economic growth applied to specific projects are more meaningful than aggregate sector analysis. Processes and products may have widely different economic implications even though identified with the same sector. One problem is that in the usual analysis industries are aggregated rather than processes. However, final assembly in Industry *A* may be much more similar to final assembly in Industry *B* in its economic implications than to the rest of Industry *A*. Labor and capital intensities, external economies and diseconomies, income coefficients, input-output relationships, consumption and savings coefficients, and export and import coefficients may vary enormously from one process to another within the same industry. Figures repre-

[8]Siro Lombardini, "Quantitative Analysis in the Determination of the Efficiency of Investment in Underdeveloped Areas," *International Economic Papers No. 9* (New York: The Macmillan Company, 1959), p. 134.

senting an industry are simply averages, with perhaps very little meaning in the individual case and with even less meaning for a given process. *It should be emphasized that the guidelines suggested below are for the management of an individual firm considering a specific project in an underdeveloped country.*

Management should look at what it proposes to do as a group of separate processes, rather than as a given package of processes (that is, a plant), in reaching a decision in reference to the degree of integration or the size of plant that is optimal. If it does this, management may find that its assumptions as to the mix of processes constituting a "plant" or "enterprise" are culture-bound. Admittedly, to examine a project in this way assumes a degree of technical and organizational inventiveness on the part of management not always present in the United States firm.

National Income Effect

... the national product (or consumption) test of a certain investment project is a calculation of the contribution of that project to present and future national product or consumption.

The calculation must be based on an accurate assessment of the project's consequences, estimated for each of a succession of years, as to value of production and costs. This assessment should include direct as well as indirect consequences and possibly secondary ones.[9]

The point of departure is the projected profit and loss statements and balance sheets of the proposed enterprise (although dependent on the nature of the enterprise, relevant test periods might be year one, five, ten, fifteen, and twenty). From this material one can derive the first approximation of the net value that will be added by the project, which — in the traditional accounting sense — is equated with the sum of the shares of the five factors of production[10] within the income of the firm, specifically:

1. *Labor* — consisting of salaries and wages, bonuses, and commissions received by the employees and wage earners of the firm.
2. *Land* — rent of land and buildings used by the firm in production.

[9]Jan Tinbergen, *The Design of Development* (Baltimore: The Johns Hopkins Press, 1958), p. 41.

[10]It is useful conceptually to consider government (including private nonprofit welfare institutions, *e.g.*, private schools) as the fifth factor of production.

3. *Entrepreneur* — net return.
4. *Capital* — interest payments on loans.
5. *Government* — taxes paid.

Taken collectively, these shares comprise the national income. In point of fact, however, the remuneration paid to labor, land, entrepreneur, and capital constitutes net value *added* by a *new* enterprise only to the extent that these factors are currently unemployed or underemployed. And taxes paid to government contribute to net value added only insofar as those taxes exceed the taxes paid by reason of the present employment of the resources to be used. Also, to the extent that the remuneration paid to scarce factors — perhaps skilled labor, entrepreneurs, capital, certain resources — understates their marginal yields, the cost to be used in deriving net value added should be greater than that shown on the firm's books. For example, the "interest rate to be applied should express the real scarcity of capital, to be derived from the marginal yield of projects as well as the marginal rate to be paid for foreign loans."[11]

On the other hand, certain costs not usually included in net value added should, under some conditions, be included. If a firm plans to engage in training programs to upgrade its labor, the present discounted value of the increased annual output expected by reason of that training should be included in net value added.[12] To the extent that domestically produced raw materials would not otherwise be used, their total cost should likewise be included. If they would be used for less valuable purposes, the difference between present cost and their estimated marginal product in the new use should be added

---

[11]Tinbergen, *op. cit.*, p. 41.
[12]For example, assume:
  a. Training expenditures of $1,000 a year per worker.
  b. Present wage of $100 per year.
  c. That training will double the efficiency of labor after five years.
  d. That the present wage approximates the marginal productivity of labor.
  e. A discounting rate of 6 percent.
  f. An average working life, after training, of twenty-five years.
Then:
  a. Investment, with interest compounded at 6 percent, would be $5,637 for the first five years, plus interest on the declining balance thereafter until the principal is recovered, or a total of $6,427.
  b. Present discounted value of the stream of incremental product ($1,000) starting after five years and continuing another twenty-five comes to $9,553.

in, unless the difference is reflected in value added via increased profit.

Closely related is the problem of assessing the external economies and diseconomies (broadly defined to include all indirect effects) of the firm's proposed operation. Consider some plus and minus items, all of which represent flows of added or decreased future income, which should be discounted to the present to establish the values of these flows in terms of present means.

Plus Items
1. The net value that will be added by economic enterprises that are likely to be stimulated by reason of the project under consideration.
2. The potential net value that will be added by freeing resources for other production through reducing per unit cost (*i.e.*, inducing greater efficiency in the production) of external goods and services by reason of the firm's added demand for them (*e.g.*, power, transport, component parts, raw materials).
3. The increased efficiency accruing to other enterprises that will use the product to the extent that the benefit is not paid for.
4. The cost of social overhead investment by the firm in the development of services that will be available to other users without full payment for the service. (Perhaps the facility would not be constructed if the enterprise did not do so — yet, having been constructed, it will render an external economy, *i.e.*, social overhead facilities which will not be fully utilized by the firm, such as a road, a port facility.)

Minus Items
1. The net value added by economic enterprises that would be replaced by the project under consideration.
2. Decrease in net value added because of increased per unit cost (*i.e.*, loss of efficiency in production) of external goods and services by reason of the firm's added demand for them.
3. Increased inefficiency accruing to other enterprises, for which the cost cannot be fully compensated for by collection from the new enterprise.
4. The cost of social overhead investment by public or other agencies (housing, urban facilities, transport) made necessary by the enterprise in excess of costs that would have been incurred to provide alternative facilities, in the absence of the enterprise.

Granted, these items are not subject to easy or exact measure, but approximations can be derived through examination of the host economy, engineering data of the input-output type, and the nature of the processes and products involved. In so doing, management should not assume the same relationships or benefits as may exist within its own country.

One should guard against claiming gains in value added that in fact are of a definitional or bookkeeping nature. For example, household chores performed by unpaid persons are not normally entered into the national income calculation. A product or device eliminating some household chore, the labor expended on which would not be spent on another productive activity, is probably not a *real* gain in national income (although one might argue that the gain in leisure may, up to a point, be socially desirable, and indeed under some circumstances induce an increase in total product; for example, where fatigue has been a limiting factor).[13] An example might be the production of canned soup, or of bread, in a society where the women-hours released would not otherwise be productively employed. Similarly, simply by moving an activity out of a nonprofit-making institution or out of a government agency where the activity has been carried in the national accounts simply at the cost of its payroll, will not constitute a net gain, except to the extent that efficiency is improved — efficiency in terms of the input-output relationship.

Inasmuch as a host government tends to look at a given project from the point of view of net *national* value added, other adjustments should be made. Items to be excluded: the cost of imported goods and services; foreign currency salaries and other payments made to foreign employees; interest, dividends, fees, and royalties paid in foreign currencies to foreign persons or entities. (It is assumed that local currency paid to foreign nationals for these purposes would be spent locally. To the extent that it would not, but would be converted into foreign currency, this amount should likewise be excluded.) Factor payments made in the production of exports, of course, constitute part of the national income and are included in figuring the net national value to be added by a projected enterprise.

Hollis B. Chenery was perhaps the first in a serious academic

---

[13]Leisure is, in fact, a gain if the family prefers the purchase of the service, plus leisure, to the previous use of income, even though it be a gain which national income accounts do not measure.

discussion to draw attention to the need for a further major modification in deriving what he dubbed the "social return on investment." He pointed out:

> . . . the fact that a high duty is levied on imports and a high price charged for domestic output does not raise the value of a product to the economy; this value is limited to the alternative cost of imports.[14]

But the cost of imports is measured by means of an exchange rate which, more often than not, is pegged at some official value. Therefore, an investment which results in exports or a reduction in imports may in fact contribute more or less to the national product than would be measured at the official rate. If, for example, the foreign currency were undervalued in terms of the local currency, both import costs and export earnings would be unduly low. Then the value added by export earnings should be increased by a percentage and the deductions made by reason of imports costs likewise increased. An example will clarify the point.

Suppose a firm in Country X imports $1,000 worth of parts from the United States. In Country X, given foreign exchange controls and resulting shortage of imports, the parts sell for 4,000 dinars. However, the official rate of exchange is only 3.0 dinars to the dollar. Consequently, the firm actually pays 3,000 dinars for the dollars with which to buy the parts, locally worth 4,000 dinars. The economy, in effect, subsidizes the firm to the extent of 1,000 dinars because of the exchange restriction.

Suppose another firm exports products worth domestically 4,000 dinars. The foreign consumer pays $1,000. The exporter is paid 3,000 dinars. In effect, this firm is subsidizing the economy to the extent of 1,000 dinars, which it would receive in the absence of exchange restrictions.

In the first case 1,000 dinars should be added to the imported cost of the product (this is what the economy is paying), and the firm's net value added adjusted accordingly. In the second case 1,000 dinars should be added to the earnings of the firm, and its net value added similarly adjusted. In 1955 Chenery estimated that a 30-percent correction of this sort should be made in determining the net contributions of a given project to the Turkish national product.

[14]Hollis B. Chenery, George E. Brandow, and Edwin J. Cohn, *Turkish Investment and Economic Development* (Ankara: U.S. Operations Mission to Turkey, Dec. 1953, typed ms. only), p. 54.

Chenery likewise indicated:

> The degree of protection of domestic industry which is warranted in the long run is determined by the equilibrium exchange rate. Domestic prices which are more than 30 per cent above the alternative cost of imports delivered in Turkey should be reduced to this level. A similar correction should be made for export subsidies in excess of 30 per cent and for industries, such as flour milling, which use domestic materials whose price is artificially high.[15]

The same sort of adjustment should be made for other enterprises with which the one under question will be linked via external economies and diseconomies, an adjustment that Chenery either overlooked or felt to be impractible.

Neither Chenery nor others have provided a formula for establishing the equilibrium exchange rate against which the actual rate is compared, unless it be simply that rate which would be established in a free, competitive market situation. The term equilibrium might be redefined so as to refer to a rate which would equalize the marginal product of goods and services within the trading countries. If one accepts this definition, there is an aggregation problem. How does one weight butter and guns to derive a single equilibrium rate in the sense in which the term is being used in this book?[16] It is suggested that an equilibrium rate might better be established for each project — or process. Such a rate may be derived by calculating the annual net national value added (as defined) by a project (in local monetary units) over, say, a twenty-year period, discounted to the present by the rate of interest at which the host country can borrow foreign exchange of the variety to be used, and dividing the result by the foreign exchange to be committed. This figure would be a rough measure of the marginal product of the foreign investment (that is, of the foreign resources to be used).

[15]Chenery *et al.*, *op. cit.*, p. 57.

[16]The problem has been stated and analyzed by A. Nove in "The United States National Income A La Russe," *Economica*, Vol. 23 (1956); by M. Gilbert in *Comparative National Products and Price Levels, a Study of Western Europe and the United States* (Paris: OEEC, 1958); and by M. Gilbert and I. B. Kravis in *An International Comparison of National Products and the Purchasing Power of Currencies* (Paris: OEEC, 1954); and by A. S. Becker, in "Comparison of United States and USSR National Output: Some Rules of the Game" in *World Politics*, Vol. XIII, No. 1 (Oct. 1960).

To summarize: Net value that may be added by a new enterprise can be approximated by:

1. Making maximum-minimum assumptions as to demand-price elasticities for factors and supply-price elasticities for products. (In so doing, one should eliminate the effect of all public subsidies — price supports, export premiums, and import tariffs.)

2. Projecting sales and costs and setting up profit and loss statements for as long a period[17] as management feels that it must maintain a given equity-debt-contractual relationship with the foreign enterprise in order to assure itself of an adequate return. (Income after that period would be of slight present value in management's eyes.)

3. Calculating the net value added by summing up the amounts to be paid to the factors used in production, plus the before-tax profit.[18]

4. Adjusting net value added so derived by:

   a. Subtracting that share of factor cost representing only a shift in factors from one activity to another (that is, include only the value of the incremental product of the factor in its new use),

   b. Adding to factor costs to the extent that they understate the marginal yields of these factors by reason of market imperfections,

   c. Adding the present discounted value of increased annual output expected by reason of company-financed training and other social welfare expenditures.

   d. Adding the cost of domestic raw materials that would not otherwise be exploited.

   e. Subtracting other external diseconomies (listed on p. 107) and adding other external economies (p. 107).

   f. Excluding the income derived from products or services that free resources which will then remain unemployed.

[17]Why not indefinitely? First, because indefinite time projections are unrealistic. Second, management selects the relevant time period by reason of business considerations. It is reasonable to use the same time period here.

[18]Include all taxes, direct and indirect. Although there is thus an income effect, it would be less realistic to exclude them.

5. Adjusting the foregoing calculations by:
   a. Excluding the cost of imported factors (including foreign personnel paid in foreign currencies).
   b. Excluding interest, dividends, fees and royalties paid in foreign currencies to nonnationals.
   c. Modifying import costs and export earnings to reflect the marginal value of the foreign currency earned.

Granted, these calculations are exceedingly difficult, and at best represent only an approximation, but reasonable assumptions make it possible for management to determine, at the very least, whether what it proposes to do falls at one extreme or the other in terms of the net value one can validly expect a project to add to the national income.

It should be recognized that the use of the net-value-added concept here differs in two important respects from its use for domestic national income accounting purposes. *First*, the concern is with the incremental net value that a given enterprise will contribute; hence, net value added is used in a more dynamic sense. Total national income is not being measured at a given moment in time. *Second*, National economies are being considered in which many resources may be unemployed; hence, full-employment concepts must be modified. On the other hand, certain resources are exceedingly scarce — particularly investable capital and social overhead. The first has to do with international economic balance; the latter, with domestic. These imbalances are relevant to business decisions, for if a firm's activity is seen as augmenting the imbalance, it will one day be vulnerable.

Balance of Payments Effect   Equilibrium in balance of payments, which is essentially an annual cash flow concept, is considered by some to be a prerequisite for sustained economic growth, such equilibrium being defined as "stable balance of payments over the relevant time period to maintain an open economy [that is, uninhibited flow of capital and goods] on a continuing basis."[19] It is seen as a self-perpetuating system, that is, one not consuming its capital resources nor dependent upon the largesse or emergency help from politically allied states. (When one looks upon military, and perhaps economic, aid as payment for services rendered — that is, political and military support — this latter qualification becomes a bit fuzzy.)

[19]C. Kindleberger in a seminar at Massachusetts Institute of Technology, Spring 1962. For further discussion, see F. Machlup, "Equilibrium and Disequilibrium," *Economic Journal*, Vol. LXVIII (March 1958), pp. 1–24.

What is probably meant is a balance between the national and world economies which permits international trade at an economically acceptable balance. Back of that equilibrium lies an international exchange rate system, money supply, interest rates, production functions, income levels, liquidity preferences, price and wage levels, supply and demand elasticities, and a variety of political factors (such as, fiscal and trade policies, effectiveness of government administrative machinery, degree of national political leverage). Changes in any one of these variables may affect the balance of payments. Both planners and managements should be aware that the traditional balance of payments concept is stated generally in annual terms. For long-run development a year is not the relevant time period, but something substantially longer. It must be a period long enough to wash out short-run variations in inventories of imports and exportables, to eliminate the effect of weather and other disasters, to eliminate windfalls, to permit an investment to set up a reverse flow, to allow induced secondary effects to appear, to balance out autonomous short-term capital movements, and to flatten out cyclical changes. Therefore, when the author uses the term "balance of payments effect" in this volume, what is meant is the anticipated average annual effect over time. It may be, of course, that in a given situation future gains (that is, in income flows) may be so heavily discounted that only the immediate effect (referring to the current year) is taken into consideration by the local authorities. However, if a country may still borrow abroad on reasonable terms, this should not be the case.[20] Therefore, it is in terms of the longer-run balance of payments effect that most host governments are likely to view the problem. Significantly, the International Monetary Fund, whose principal job it is to maintain liquidity through temporary periods of balance of payments disequilibrium, has set a maximum of five years on its financing.[21]

Given perfect mobility of factors, the balance of payments effects cannot be differentiated from the net-value-added concept in the dynamic and modified sense in which these terms have been used

[20]Admittedly, the effect on annual flow during some periods may appropriately be weighted more heavily than during others. For instance, if foreign exchange were expected to be very difficult during the next decade, the impact then may have far more importance than that later. Moreover, because the further future is uncertain, it is appropriate to weight the near future more heavily in arriving at an evaluation.

[21]Address by Per Jacobsson, *International Financial News Survey*, Vol. XIV, No. 37 (Sept. 21, 1962), p. 303.

above. The one is an integral part of the other. For example, a persistent balance of payments drain arising out of the international transactions generated by an enterprise would adversely affect the level of net value added (*over time*) by that enterprise. In fact, such a drain is precisely equivalent to a reduction in the national value contributed because the economy could recoup the foreign exchange loss by shifting resources from production of goods for domestic use to production for export. If net value added is taken as a flow over successive periods, then there is no reason to consider the balance of payments effect separately — provided factors are perfectly fluid. However, they are not; both time and money attend the shifting. And many, given their specialized or localized nature, cannot be shifted at all. An actual loss will be incurred if the shift takes place prior to full depreciation. Furthermore, a persistent balance of payments drag may arise out of a structural disequilibrium, to which a foreign-inspired enterprise may contribute. An example would be the channeling of local resources, including foreign exchange, into a skewed development so that the economy rests on a single or few products, the supply of which is inelastic except over the very long run and the demand conditions for which are subject to changes beyond the influence of the producing country. Therefore, it is suggested that it is appropriate to consider the balance of payments effect separately over the moderate run (say five to ten years) as representing a distinct gain or loss. And it is so considered by many governments. Even though a project may release resources, increase investment, up incomes, and eventually lead to a net credit on the balance of payments (depending on export and import-income elasticities), loss may, nonetheless, occur in terms of the nonavailability of the foreign exchange consumed. This exchange might otherwise be used to purchase the substance of alternative investment projects that would contribute immediately to foreign exchange earnings. In the shorter run the cost of borrowing that foreign exchange lost should thus be charged to the using enterprise, for it is a rare underdeveloped country that does not suffer from a chronic foreign exchange shortage.

That the balance of payments effect may well take time to work out is demonstrated in the following. Assume an enterprise using foreign exchange that will produce a commodity or service sold entirely to the domestic market. The product is not an import substitution in that present domestic supply is adequate for essential domestic consumption, and imports above this level are blocked.

What may happen to produce a long-run credit impact on the balance
of payments?

1. More efficient use of scarce resources may eventually release
   exportable resources, or resources usable in producing exportable products.

   Examples
   1. More efficient use of local fuels for power generation,
      thereby releasing fuels for export.
   2. More efficient use of land for production of a locally
      consumed crop, say wheat, thereby releasing land suit-
      able for the production of a crop that can be processed
      into an exportable product, such as sugar beets.
   3. More efficient use of skilled labor, through automation,
      thereby releasing it for use in the production of an
      exchange-earning industry.
   4. More efficient use of capital, by shortening the time of
      production or reducing inventories, thereby releasing it
      for use in developing exchange-earning industry.

2. Resource development may make possible the establishment
   of other enterprises which are exchange earners or savers.

   Example
   1. Production of a nontradable resource, such as hydro-
      electric power, thereby making possible externally
      competitive industry.

3. Lowered service costs, thereby making other production
   externally competitive.

   Examples
   1. Improved domestic transport.
   2. Improved storage.
   3. Improved market organization.

4. Lowered product costs, thereby making using industries externally competitive.

5. Increased incomes, thereby increasing the propensity to save
   and leading to investment in exchange-earning or -saving
   activities (if marginal propensity to consume additional income is less than unity).

6. Lowered factor costs because of increased demand, thereby making factor price externally competitive (in a decreasing cost, competitive situation).

7. Production of a popular consumer product in which the income-demand elasticity is positive — a "superior good" — thereby producing a reduction in demand which lowers the prices of certain exportable goods into the externally competitive range (for example, soft drinks in some countries).

8. Direct stimulation of other industries producing exchange-earning or -saving products.

   Example
   1. Technical assistance and purchase contracts given to stimulate local suppliers, thereby generating the production of new products which are exchange earners or savers.

9. Encouragement of diversification into industry in which product supply is less vulnerable to an unpredictable natural event (such as, weather, exhaustion of a mineral) and more elastic (that is, responsive to price) and for which overseas demand is more elastic in respect to price decreases, less elastic in respect to price increases, and less elastic in respect to the level of national income of the importing country.[22]

   Examples
   1. Increased demand for a locally manufactured good, thereby causing a shift of resources, for example, diversion of local investment from increased rubber plantings to rubber products manufacture.

   2. Increased demand for annual crops, thereby causing a shift out of perennial crops, for example, from a tree crop to vegetables.

It can be seen that even though an enterprise is directly responsible for a net outgo of foreign exchange, its induced impact could be

[22]Many primary commodities are believed to have a higher supply elasticity upward than downward (it is easier to shift resources into production than to shift them out) and a higher demand-price elasticity upward than downward (the quantity purchased does not increase as much, proportional to the change in price, when price falls as it decreases when the price increases.

such as to reverse its rating. Or, a net foreign exchange earner might generate a long-run drag. The difference between an enterprise producing an immediate and direct *plus* impact on the balance of payments and one that does so only at some later date, given a chronic foreign exchange shortage, is the cost of borrowing. But, even taking into consideration the possibility of these time-delayed and indirect balance of payments effects, if management cannot establish *beyond reasonable doubt* that what it proposes to do will, at the very least, have a neutral balance of payments effect, the project is vulnerable to adverse reaction in that it contributes to a structural imbalance in respect to the international economic relations of the host country.

If it is suspected that a projected enterprise will have a neutral or negative balance of payments effect, management would do well to re-examine what it has in mind. Several rules may be suggested.

First, a foreign owner who capitalizes locally available resources — or capitalizes imported resources for which local substitutes are feasible (even though development of these resources be required) — should examine his project with particular care. And he should do so periodically. Once it is suspected that the same activity could be carried on with available local resources, including human skills, the foreign equity may be challenged. At this point, the host society is making available foreign exchange to pay the foreign owners without economic justification. The marginal product of the foreign exchange in this particular use is thus reduced to zero. An alert management will admit local equity well before this critical point is reached.

Second, if the firm's activity constitutes a significant part of the total economy of the host country, it should be wary of creating undue dependence upon a single activity or product, or a group of related activities or products. Such concentration may lead to structural imbalance[23] and persistent balance of payments deficits. Geographical and/or industry diversification is then in order. What is "a significant part" in this context? This query may be answered by asking oneself what would have happened if the local resources used by the firm had been otherwise employed. Would the result have been significantly different?

Third, a firm should make certain that all of the foreign exchange

[23]As used here, structural imbalance refers to an allocation of resources to uses in which their marginal utility — in reference to national growth — is less than it would have been in other uses. Because of the cost and time in shifting resources from one use to another, the imbalance may be a persistent one.

arising out of a foreign operation (other than representing an acceptable profit) is made available to the host country. In a country where foreign exchange controls operate, foreign exchange transactions are generally undertaken by a public agency, although in some cases authority is given to a private interest to export and retain part or all of the foreign exchange earnings, sometimes as an export incentive device. Even in the absence of such authority, when the foreign company is exporting to an associated company located elsewhere it becomes virtually impossible for the host government to be sure that it is receiving all of the foreign exchange earnings in fact generated by the export. The foreign company can sell to the associated company at an abnormally low price and the latter sell at a much higher price. Meanwhile, the product may have been processed or mixed with other goods. A scarce resource — foreign exchange — may thus be lost, and the host government can be expected to react vigorously whenever it sees any alternative or effective leverage at hand.[24] A firm owned by nationals of the country in which the firm operates can be expected — unless capital flight or overseas investment is intended — to repatriate these foreign currency earnings in the form of imported goods and services. There is no reason to expect that the foreign-owned firm will do so unless it has a deliberate policy of using foreign currency earnings over and above those required for repatriation of profit and capital (often subject to governmental agreement) for the purchase of needed capital imports.

Public Revenue Effect Like the balance of payments effect, the public revenue effect really cannot be separated from the net-value-added criteria in the dynamic sense in which it has been defined here. In the long run both the balance of payments and public revenue effects of an enterprise will make themselves felt on the net value added (viewed as a flow over successive time periods) by that enterprise to the national economy. Contributions to public revenue (and ease of collection), as well as public costs set up by an enterprise, are included in the calculation of net value added. However, similar to international structural imbalance which may be created by projects which set up a sustained drain, projects which set up a persistent drain on public resources may lead to a domestic structural imbalance as between social overhead and direct productive facilities. Therefore, it seems reasonable to consider the public revenue effect as something

[24]The many disputes between the oil companies and the oil-producing countries constitute examples.

separate. When such an imbalance is created, resources are wasted because of their underemployment — or inefficient employment — and their immobility in terms of use.

To determine the public revenue effect, management should consider not only the taxes it pays (or indirectly induces others to pay) but also the following:

1. The firm's share in the losses (or profits) incurred by public services which it buys.

2. The costs that a firm incurs for services provided by the firm itself which are of far-reaching consequence and would otherwise be undertaken by a public agency (basic education, generalized technical training, public health, housing, provision of urban facilities, maintenance of law and order).

3. The cost of public housing, social welfare and urban facilities required of public authority by reason of the firm's operation.

4. The ease (that is, relative cost) of taxing the net value added by the firm (for example, a capital-intensive enterprise generally may be taxed more easily — that is, tax collection is less costly — than a labor-intensive one; the bulk of the tax is collected from fewer persons).

5. Dividends paid to public owners (that is, to governmental entities) or, goods, prices, license, management and royalty fees paid by the government to private owners in excess of net value added to the economy by the services or goods being provided.

If it cannot be established beyond reasonable doubt that the projected enterprise will have at least a neutral public revenue effect, it seems likely that it will consume more social overhead than it will supply, thereby pushing in the direction of imbalance and wasted, or inefficiently employed, resources. If the host government finds difficulty, as many do, in capturing adequate resources to provide what seem to be minimum social overhead requirements, management can anticipate difficulty once the situation is noted — perhaps in the form of higher factor prices, services denied, or higher taxes. In the first and second cases, the firm itself may have to provide social overhead services, the cost of which may be nearly prohibitive unless the company wishes to integrate horizontally on a grand scale. Power, housing, and general technical training are three possible areas of concern.

It may be charged that double-counting occurs in that such an effect is already included in the external economies or diseconomies, which are part of the net-value-added calculation. However, there is a distinction. The net-value-added concept relates to the *aggregate* net impact of an enterprise on the national economy. Here the concern is with its impact on the *balance* between social overhead and direct productive capacity and on the cost of shifting resources (including the waste of those not subject to shifting) when imbalance arises between these two sectors, an imbalance which limits — or renders more costly — the generation of real income. Granted, if one took a long enough and broad enough view of the value-added effect, these structural imbalances would be included, but the value-added concept has not been extended that far. Also, decisions relating to the allocation of resources to social overhead may be conditioned at least in part by goals and values held by society of a noneconomic nature (those not reducible to a monetary measure).

A management, forewarned that its enterprise will be a net consumer of publicly financed services, would be well advised to accept at least part ownership by a public agency. External social economies and diseconomies are then internalized in the sense that they form part of the calculus for policy and investment decisions.

Additionally, a firm should stand ready to prove beyond reasonable doubt that its associated foreign firms are profiting from the relationship to the same extent that would be true were the transactions conducted between entirely unrelated enterprises. Through cost and price manipulations it is simple to minimize the profits shown by foreign associates, thereby *reducing the tax base* of the foreign government. So long as the foreign tax percentage is less than that charged by the home country, say the United States (and the foreign taxes qualify as tax credits), then there is rarely any purpose in reducing foreign profits by intercompany transactions carrying subnormal margins. However, if the owner of the foreign company be a Swiss, Panamanian or Liechtensteinian subsidiary of the United States parent, profits untaxed in the country of origin may be invested by the parent elsewhere, likewise with little or no tax erosion.[25] They may

[25]Even under the 1962 tax legislation, no United States taxes may be paid if the foreign enterprises are organized as subsidiaries of United States-owned less developed-country corporations. In this case, income is operating income, not holding company income which is now subject to immediate United States taxation.

even be returned one day to the United States via the capital gains route, in which case the United States tax burden is lighter than that prevailing in many underdeveloped countries. Any firm operating in this manner is clearly operating contrary to interests of the host country in that it is paying less taxes than a comparable firm owned by nationals of the host country. Given the critical shortage of social overhead capital resources in many areas, such practices are even more detrimental than would be true in the more developed countries.

Growth-generating Effect In estimating the net-value-added income, balance of payments, and public revenue effects of a given enterprise, the time span that one chooses is both relevant and material. It may be so in reference to product usage, to industrial linkage effects, to social welfare effects. The production of Good *A* may lift the national income more in the short run than would the production of Good *B*, even if the calculation of net value added by the two were modified as indicated in the preceding discussion. In the longer run it is perfectly possible that the larger gain in national income would flow from Good *B*. The same might be said of foreign exchange and of public revenues. A classic case in point would be the comparison between a cosmetic project and a pharmaceutical enterprise. The full impact on national income of the latter — via improved health and energy level — may take a fairly long time to work itself out, but eventually be greater, even if discounted, than the former project. Another case in point: assume equal amounts spent on soft drinks and on agricultural or industrial research. Which contributes the most to national income? Now? Five years from now? Twenty years later? Obviously, even the suggested modifications to the net-value-added, balance of payments, and public revenue concepts do not make them truly dynamic measures of the impact on the *growth* process, which in the long run has to do with (1) placing resources in the hands of innovating entrepreneurs, thereby augmenting the productive capability of the innovator, and (2) encouraging growth in the number and quality of innovators. Foreign business interests which can demonstrate their importance in these two respects may anticipate a favored position in the long run.

Allocational Effect It should be borne in mind that the governing elite of many underdeveloped societies are concerned primarily with accelerated and sustained growth, only secondarily with short-term additions to consumers' real incomes. In other words, future income (or consumption) is discounted at very low rates.[26] This fact is relevant to the selection of appropriate discount rates to use in making the estimates previously suggested.

Furthermore, if long-run growth be the major concern, it becomes important, then, *who* receives the incremental income, the foreign exchange, and the public revenues, and what is done with these resources. Take the incremental income, or net value added: if most goes to labor, say in a labor-intensive project, the propensity to consume the added income may be relatively high. If, on the other hand, the bulk goes to entrepreneurs and financiers — as would tend to be the case in the more capital-intensive enterprises — the propensity to save and invest in productive enterprises may be relatively high. (Also, it may be more difficult and costly to tax away the incremental income of labor-intensive enterprises than in capital-intensive ones.)

A foreign investor can anticipate a cross fire between the *political* interest in maximizing the number of persons employed, in distributing income more equally, and in increasing immediate consumption and the *economic* interest in maximizing the net value added *over time* by the investment of a given amount of capital (which in a capital-poor country tends to be in more capital-intensive enterprise). The first, the political interest (in driving toward maximum employment, a more equal distribution of income, and higher immediate consumption — tends to emphasize labor-intensive enterprise. The second, the economic interest (which pushes in the direction of a more skewed income distribution and a higher level of saving) tends to encourage capital-intensive industry.[27] The foreign investor should be aware of these cross currents and try to assess what he proposes to do in light of the convictions expressed by the elite of the host country, which, for

[26]It is recognized that a desire for a (1) high (relative to the current) level of future income is distinct from (2) a desire for a high rate of growth in income. But, neither becomes reality without the other. Therefore, even if one were to adopt a high growth rate as the real goal, he thereby necessarily reduces the importance of present income as related to levels of income of various future periods, the difference between which represents the desired growth rate. In effect, he is discounting that higher future income to the present at a lower rate than would otherwise be the case. Therefore, for the purposes here, the choice of goals is irrelevant.

[27]Similar views are expressed by Walter Galenson and Harvey Leibenstein in "Investment Criteria, Productivity and Economic Development," *Quarterly Journal of Economics*, Vol. LXIX, (Aug. 1955), p. 358, although they did not make explicit the implications of the conflicting economic and political interests related to labor- and capital-intensive enterprise.

reasons discussed below, are — in the long run at least — likely to be dominated by the economic interest.

On the labor-intensive versus capital-intensive argument, Walter Galenson and Harvey Leibenstein add some further points which are useful to consider in analyzing the implications of a given project.

> Failure to introduce capital intensive techniques at the outset of the industrialization process may create insurmountable institutional barriers to modernization.[28]
>
> Establishment of the highest initial productivity of labor will minimize urbanization costs by bringing into the industrial labor force a minimum of workers.[29]
>
> The longer the life of the capital, the longer the period of time during which no replacements have to be made, and hence the greater available output per man [also, per unit of capital] during this period than with capital of shorter life. . . . [T]he longer the average life of capital, the smaller is the proportion of gross investment needed for replacement [under conditions of growth].[30]

Another point relevant to the capital-intensity–labor-intensity controversy: among the most capital-intensive activities of all are various public welfare enterprises (education, housing, resource conservation, public health, power and communications), enterprises in which the pay-off is generally very long or far removed in time from the period of heaviest investment.[31] Resource development — including agriculture — would probably come next, then basic industry, intermediate industry, and, finally, consumer goods industry, which on the average is the most labor-intensive industry (and least capital-intensive) of all.[32]

[28]*Ibid.*, p. 359.

[29]*Ibid.*, pp. 360–361.

[30]*Ibid.*, p. 362.

[31]Admittedly, high short-run returns may also be generated. The capital-intensity of a given investment depends on the specific circumstances. Ranking may then shift with circumstances and times.

[32]W. Leontief, "Factor Proportions and the Structure of American Trade: Further Theoretical and Empirical Analysis," *Review of Economics and Statistics*, Vol. xxxviii, No. 4 (Nov. 1956), pp. 386–407. With the exception of public welfare activities, with which he does not deal, Leontief ranks these activities in this order.

According to Schultz, the United States investment in education was $7,140 per person in the labor force in 1957 (*i.e.*, direct private costs, plus earnings foregone, but not including normal consumption). This amount was 34 percent as much as was the total formation of physical capital during the year.[a] If one divides this $7,140 by current output per person in the labor force in 1957, or by

Whether capital-intensive or labor-intensive undertakings are given priority by a host government depends very largely upon whether the emphasis placed by a society is on short-run income (and consumption) or on long-run development. Where the emphasis falls depends on the rate at which the society discounts future consumption (or output). The question is: Who acts for society?

To some students of politics it seems likely that within the foreseeable future the principal social actors in many of the emerging countries are likely to be strongly authoritarian elite groups, often with a military tinge, which will emphasize growth rather than immediate consumption. If so, the foreign enterprise that can identify itself solidly with the long-run growth of the host society will occupy the most secure position, but it will do so only as long as the foreign interest is seen as contributing something at least equal in worth to that being taken out of the economy. In any event, concentration on capital-intensive activity is no assurance that a foreign investor is in a growth-generating activity. It is only one measure.

Innovational Effect As many economists and sociologists recognize, there is no neat correspondence between sustained growth on the one hand and capital intensity and/or savings on the other.

roughly $6,400,[b] one derives a capital coefficient (capital stock/output ratio within a period) for education of 1.10. The problem is that most of the current educational investment does not contribute significantly to *current* output. The pay out is delayed several years. It would be more realistic to take Schultz's $7,140 and divide it by the present value of the incremental income anticipated in the future by reason of the present investment in education. The capital requirement so derived could not reasonably lie below the United States *economic* activity with the highest direct capital coefficient — namely, agriculture, with a requirement of $1.6114 for each dollar of current output.[c]

[a]Theodore W. Schultz, "Capital Formation by Education," (A.E.R. Paper No. 5807, revised, Feb. 4, 1960, typed ms.), p. 26.

[b]Based on figures given by Paul A. Samuelson, *Economics* (4th ed., New York: McGraw-Hill Book Company, Inc., 1958), p. 204.

[c]For example, assume that the average annual educational investment in the United States is $5,000 per employed worker (rather than Schultz's $7,140, which is likely to be close to $10,000 now). Assume also that this investment will generate increased productivity valued at $5,000 (in real terms) beginning eight years from now (half of a sixteen-year, college-topped education). This stream of added future product (or income), if discounted at 6 percent, is equal in value to an annual income of $3,137 beginning at the present. Therefore, the capital coefficient would approximate 1.6. But bear in mind that minimum assumptions have been used. If the $10,000 figure were correct, the capital coefficient would be roughly 3.0.

Implicit in the foregoing discussion is the generation of additional income, which is saved and ultimately invested in *productive* enterprise. Characteristic of the underdeveloped society is massive nonproductive spending (equated with expenditures more than adequate to sustain a socially or politically acceptable consumption level in terms of food, clothing, and shelter). The expenditures referred to are those entailed by war, ostentation, ceremonials, the accumulation of inventories of nonessentials. Such expenditures provide no assurance of future growth. The central question is: Does an enterprise induce greater domestic investment of its value added in productive enterprise? Or, put in another way, does the enterprise tend to expand and support the technically and economically innovating elements among the local population? Possible measures of this criterion are:

1. The degree to which the enterprise expands, and upgrades the social recognition of, local technical and organizational skills (for example, training of local nationals and their employment in responsible positions).

2. The degree to which it places resources in the hands of local innovating elements, whether public or private (for example, encouraging local equity participation).

3. The degree to which it induces a recognition of the value of literacy (for example, via hiring policies, promotion, bonuses).

4. The degree to which it induces the physical mobility of individuals (for example, labor concentration).

5. The degree to which it induces dissatisfaction with traditional agricultural methods (for example, via demonstration of improved methods).

6. The degree to which it induces locally oriented research and resource exploration.

7. The degree to which it stimulates the expansion of a local middle class (for example, via development of local supplies of goods and services).

8. The degree to which it stimulates the growth of a cash economy (for example, increased demand for cash crops), thereby expanding market communication.

These things do not lend themselves to concise mathematical measures, but approximations can be made. If a firm finds itself weak in these several respects, it would be well advised either to alter its policies and structure or to anticipate powerful pressures once another manner of operating is envisioned by the local authorities. In terms of its own interests (that is, continued access to market, security of assets, and so forth) the foreign firm should be sufficiently alert as to anticipate the local authority in this area. One way for the foreign firm to establish a clear identity with economic innovation is to concentrate on those activities in which the transmission of skills is of obvious importance.

Impact on Political Development[33]

A foreign firm that does not measure up in economic terms to what the local political authority expects (or feels desirable) may anticipate political pressure against its interests. In addition, and quite apart from these economically induced political feedbacks, the firm should be aware of the more direct political consequences of its entry into non-Western environment. In the opening chapter the differing relationships that have existed in the past between Western enterprise and non-Western societies were analyzed in essentially political terms, for the political response represents the totality of the response generated by a firm's activity. In the final analysis, response takes the form of the host society's collective reaction to foreign enterprise. The nature and timing of that reaction was very largely a function of political relationships — the capacity of one group to influence the behavior of the other.[34] The means of exercising that influence are economic, legal, coercive, persuasive. In this section the modern era will be examined using the same analytical tools.

Modern Nationalism and Western Enterprise   Inasmuch as the rise of nationalism — both economic and political — in the newly independent nations characterizes the post–World War II era, it is useful to look closely at its rationale. The true meaning of nationalism in this context has to do with the criteria on which basic decisions are made. Consideration of national interest (that is, universalistic norms

[33]Political development is defined in Chapter 1, pp. 43–44.
[34]For a definition of politics, see Quincy Wright, *The Study of International Relations* (New York: Appleton-Century-Crofts, 1955), p. 130.

within the nation), however well- or ill-defined, tends to predominate, not the personal interest or that of specific interest groups. Political functions thus tend to become more universalistic in scope and to reflect more affectively neutral norms in the nation, though not yet the international arena. And the process of political socialization (identification with a given political culture) expands to include the entire indigenous population of the nation state. At the same time, the process of political recruitment often remains inadequately developed, which fact means that political change appears sporadic and disorderly, if not violent. Of Latin America, one study declared:

> What seems to worsen the investment climate and to deter new investment is not the hostility of [local] businessmen or governmental corruption, but the coming to power of radical reform governments. Since Latin American radicalism is not only likely to stay but is also a noisy and often harsh instrument for institutional changes which many of these countries need if they are to develop solid cohesion and economic dynamism, this reaction of American investors, though understandable, is unfortunate.[35]

Perhaps in part because of past interference by Western governments and Western enterprise in the evolutionary development of the process of political recruitment (that is, participation in the legitimizing of political authority), political change in many of the newer nations is inescapably equated with violent revolution and the emergence of charismatic leaders. In the modern context, a successful revolutionary leader must ultimately gain acceptance by appearing to embody the nation within his own personality and convictions, for interest-aggregating and -communicating functions are only inadequately differentiated. Rather, they tend to be exercised by powerful and appealing political personalities. And, partly because of the record of collaboration with previous colonial regimes that many bureaucrats have, the charismatic leader tends to be suspicious of them and to retain virtually all decision-making authority in his own hands. Indeed, where the process of political recruitment is so unstable that political leadership can be changed only by violent, extralegal means, it is perhaps unreasonable to expect the development of affective, differentiated rule-enforcing and rule-adjudicating functions. The administrator is understandably disinclined to make

[35]*United States Business and Labor in Latin America* (University of Chicago Research Center on Economic Development and Cultural Change, Comm. on Foreign Relations, S., 86th Cong., 2d Sess., Jan. 1960), p. xi.

decisions or to identify too closely with the rule-making authority. His survival may depend on his ability *not* to act independently, or perhaps not to act at all.

Government thus remains personal and political functions non-specific (that is, not differentiated, diffuse), which renders it exceedingly difficult for the political authority to cope effectively with the complex problems of internal development and international relations thrust upon it with independence. The frustration and emotional outbursts against those seen as responsible for the problems — namely, the foreigner — may be more violent than would otherwise have been the case. And Western enterprise not infrequently becomes the convenient scapegoat against which to spend the pent-up fury of both social discontent and national frustration. Western enterprise remains on the scene after Western governments have withdrawn and can no longer be attacked directly.

Western business efforts to maintain control over its overseas activities after the withdrawal of Western political power has often led to a deliberate structuring of enterprises so as to assure control either by limiting information, by restricting access to decision-making centers within management, or by making the foreign enterprise a captive of the home industry by limiting its function to intermediate activities, such as assembly or otherwise processing of foreign-supplied materials. Therefore, managerial and organizational skills in the measure needed to sustain development were not transmitted. Only since World War II has there been a serious effort by Western enterprise to develop local managements and highly skilled local technicians. Possibly, previous effort would have been foredoomed to failure in view of the relatively low level of achievement motivation in the traditional societies.

Nonetheless, there seems to be a politically compelling national need in the non-West to close the gap in material well-being. The sense of national inferiority, generated in part by the closed-door policy of Western enterprise, must be assuaged. It appears likely that "the sacrifices which economic growth requires, particularly in the early stages of economic development, can only be imposed and borne in the name of powerful ideologies: nationalism, in the sense of rising national consciousness and solidarity, has often proven capable of calling forth such sacrifices."[36] Some have objected to the use of the

---

[36]*United States Business and Labor in Latin America, op. cit.,* p. 61.

word "sacrifice" in this context. Sacrifice is indeed a meaningful concept when there is a gap between immediate potential consumption — that is, that which is both popularly desired and technically possible, given the resources at hand — and actual consumption. That this gap represents in the minds of many people a sacrifice of present consumption for future welfare appears in the political literature of many non-Western societies, where the political elite call endlessly upon their people to "tighten their belts," "to work for their children," to look toward the "golden era" ahead despite present hardships. (I personally have lived in a society (Turkey) that was full of this kind of propaganda. I have heard it likewise in Korea, Yugoslavia, Egypt, and elsewhere.) Whether or not the people were in fact sacrificing consumption that they would otherwise enjoy is irrelevant; they *believed* that they were. Indeed, in some instances, it seems unlikely that the public was in fact saving any more than was customary. The "sacrifice" came from maintaining the same level of savings in the face of heightened consumption desires and expectations.

In some cases the charismatic leader has deliberatively elevated accelerated economic development to the level of a political ideology and merged it with the nationalistic ideology itself, thereby substituting nonmaterial motivation for the material reward of increased consumption which such a society must temporarily forego. A responsible leader of this type necessarily undertakes a vigorous effort of nation building, inherent in which are two major tasks: (1) a deepening of political socialization (identity with a political culture) and (2) a broadening of political recruitment (legitimitizing of political authority). To be successful he must concentrate on elements of cohesion and similarity and de-emphasize all politically significant symbols of internal difference. Western enterprise tends to be a victim unless it succeeds in so thoroughly building itself into the local society as to be effectively localized — that is, nationalized in the sense of being so closely identified with national political and economic interests as not to be sharply distinguishable from them.

One of the frequent by-products of nation building in this sense is a felt need on the part of the political elite to even out differences in levels of development *within* the nation. Industrial and agricultural development may be forced into the more isolated, more primitive parts of the country so as to bring about a greater sense of interdependence and of identification with the rest of the nation. An enterprise that contributes to this process may be viewed as more desirable than one that contemplates a more developed urban site. Hence, the political vulnerability of the former may be somewhat less.

National opposition to alleged exploitation by Western business, at some places and times, appears to have contributed significantly to the nation-building process, although not necessarily contributing to economic growth in any immediate sense. Mexico's fight with the oil companies, Iran's struggle with Anglo-Iranian Oil, and Egypt's campaign to oust the Suez Canal Company surely added to the intensity of the political socialization process in these countries. One student of the Anglo-Iranian oil problem wrote:

> The peasant support of political nationalism in 1951 [in Iran] was as much the product of a reaction to years (or centuries) of oppression by landlords and inefficient governments as it was a reaction to abuse by foreign commercial enterprise.[37]

Social Change Induced by Western Enterprise   The inherent danger in the intensification of political socialization without a parallel broadening of political recruitment is mirrored in the extreme case of South Africa. The role of Western enterprise in this instance is significant.

> Social changes and industrial developments in South Africa are the most serious threat to the present system, which is based on the assumptions that racial groups can be mutually insulated from competitive and "contaminating" contacts and that the position of these groups can be fixed and enforced by legislative and administrative action. While this might have been possible in static rural societies, South Africa is no longer rural. . . . The labor demands of the mines and of a burgeoning industry constantly draw Africans into the vortex of urban and industrial life. . . . Both Europeans and Africans are being drawn into a complicated industrial order. Complete separation is obviously not possible, and restrictive regulations for industry based on rigid concepts of caste are extremely difficult to enforce. Industry has a vested interest in more flexible arrangements and, with the growing scarcity of skilled labor, does not look with favor upon government edicts which define skills and jobs in racial terms.[38]

The pressure exerted by modern industry in the direction of inducing more universalistic, affectively neutral, achievement-oriented norms,

[37]A. W. Ford, *The Anglo-Iranian Oil Dispute of 1951–52* (Berkeley: University of California Press, 1954), p. 16.

[38]W. O. Brown and H. Lewis, "Racial Situations and Issues in Africa," in *The United States and Africa*, Walter Goldschmidt, ed. (New York: American Assembly, Columbia University, 1958), p. 152.

in the surrounding society is apparent in this extreme case. Serious conflict between the norms applied within business institutions and those defining the political functions may well contribute to political upheaval. It is generally agreed by informed observers, for example, that the operation of the Arabian-American Oil Company in Saudi Arabia is having the effect of creating a modernizing middle class of revolutionary potential. So long as political evolution (in terms of socialization and recruitment and the values applied by the rule-making, rule-enforcing and rule-adjudicating institutions) is contained, the more violent the eventual change is likely to be. Western enterprise has thus helped immeasurably to join the issue in violent conflict by first interfering with political development and then accelerating the development of differentiated economic functions at such a rate that political development is outpaced.

A critic might respond, however, "If Western business is such a powerful modernizing influence, why then are revolutionary groups inclined to be so hostile to Western business?" A good question, but answerable. First, in order to exist at all in many areas, Western businessmen have been forced to make deals with essentially irresponsible and/or dishonest political leaders. In the process it was difficult not to become identified with these older, traditional regimes that preceded the appearance of political leadership more sensitive to national interest. Second, in the face of an inadequately developed political culture in many areas, Western enterprise has taken upon itself many political functions. These, it has been reluctant to give up to new, untried political institutions of the host society. Western enterprise was thus seen as a competitor in the political arena. Third, revolutionary leaders in many areas were convinced, at least initially, that many of their ills stemmed from Western political interference, which, given the record, seems a perfectly reasonable — albeit, often mistaken — assumption to make. After all, Western politics had become identified with attempts to maintain the shattered status quo. Because the business and political functions were not differentiated in Western enterprise in many areas until very recently, if at all, this politically generated resentment and frustration extended to include Western enterprise. Fourth, as independence is gained and Western political authority withdrawn, very frequently Western enterprise remains on the scene. Resentment generated by the previous foreign political regime is then directed toward the Western interests remaining (that is, business). Fifth, the modernizing effect of Western business was not necessarily a popular one; many resentments were generated. The success of a revolutionary regime in a non-Western state tends to be inversely related to the degree to which traditional institutions and attitudes are upset until its power is consolidated — a process that may take a number of years. In the meantime, attention from the revolutionists' true aims is often diverted into zenophobic tendencies. Sixth, not all revolutionary regimes have turned on Western enterprise. The republican Turkish administration of the 1920's made a serious effort to attract more private foreign investment, explicitly because of its modernizing effect. Also, one should note the concessions offered by many of the new independent states to the foreign entrepreneur.

It is generally true that with the increased employment of local nationals at all levels within an enterprise — or in support of the enterprise — Western business has greatly stimulated the process of West-East acculturation. Adding momentum to the process has been the tendency toward urbanization. Those caught up in this secondary process are not only required to assume different values in order to make a living, but they are pulled physically out of their traditional social environments. It is reported that "studies show that throughout Africa the natives who have lived for long in the city never really readjust to the rural area." Native informants report that once they become accustomed to European ways, they cannot "accommodate to the 'uncivilized' way of rural people." The same report goes on to observe that "the villagers are distrustful of those who have 'followed the Europeans.' " One informant put it this way, "My village people like you to come back for a few months, but if you stay for good, they will poison you."[39]

It has been observed in reference to southeast Asia that, "the process of urban growth, the changes in social stratification, and the emergence of more secular norms of behavior all reflect in large part the impact of Western commercial and economic institutions on the region."[40]

Western enterprise, both deliberately and otherwise, has in the past tended to draw about it local nationals who had already withdrawn from the traditional culture (the "modernists"), or who were in

[39]Walter Goldschmidt, "Culture and Changing Values in Africa," in *The United States and Africa, op. cit.,* pp. 180–181.

[40]Pye., *op. cit.,* p. 104.

the process of so doing (the "transitionalists").[41] One writer reported:

> In many of the underdeveloped countries, foreign firms are almost unique in being able to offer a well-paid career in private business which is socially rewarding, respectable, and usually better paid than the Civil Service or armed forces. . . . Moreover, a career in [such] . . . enterprise is one with full opportunity. This contrasts favorably with that in the communal, family-dominated, local business whose practices in any case are often not considered respectable by the old or newly-emerging professional class.[42]

The traditional entrepreneur is not likely to attract the local professional man precisely because achievement-motivated individuals realize that opportunities within these firms are limited in that norms remain affective. There is thus the danger that Western enterprise may isolate itself from effective communication with the traditional culture and, in so doing, may bring upon itself hostility. For example, "Latin American businessmen, as a rule, prefer [to accept] foreign enterprises which do not enter into serious competition with them or radically upset existing business practices and labor policies."[43] At the same time, Western enterprise may be interfering with the political recruitment process by pulling many of the most competent "modernists" and "transitionalists" out of the traditional society, and thus alienating them from the local political culture. Not only are these firms likely to be more achievement-oriented, they often can offer higher salaries and more cosmopolitan careers.

One way around this dilemma, found by such enterprises as Arabian-American Oil Company and Sears Roebuck de Mexico, has been to undertake to surround the enterprise with a variety of local, *independent*, ancillary services and industries. The result is the creation of a modern, *indigenous* middle class. Anthropologist Carleton S. Coon has reported that to Aramco's program of local contracting for all services not directly related to the production and transport of oil "belongs much credit for stimulating new productive ventures of a rising capitalist middle class in eastern Saudi Arabia, for helping to

---

[41]These terms are borrowed from Daniel Lerner, *The Passing of Traditional Society* (New York: The Free Press of Glencoe, 1958).

[42]J. S. Fforde, *An International Trade in Managerial Skills* (Oxford: Basil Blackwell, 1957), p. 107.

[43]*United States Business and Labor in Latin America, op. cit.*, p. 51.

raise the standard of living of a whole province, and for the pro-
American attitude of many Saudi citizens."[44]   In part as a result,
Aramco has lived through the Iranian oil upheaval, the Suez Canal
crisis, and the United States landing in Lebanon.   A major complaint
against the British oil interests in Iran by local nationalists was the
horizontal penetration of the oil company itself into a wide variety of
ancillary services.   Initially, there was much opposition within
Aramco and Sears' managements to this time-consuming and relatively expensive manner of providing the company with necessary
services.   Possibly, it would have been cheaper and easier for these
companies either to have done these things themselves (as similar
companies elsewhere had done and are doing) or to employ foreign
contractors.   But by this policy of *local* contracting they have induced
an internalizing of new values by a new middle class, which identified
with the interests of the firm but was not part of it.   By remaining
personally independent of the foreign company, the individuals involved are not blocked from performing effectively in political roles
within the necessarily nationalistic environment, nor are they as likely
to become alienated from their own culture.

One study of the Latin American scene has recommended that:

> United States firms and their subsidiaries in Latin America should con-
> tinue their activities in health and sanitation, education and training, and
> related fields to improve the productivity of employees and the welfare of
> their families.   Where public programs serving their employees in these
> fields are underway, the business firms should participate in them, and if
> feasible seek to achieve integration of the public and private activities.[45]

From the point of view of political development, the above may be
very poor advice.   Too many foreign concerns have, in line with
traditional practice carrying over from the previous era, usurped local
governmental function.   Granted, it is often less time- and money-
consuming to continue the obligations of the paternalistic employer
rather than to rely on others.   But once a nationally responsible
political authority emerges, and some semblance of specific, differentiated, political institutions develops, the Western enterprise should
probably undertake a concerted effort to rid itself of all of these extra-

[44]C. S. Coon, "Operation Bultiste: Promoting Industrial Development in
Saudi Arabia," in *Hands Across the Frontiers*, Howard M. Teaf, Jr., and Peter G.
Franck, eds. (Ithaca: Cornell University Press, 1955), p. 309.

[45]Laird Bell (chairman), *Technical Cooperation in Latin America* (Washington: National Planning Association, 1956), p. 132.

business activities. Public health and basic education should be a function of the public authority. If the Western enterprise is seen as competing for public favor with the local government in these fields, it becomes vulnerable to political reprisal. It opens itself to the charge of interference with the process of national political development. The wiser policy would be the exercise of subtle pressure on local individuals, local groups, and the local government to assume responsibility for these activities. Perhaps technical assistance, loans, and other forms of support might be given, as has been done by Aramco in Saudi Arabia and Sears Roebuck in Mexico.[46]

Another example is that of the Rhodesian Anglo-American Limited, the chairman of which reported:

> Our investments showed a net increase of £1,809,490, after writing off £159,737 mostly in respect of interests in prospecting companies. The largest single new investment was a loan of £500,000 to the Federal Government [Rhodesian], which forms part of loans totalling £5.1 m. being made over a period of twelve years by companies in the Anglo-American Corporation Group in Rhodesia, to assist and accelerate the development of the Federation's resources particularly in the rural economy. In view of the Group's special responsibilities in Northern Rhodesia at least £2 m. is to be spent there.[47]

It is the nonbusiness activities which United Fruit has been involved in such a large way — police, retailing, public health, education, transport, and so forth — in several Central American countries which have come under political attack. These activities, although politically functional during the Exploitative and Concessionary Eras, have become clearly dysfunctional from the point of view of local political development. In a sense, it is in competition with local governments.

Part of this same problem is exposed in the elaborate public relations efforts undertaken by some Western firms to establish their signal importance to the continuing well-being of the host countries. Such publicity almost demands that the local political authority deny

[46]The ramifications of the Sears development in Mexico are outlined by Richardson Wood and Virginia Keyser, *Sears, Roebuck de Mexico, S.A.* (Washington: National Planning Association, 1953).

[47]Chairman's statement, Rhodesian Anglo American Limited, *New York Times* (Oct. 21, 1962), p. 49. For a more detailed account of the changing relationship of this enterprise to its community, see Hortense Powdermaker, *Copper Town: Changing Africa — The Human Situation in the Rhodesian Copperbelt* (New York: Harper & Row Publishers, 1962).

the alleged importance. To point out that foreign enterprise is responsible for 50 percent of the revenue of the Venezuelan government is unfortunate, if true. Such a situation means that decisions affecting the financial resources of the government in an important way are not only being made by a nonpolitical body, but, in addition, by a foreign entity. That the decisions are beneficial or otherwise is irrelevant.

The Problem of Role Conflict   It is revealing to examine the roles occupied by the Western businessman in the newly emerging states and the conflict among those roles. First, he represents a Western management. As such, he is required to structure the foreign enterprise so as to yield maximum profit. Being at the base of operations and hence usually more knowledgeable of the local political culture than those at a higher level in the home office, he is acutely aware that practices yielding the highest profit in the short run may endanger the company's assets in the long run. The longer many of the modern, professionally trained businessmen remain abroad, the more deeply aware they become of the genuine interests of the country of their employ, sometimes more so than national political leaders themselves. And so, at least in emotional terms, they become involved in local political choices. As a foreign national, the individual businessman is also an unofficial representative of his own country's foreign policy. As a professional manager or technician, he is concerned with his own standing in the profession. To maintain that standing, he may be restless about remaining overseas too long. His various roles may be summarized thus:

Role	*Measure of Success*
Stockholders' representative	Maximum profit, short term
Management's representative	Conformity with policy, low cost operation
Management's country specialist	Maximum profit, long run (*i.e.,* security of assets and market position)
Resident in a foreign country	Identification with national interests of host country
Innovator — modernizer	Local acceptance
Foreign citizen	Identification with national interests of home government
Member of a professional group	Prominence in professional associations, principally at home

Role	Measure of Success
Member of local business	Identification with interests of that community
Member of a local foreign community	Identification with the interests of that community

Obviously, many role conflicts other than those discussed can arise. It is equally apparent that when role conflict is laid on top of ethnic conflict, serious difficulty may be reasonably anticipated. These conflicts may be internalized or externalized by the individual caught up in them.[48]

A case study of an American-Turkish enterprise is revealing.[49] It was found that the Turkish supervisors often demonstrated an undue pride in their positions and accomplishments, possibly a function of the scarcity of industrial management positions and the highly developed sense of social status characteristic of traditional Turkish society. The system tended to yield men highly sensitive to rank and to symbols of that rank, such as the size and location of offices, rather than to demonstrable achievement. As a result the American manager was reported as often frustrated and puzzled by what he observed of his Turkish associates. His reactions seemed to be polarized around two extremes. Either he acted in a domineering manner and "subjugated" the foreign nationals, or he tried so hard to be a "good guy" that he failed to exert a beneficial influence. By "beneficial influence" in this context was meant the effective transmission of managerial skills and appropriate values.

Many cases of serious conflict between American managers abroad and their home offices could be cited, or between those in charge of organizing a foreign project and top management. One instance was the organization of the Merck project in India, during which the American team sent to India to study and negotiate came to feel very strongly that the company should enter into a joint manufacturing venture with the Indian government. Top American management refused, apparently on almost doctrinaire grounds that indicated little sensitivity to the differences in the Indian situation from the American — that is, the critical nature of the products

[48]For a further treatment of these conflicts of interests, see Richard D. Robinson, "Conflicting Interests in International Business Investment," *Boston University Business Review*, Vol. 7, No. 1 (Spring 1960), pp. 3–13.

[49]C. W. Skinner, "Management Problems' Slow Progress Abroad," *Virginia Law Weekly*, Vol. xii, No. 23, April 22, 1960, p. 7.

involved, the inadequacy of supply, and the resulting need for public control of distribution.[50]

Such conflicts as these may seriously interfere with the effective transmission of skills and values. A further problem challenging some of the more thoughtful members of the international business community is the suspicion that certain values long held in at least verbal awe in professional management circles may not be universally valid. The concept of complete neutrality in interpersonal relations may not, after all, be conducive to the most effective communication within a large organization. The Japanese experience would indicate that at least some modification of the neutral and achievement norms may generate greater efficiency, at least under some circumstances or in some cultures. In short, there is a growing awareness that additional research is needed before proceeding any further in the attempt to "modernize" foreign business associates.

This admonition is an echo of that made by James Abegglen in his study of the Japanese factory. He reports that one of the major differences between the organization of the American and the Japanese factory lies in the greater "individualization or impersonalization" of human relations within the former. He observes:

> The apparatus of modern production in the West depends heavily on the assigment of individual responsibility, on individual incentive programs, on job evaluation of the individual employee, and on a system of rewards in which individual competence and energy will be recompensed. In all of these respects the difference from Japan is marked. Individual responsibility is avoided, incentive systems have little relationship to individual output but, rather, depend on group success, and the motivating of energies appears to depend on the individual's loyalty and indentification with the group and his superior.[51]

Abegglen, noting the "considerable industrial success" possible under the Japanese system, concludes: "Rationalization and impersonalization are not, the Japanese experience seems to argue, necessary to the adoption from the West of an industrial economy."[52] The point

---

[50]Richard D. Robinson, "Merck & Co., Inc., in India" (Harvard Graduate School of Business Administration, 1959, Business Cases ICR 183 and ICR 184). A shorter version appears in R. D. Robinson, *Cases in International Business* (New York: Holt, Rinehart and Winston, Inc., 1962), p. 100.

[51]James C. Abegglen, *The Japanese Factory* (New York, N. Y.: The Free Press, 1958), p. 140

[52]*Ibid*, p. 141.

is that the greater ease of effective communication within the more affective and group-oriented Japanese structure may more than offset the technical inefficiency of not necessarily maximizing the productivity of individuals by impersonally matching ability and challenge.

Local Integration   A way to obviate some of the conflicts may be to combine roles through a variety of devices designed to bring about a high degree of local integration. Some Western firms have moved far in this direction. By so doing, the foreign associates are more likely to be cast in the role of a transmitter, that is, one who moves from one culture to another and consciously tries to change *both*. Such a role is in contrast with the amalgant role, which is assumed by one who is at home in both cultural worlds, but makes no attempt to change either.

Local integration may take a variety of forms, many of which are not necessarily mutually exclusive:

1. Intensified public relations to stress the importance of the enterprise to national development.
2. Assistance to local public authorities (such as, loans, technical assistance, use of facilities, and so forth).
3. The employment of local nationals in specialized and supervisory roles.
4. Contracting for all possible ancillary services with independent, local businessmen, who may or may not be assisted by the company.
5. Processing of locally procured materials and production for the local market.
6. Organization of joint ventures, in which local capital participates on a minority basis or a widely held majority basis (thus securing control for the minority foreign interest).
7. Local management, but with continued foreign financial and policy control.
8. Local majority ownership, but with a management contract held by the foreign associated company.
9. Local ownership and management, with only a minority ownership held by the associated foreign concern, together with perhaps some form of contractual relationship (license, technical assistance, sales).
10. Representation in the parent foreign firm by members of the associated local group board membership).

11. Participation by the local group in the ownership of the parent foreign firm.

It will be noted that as one moves up the ladder of integration, roles tend to be combined. And they tend to change in character from the amalgant to the transmitter. True integration involves the deliberate structuring of the relationship so as to encourage a feedback from the host culture into the management of the firm, preferably at the parent firm level. Obviously, many practical commercial, financial, legal, and national political factors enter in the judgment as to what is practicable and desirable under specific circumstances. But generally, the greater the feedback into the associated Western enterprise at its home headquarters, the greater will be its constructive impact on the host culture, and the greater will be the security of its assets and market position. If individuals at policy-making levels are thus identified with both cultures, they are much more likely to open up effective communications and to change attitudes and practices at both ends so as to enhance efficiency and eliminate conflict.

Some managements are sensitive to the need for integration. Within such firms, the attitudes of both the local and foreign managements tend to become increasingly *de*-national for they no longer identify completely with either national culture.

Political Vulnerability — A Summary An enterprise may be politically vulnerable for a variety of economic reasons. To summarize, these reasons are:

1. A minimum contribution to net national value added either because of the shifting of already employed resources or because of the generation of external diseconomies.
2. A persistent net drain on foreign exchange resources (as previously defined) arising out of the capitalization of locally available resources in the foreign equity or the insistence by foreign owners of an ownership share larger than the proportional contribution made by them (measured against the potential local contribution).
3. A persistent net drain on public revenues and services (as previously defined), coupled with a management refusal to enter into a joint venture with a public agency.
4. A weak or neutral effect on national economic growth (as previously defined) — in terms of resource allocation or encouragement of innovation.

Closely associated with these causes of adverse political pressure is the injury to a local enterprise by the incursion of more efficient, foreign enterprise — *even though displacement may mean a net gain in national product.*

> Sometimes American investors, exercising free enterprise, drive the local firms out of business by their superior methods and know-how. This is not a triumph for American technology. The local firms might have done as well if we sent technicians and advanced capital. Foreign capital that displaces internal capital is not welcome.[53]

Other, essentially *noneconomic* measures of political vulnerability relate to the sheer size of an enterprise as projected against the total economy of the host society. In event of large relative size, these factors become blown up:

1. Seat of decision-making (also nationality of decision-maker).
2. Public awareness of the firm's activities (that is, the degree of pervasiveness).
3. Relation with previous, now unpopular, political regimes.
4. Relation with mother country's political interests and activities.
5. Size of payroll (for example, capital intensive projects may be somewhat less vulnerable politically).
6. The amount and sort of local resources used (for example, land is particularly vulnerable).

An additional set of criteria, relating to the product, are suggested by the following questions:[54]

1. Is the product ever the subject of important political debates in respect to adequacy of supply? (Sugar, salt, kerosene, gasoline, foodstuffs, transport facilities, public utilities, tires, medicines, for example.)
2. Is the production one on which other industries rest? (Cement, steel, power, machine tools, construction machinery, and so forth.)

[53]Herbert L. Matthews, "Diplomatic Relations," in *The United States and Latin America* (New York: The American Assembly, Columbia University, 1959), p. 170.

[54]Discussion of political vulnerability of product is taken from Richard D. Robinson, "The Challenge of the Underdeveloped National Market," *Journal of Marketing*, Vol. 25, No. 6 (Oct. 1961), pp. 24–25.

3. Is the product one in which effective competition is difficult in small national markets?
4. Is the product one held to be essential, either economically or socially? (Key drugs and medicines, laboratory equipment.)
5. Is the product important to agriculture? (Farm tools and machinery, pumps, fertilizers, seed, and so forth.)
6. Is the product of national defense significance? (Communications equipment, transport equipment, for example.)
7. Does the product include important components that would be available from local sources? (Labor, skills, materials.)
8. Is the product one for which competition from local manufacture may be reasonably expected in the foreseeable future?
9. Does the product relate to channels of mass communication media? (Newsprint, radio and television equipment.)
10. Is the product primarily a service?
11. Does the use of the product, or its design, rest upon some legal requirement?
12. Is the product potentially dangerous to the user? (Explosives, drugs.)

If each of these questions were answered on a ten-to-one scale, from a strong "yes" to a strong "no," the lowest scoring products would be among those least vulnerable to political pressures. (It is often useful to ask how foreign ownership of a given industry or product would be treated in the parent nation.)

Political vulnerability may lead to labor agitation, public regulation (price fixing, allocation quotes, and so forth), nationalization (in the sense of restricting ownership to local nationals), or socialization (public ownership) on the one hand — or on the other hand, to favoritism and protection. Which way the pendulum swings depends largely upon the sensitivity and foresight of management in responding to political pressures before they become irresistible, also upon the effort management makes to relate its product to the specific needs of the market in respect to both design and impact.

Goods deemed to be essential (for example, high numerical scores in questions 2, 4, 5, 6, and 9) often receive first claim to scarce foreign exchange in respect to importing. Likewise, these same products, if made within the country, often receive a high degree of encouragement and protection, up to and including government guarantee for the repatriation of profits and capital and an official prohibition against competing imports. Therefore, other than the possibility of nationalization or socialization, the risk of investment abroad in the production of essential products is substantially less than that incurred in the case of less essential products.

Conclusion

Various measures or criteria have been discussed which are (or will be) used — explicitly or implicitly — by non-Western governments in viewing what Western business interests do locally. It has been observed that long-run security of market position and business assets rest on management's ability to think in similar terms and to so structure overseas enterprises as to identify them with the national interests of the host societies.

The economic measures suggested are the net-national-value-added, balance of payments, public revenue, and growth-generating effects — the latter being a combination of allocational and innovational effects. Although overlapping to some degree — and theoretically part of the same general system — these measures are nonetheless operationally distinct, given the tools outlined and the mental processes described. Until someone erects a convincing model encompassing all of these variables, with a given project as the input and a growth rate (both short- and long-run) as the output, it is necessary to work in this piecemeal fashion. One doubts, in fact, even the theoretical basis for assuming a single, continuous system, given the different interpretations as to what constitutes growth (for example, the problem of psychic income and immediate income versus future income) and changes in the time horizon. If a people increase their literacy from say 20 percent to 50 percent but with no significant gain in national product as usually calculated, has the country grown in the per-capita income sense? It depends, it seems, upon the satisfaction derived from the achievement of literacy and the incremental product that may be anticipated years hence by reason of that literacy. Neither of these effects would be reflected in the first three sets of suggested criteria because of their rather limited time dimension.

It seems quite clear that the political vulnerability of a given enterprise is a function of all four of the measures examined, taken separately and in concert, plus certain noneconomic measures of political impact which relate to (1) a firm's operational policies, (2) the structure of the enterprise, (3) the size of the enterprise and (4) the nature of the product.

The problem remains, however, as to how these four economic measures can be combined to provide a first approximation of political vulnerability. It is contended that a Western-sponsored project must successfully pass each one of these measures. That is, a low rating (low relative to other feasible uses of the same resources) in terms of any one of the criteria may generate a high level of political vulnerability. Consider (1) the interlocking nature of the criteria and (2) the differing time dimensions (that is, one calculates net value added, balance of payments, and public revenue effects over the intermediate run,[55] probably not more than ten years, whereas the allocational and innovational effects relate to the very long run). If a project fails badly in respect to *any one* of these criteria within the foreseeable future (that is, that time span relevant to the manner in which members of the host society — particularly the elite — evaluate and react), it will eventually set into motion events that will generate feedbacks that will render an adverse measure against all the criteria. Hence, the enterprise can anticipate political vulnerability as soon as these relationships are realized. For example, a weak allocational or innovational effect will, in the long run, produce a negative effect on net national value added, balance of payments, and public revenue. The effect may be negative only in relation to the result that could be expected reasonably from an alternative use of resources. That is, if a management cannot justify a project and its participation in it[56] in terms of all four sets of criteria, then it should restructure that project in respect to employment of resources, ownership, control, management, profits and fees, or personnel. If the project still does not measure up, the firm should refrain from involvement.

Finally, even if the project and the manner of the firm's involvement passes this test, management should examine the political vulnerability of the enterprise generated by its operational policies, its structure, and its size (relative to the host economy) and by the nature

[55]Defined as not long enough for any significant structural changes to have taken place in the economy, *i.e.*, the maximum length of time over which any firm quantitative estimates can be made.

[56]Possible ways of participating: debt financing, equity financing, joint venture, mixed venture management contracting, contract manufacturing, leasing, licensing, technical assistance contracting, a combination of any or all of the foregoing.

of the product. One test is to reverse the roles and postulate a foreign-owned enterprise of a similar nature and relative size (that is, relative to the host economy) in the parent country. What would its political position be?

Some readers may object to these generalizations on the ground that a large percentage of international investment — in the traditional financial sense — would be ruled out. That is precisely the point. It is the author's conclusion that the choice of projects by Western business in general and the manner in which business relates itself to many of these projects (ownership, control, management, personnel) threatens to set up a massive conflict of interest between the developed industrial states of the West and nonindustrial societies of the non-West.

Other readers may point out that a mathematical model has not been offered. This has not been done primarily because it is the author's conviction that personal judgment enters into the picture at so many levels that a mathematical model might be misleading. What has been described is a conscious mental process by which management might arrive at a much sounder measure of the political vulnerability of what it proposes to do overseas than has been the case.

If one thus utilizes the analytical concepts and tools of modern economic and political theory, it is possible to define national interest and at least derive a first approximation of the impact of a proposed enterprise on the host country. In the final analysis, this means an over-all assessment of the political vulnerability of the enterprise, which may be equated with the degree of nonbusiness risk. If that risk can be reduced through the application of more refined measures than now used by management, then the rate at which management discounts its future earnings from overseas enterprise may likewise be reduced. In such an event, Western business moves into a position of being able to consider a much wider range of involvement in the development of Africa, Asia, and Latin America.

▶ ▶ ▶ ▶ **4**

Environmental Dimensions of
the Firm: Company Policy[1]

[1]The generalizations made in Chapters 4 and 5 are the result of a three-year study (1956–1959), by the author, of 172 American firms in respect to their foreign interests. There is no claim that this sample is representative of the entire universe of United States business, but there was a conscious effort to include a wide variety of firms in terms of size, age, industry, organization, diversification, exports, foreign experience, complexity of product, labor and capital intensity, skilled labor requirement, product servicing, value of product, and so forth. Thus, the range of American business attitudes and experiences reported is fairly inclusive, but the incidence of given policies and experiences on the basis of this sample is not necessarily statistically representative. Therefore, no numerical tabulation is included; it would be misleading to do so.

It is all very well to define the criteria by which a Western firm might measure an international business relationship in order to ascertain the economic and political impact and thereby resolve, in an approximate way, whether or not what it proposes to do is functional from the point of view of the host society. The trouble is that such a discussion assumes on the part of management the willingness and ability to:

1. Look at and evaluate foreign projects.
2. Consider these projects in terms of the interests of the host societies.
3. Adapt process and products to the foreign environment.
4. Search out and examine a variety of alternative projects simultaneously.
5. Structure the enterprise in the most appropriate manner (that is, in reference to ownership, control, financing, choice of foreign associates, and so forth).

In other words, the previous discussion assumes a policy and organizational environment that provides the firm with the degree of flexibility and international-mindedness required to apply the criteria

146

developed in Chapters 2 and 3. The truth of the matter is that such an environment rarely existed, at least among the United States firms examined by the author.

Company policy is obviously relevant to decisions relating to the choice and structuring of overseas enterprises. For purposes of discussion, these policy variables are divided into ownership, growth, product and process design, and investment. A policy, of course, may be made explicit or it may be implicit in the company record.

Ownership Policies

Of the total direct investment [overseas, by United States firms] of $25 billion [in 1959], nearly three-quarters was in enterprises in which the U.S. equity ownership was 95 per cent or more (including foreign branches), and 20 per cent was in the ownership range of 50 to 95 per cent. Only 5 per cent of the investment was in enterprises in which United States equity participation was less than 50 per cent.[2]

It is revealing and significant to examine the attitude of company executives in the United States toward foreign control of, or participation in, international joint and mixed ventures.[3] Such an assessment is revealing because it underscores the importance of unsupported personal opinion in foreign investment decisions. It is significant because it reflects a general lack of management concern for the interests of host countries.

Fixed attitudes in respect to such undertakings are compounded largely of prejudice. This fact was borne out in the author's 1956–1959 inquiry in that opinion among executives on the merits of 100-percent United States industry-owned subsidiaries, joint and mixed ventures seemed to be divided and could not be correlated with any objective

[2] *U.S. Business Investments in Foreign Countries* (Washington: U.S. Department of Commerce, Office of Business Economics, 1960), p. 6.

[3] For our purposes here an international joint venture is any undertaking in which individuals or legal entities of more than one nationality form a continuing, profit-seeking relationship in which the partners share to a greater or lesser extent in the risks of the undertaking. Such an enterprise may or may not involve sharing equity, for various types of contractual relationships likewise fall within this definition. By mixed venture is meant an enterprise in which a government participates in ownership. Discussion of this subject follows closely the author's article "Management Attitudes Toward Mixed and Joint Ventures," *Western Business Review*, Vol. VI, No. 1 (Feb. 1962).

business factors. Some firms looked for joint ventures; others avoided them. Some looked only for contractual relationships without equity interest on their part. Furthermore, the record of companies that had gone abroad only on the basis of 100-percent-owned subsidiaries as against those that had been willing to participate in joint and mixed ventures (including those based on contract, without equity) was by no means conclusive in demonstrating the superiority of one type of relationship over the other. Much depended upon specific circumstances. And, as has been argued in the preceding chapter, the degree of "jointness" of a foreign project should logically rest on the relative contributions made — or which could be made — by foreign and local interests. In no case did a firm relate its policy to this factor. Therefore, the selection of a *general policy* applicable *at all times* and under all circumstances, in regard to joint and mixed ventures and contractual relationships, could only be attributed to prejudice — or opinion, if one prefers — held by those determining company policy.

It was also significant that on no occasion did a company official comment upon the different meaning of "control" once one began operating across an international frontier. What did "control" mean under circumstances where recourse to local commercial law could be slow and heavily biased toward national and local interests? Effective control could be lost very easily through the encroachment of local law, government enterprise, and political discrimination. Majority ownership did not always mean effective control. And what did ownership control mean where the management consisted entirely of local nationals? One could anticipate that in fact control could be assured only so long as the policies of the firm coincided with the interests of the host governments and of local associates. If conflict arose, control could be lost with or without ownership, contractual relationship, or American management.

One Hundred-percent Ownership   An inflexible policy against entering any joint or mixed ventures was nearly always a veneer covering basic distrust by United States businessmen, and possibly dislike, of non-Americans. In casual conversations with company officials this fact was clearly revealed; there was a striking correlation between policy and general attitude vis-a-vis non-Americans. It might be worth-while for a management having such an inflexible policy to examine the real motivation and reasons for the adoption of that policy. In any event, such an inflexible policy seemed a very poor basis on which to enter international business, a thesis that will be developed in the following pages.

Managements insisting on 100-percent ownership *under any and all circumstances* gave a variety of reasons for their policies. These could be clustered under the following:

1. Interference in management by a minority interest.
2. Inadequate protection for the firm's products afforded by mere patent and trademark control.
3. Lack of confidence in the ability and integrity of foreign business groups.
4. Unpleasant past experience.
5. Need to maintain complete quality control.
6. Desire to follow a rather unusual personnel policy.
7. Conflict of interest between the American and foreign companies (*e.g.*, pricing of parts and materials, use of profits).
8. General distrust of foreign partners.
9. Danger that the company might be edged out of a joint venture by the foreign partners.
10. Possible difficulty in maintaining equity.
11. Belief that it was unfair to expect anyone to participate in an enterprise over which they had no control either in respect to profits or management.
12. The family nature of local investment.

A significant contrast in attitudes toward degree of foreign participation was provided by the approach by two firms to Japanese ventures, both manufacturers of rather complex industrial products. An executive of the first said very frankly, "We would build in Japan if we had control over sales." Management feared possible Japanese competition were it to permit a Japanese company to manufacture its products. In this case 100-percent or majority ownership by a foreign company was ruled out by the attitude of the Japanese government. A possible licensing deal with a Japanese firm, or a minority investment, died primarily because of management's fear of Japanese competition. The approach of the second company was somewhat similar in that during the initial phases of negotiation, management insisted on at least a 55-percent interest in a jointly owned company, plus a royalty equal to 15-percent of the total sales of the new company. After a year of negotiation and study it became clear that it would be more profitable for both parties if the United States firm would merely take a direct royalty of say 10 percent from the Japanese manufacturer and eliminate the proposed third company altogether. Eventually, as mutual confidence grew between the managements of the two companies, this scheme became the basis for final agreement. An executive in the American firm observed that the demand for control over the Japanese operation had eased as the American management came to know the Japanese management better.

In the latter case, as part of the final agreement, the United States firm named the Japanese manufacturer an "operating associate" of the former's international sales organization. The Japanese territory was to be world-wide, and the United States firm's international division was to "make every reasonable effort to encourage purchase from Japan, particularly when current availability, lower delivery costs, and faster services exist." The Asian area was to be considered as a nonexclusive territory for supply by the Japanese. All sales originating in territories outside Japan were to be handled through the United States firm's international division. Such orders calling for manufacture in Japan were to be placed with the Japanese company by the international division, with necessary shipping instructions. The Japanese company would then bill the division at prices indicated on the United States company's wholesale list. The Japanese firm agreed to pay the United States firm, for technical assistance rendered, 8 percent of the sales price for American-designed products manufactured by them, such payment to be in dollars. Thus, with adequate confidence between managements of companies located in different countries, the fear of unfair competition by the foreign associated company might dwindle to insignificance. Furthermore, arrangements could be devised which provided for the servicing of foreign markets to the mutual advantage of both companies, although admittedly a weather eye should be focused on United States antitrust provisions while doing so.

Acceptance of Minority Foreign Equity Another group of companies, about equal in number in the survey to those which demanded 100-percent ownership, insisted on majority control only. The difference was significant in that it often seemed to reflect growing management sensitivity to the realities of international business.

Statements by executives in support of majority — but not complete — ownership of foreign enterprises underscored the highly personal or nonbusiness nature of many decisions. One executive commented, "We are continually struggling with the question of local participation. We feel that we should not be operating 100-percent-owned subsidiaries, but we would be unable to stomach not having control of our subsidiaries. . . . We feel that our participation is sort of a guarantee to other investors" (because of the firm's reputation, size, and so forth). Another reason for insisting on at least majority control was that the investment policy in underdeveloped countries was so different from that of the United States, particularly in respect to anticipated return on investment.

In another company an executive explained that though each one of his firm's foreign operations was wholly owned, in principle, the firm was prepared to sell minority interest to local investors. He then added

> We were prevented from doing so in Uruguay due to some archaic law they have. And we were prevented from doing so in the Argentine by Peron. We have a Brazilian subsidiary in which the public owns 48 percent of the stock. There was a curious thing about that; the buyers wanted a guarantee that [we] . . . would remain in control. We refused to give that guarantee, although we indicated that we had no intent of withdrawing.

Later, he commented, "The real problem of foreign investment is management." The firm was decentralized, and there were local boards and resident managers in all of the subsidiaries abroad. Although the company employed 4,000 persons overseas, there were only sixteen Americans employed.

Company *L* executives at one time had talked with their Filipino representative about the possibility of manufacturing in the Philippines. It developed that the Philippine government did not wish outsiders to have controlling interest. As a result of this fact, plus certain other considerations, management recommended to its board to go ahead on a technical assistance and management contract basis only, and the recommendation was accepted. Under the agreement the American firm accepted responsibility for every function including management, plant construction, and training of personnel, and the supply of necessary technical know-how. The company also was given the option either of accepting a cash fee or being paid fully or partially in stock. It could, if it so chose, take a minority interest in the Philippine company anytime during the first five years of operation. In this case the American company initially had no cash equity in the Philippine enterprise, apparently because of the former's inability to secure a majority interest, though it did assume management control for a limited period of time.

Executives of a drug company felt that the principal reason their firm had not gone into India on a direct-investment basis, as its

Indian distributors had been urging, was an Indian requirement that 51 percent of the Indian firm be owned by Indian nationals.[4] This, they felt, would place the company's interest in a very vulnerable position in that the parent company would necessarily have to divulge its formulas and processes to the Indian subsidiary. The Indian majority interest could then squeeze the American firm completely out of the picture, in which case it would lose both its investment and the Indian market.

Alongside these rejections of investment projects by reason of official pressure for majority local control could be laid the experience of *P*, one of the few American firms which had been able to secure recent permission for a fifty-fifty participation in a Japanese enterprise. Management had held out for such a deal. The Japanese were so interested in some of *P*'s products that they finally gave permission. Although officially the company was organized on the basis of 50-percent participation by *P* and 50-percent participation by its Japanese partners, *P* actually had voting control on the board of directors of the Japanese company because one of the Japanese directors lacked voting power. This arrangement was accomplished by establishing a low initial capital, split fifty-fifty. The company then called for a second capital installment, and the Japanese deliberately defaulted on 1 percent of their investment, thereby giving control to *P*. This financial maneuver took place before production had started and by prearrangement between the Japanese and American partners. In this case, cross-licensing arrangements with other companies — some of them involving products to be manufactured in Japan — required *P* to have absolute control over any associated companies making use of the licensed processes and products.

Company *P* was not the only American firm to find a way around official restrictions. Another example was Company *M* in India. Investment by this firm was to be between $100,000 and $200,000, and, in addition, it was to provide technical assistance to the Indian subsidiary and receive royalties in return. Through a majority interest the Americans were to have management control. The Indians then

[4]This is not quite correct. The Indian government did not object to the control of a concern by foreign capital for a limited period, if such were found to be in the national interest. The point was that each case would be dealt with on its merits. As a matter of actual practice, however, most foreign companies at this time were not permitted absolute control of Indian enterprises, although in the 1960's there has seemed to be some weakening on this point.

threatened to force local control. A way out for the American company was provided by a friendly Indian concern which offered to become a sham majority stockholder. On paper, the United States firm owned only 49 percent of the Indian company, but in reality it effectively controlled the Indian enterprise with the connivance of its Indian partners. An executive declared, "Of course, they could turn against us, but this was the best we could do."

Desire for Foreign Equity Interest   An executive of another company, in outlining a number of factors that are held to be important in inducing favorable action by management on a given foreign investment proposal, mentioned first the necessity of finding a set of suitable partners. His management generally desired a minority interest by local investors. "We feel enterprises are more secure if we're not alone," he explained. It was likewise a policy of the Company R to have a local associate. The president of this latter company said, "We want to come to a country and add to it, not take away."

Thus, there are managements which *actively desire* foreign minority partners, an attitude quite different from mere acceptance of such partners when 100-percent ownership became impossible. And generally, one might add, the trend seems to be in the direction of joint enterprise by choice. The Kalmanoff study of joint ventures in Colombia concluded:

> The trend of formation of joint ventures . . . has intensified since the War, and there has been a pronounced increase in the trend during the last five years. To some extent, this is a reflection of the increased pace of industrialization in the country, and, in connection with some of the more recent projects for local assembly of durable equipment, it also reflects the formation of local industries in response to import prohibitions and restrictions. The trend also indicates an awareness, on the part of both domestic and foreign investors, of the advantages to be derived from their association in common ventures.[5]

The Newman study of joint ventures in Cuba reported:

> While joint ventures were rare before 1950, they have become very common in many fields in the past seven years. Moreover, they are likely to become even commoner in the future.[6]

[5]George Kalmanoff, *Joint International Business Ventures in Colombia* (New York: Columbia University, 1957, mimeo. only), p. 10.

[6]Philip C. Newman, *Joint International Ventures in Cuba* (New York: Columbia University, 1958, mimeo, only), p. 36.

Newman's observation points up an advantage accruing to joint ventures; in the case of expropriation, one stands to lose less.

Policy shift in respect to ownership of foreign subsidiaries was reported by a large diversified company. The president of one of its divisions explained that management much preferred to own subsidiaries on a 100-percent basis, whether within the United States or not. "Most of our foreign subsidiaries are wholly owned, but we are learning and are willing to take in local participation," he stated. The company was even changing some wholly owned subsidiaries into public corporations and selling stock locally. Its Indian enterprise was an example. Management apparently was coming to the view that foreign companies should invite public participation in India as a protection against nationalism, and possible risk of expropriation. The observation was made that the Indians were involved in at least two conflicts: (1) the desire to retain their own natural resources as against the need for their exploitation, and (2) nationalism as against the need for foreign capital.

The board chairman of another large company explained that the founder had been "quite an internationalist." In setting up companies in England, France, Belgium, Switzerland, and Italy he had invited local ownership. As a result, the American parent company ended up with only a little over 50-percent interest in these ventures. Public participation in these, the chairman indicated, had interfered with the proper management of the companies to a certain extent; at least it had complicated matters. He did not elaborate. On the other hand, the director of the company's international division felt that there was distinct advantage in local participation. Even where local participation did not then exist he would be in favor of such participation within a relatively short period of time. The firm's Turkish subsidiary was 100-percent owned by the parent company; the German company, 97-percent; and all others, over 60-percent. He would be in favor of giving 30-to-40-percent local interest in the Turkish subsidiary in a few years' time. The reason for holding off that long was that he did not wish to impose on anyone the "problems of childhood" of the Turkish subsidiary. It would be a mistake to have local capital in at the start, he felt.

In explaining the rejection of a Philippine project because of the Philippine insistence upon majority control, the president of another company observed, "We want to control our own business." Later, he reflected, "I don't blame the Brazilians or the Filipinos for feeling the same way."

It was true; some non-Americans did feel the same way. In a report on a Colombian project, an executive of a chemical corporation wrote:

> During my visit, *P* . . . [the prospective Colombian partner] was adamant in maintaining that they were interested in a 50-percent participation in a new company. This position, quite different from that expressed in the correspondence with us, was expressly taken because of a fear of two things should they be minority stockholders:
>
> (a) That the new company would be forced to purchase all its raw materials from [us] . . . regardless of competitive prices. I assured them that we have no intentions of requiring a Colombian company to buy technical material from us but that we would request that [our company] . . . be given an opportunity to meet the prices on any bid.
>
> (b) That they might lose their equity in the company if we should want to double or triple our investment and had insufficient capital to participate in the increase. I indicated that we would be agreeable to a contract which required approval of minority stockholders prior to increase in the company's capital.

The author of the report said:

> My conclusions in this regard (and these were left with Mr. *P*. . . .) were (1) in no circumstances would we favor a fifty-fifty proposal; (2) if we were to invest money in Colombia we would want a majority position in the company; and (3) if *P* . . . wished to maintain control, we could discuss the possibility of our participating to the extent of 15 percent to 20 percent in exchange for the use of our name, for technical assistance (both in production and in sales), and for the use of patents. Under these circumstances we would not invest capital.

Some managements had sought local participation in certain countries, although not in others. An executive of a manufacturing company pointed out that local participation in a Brazilian project was opposed by his firm because Brazilians expected at least a 15-percent return immediately; they were not willing to wait. This tendency was strengthened by their ability to realize high short-term returns from real estate investment, particularly in apartment houses. Further, local investment would not be a mass investment but would be based on a few large family fortunes. This type of investment ran the risk of introducing uncertainty in management as key persons died and control fell into the hands of those knowing nothing of the business and having little interest in it. Rationalization? Perhaps. Majority ownership in Willys-Overland de Brasil, an affiliate of Willys Motors, Inc., was held by more than 15,000 Brazilian stockholders.[7]

Occasionally a management did desire local participation but found it difficult to secure. One company had pushed hard in order to permit Canadian participation in its Canadian sales and service subsidiary. But, as one executive explained, it would have been necessary to capitalize the business at perhaps double what the firm had put into the subsidiary in order to permit significant local participation. Even in 1956 earnings would not have given enough return on the higher capitalization; hence, it was impossible to increase it. Personally, this executive would have preferred local Canadian participation, but only when earnings were high enough to enable the company to get adequate returns, plus the return on the 40-percent or 45-percent of additional stock.

In general, it seems that a steadily increasing number of American executives are coming to realize the essential fairness of the position that local interests should be permitted to participate in enterprises launched by foreign groups in their respective lands. The United States Department of Commerce reported that as of 1959 there seemed to be "a tendency for newer enterprises to have a somewhat larger proportion of foreign equity proportion."[8]

The Friedman-Kalmanoff study of joint ventures concluded:

> As private direct investment in the less developed countries has increased, the use of the joint venture form of investment has also increased.... In Latin America, joint ventures appear everywhere to be gaining importance.... Among the countries in the Far East and Middle East, there appears to be an even greater emphasis on joint ventures than in Latin America.[9]

Perhaps the problem had been brought home to American management particularly by Canadian pressure. A concise statement of the Canadian attitude, prepared in 1955 by the Canadian Manufacturers' Association, is as follows:

[7]See International Finance Cooperation, Press Release, No. 16 (July 11, 1958), for details of this joint venture, in which the IFC is an investor.

[8]*U. S. Business in Foreign Countries, op. cit.*, p. 6.

[9]Wolfgang G. Friedman and George Kalmanoff (eds.), *Joint International Business Ventures* (New York: Columbia University Press, 1961), pp. 37–38.

A large proportion of Canada's manufacturing enterprises are controlled by nonresident head offices, chiefly located in the United States. Some of these enterprises enjoy a large degree of autonomy and have tended to become "naturalized" Canadian companies, but, at the other end of the scale, many exist simply as branch assembly or manufacturing operations with little effort or opportunity to develop a responsible national outlook. Such companies may operate under policies which bear little relation to the social needs of the communities in which they are located; some contribute little in the way of capital investment, import all their needs of materials or components, and may be closed down or withdrawn on short notice.

At the end of 1953 nonresidents controlled 4,253 Canadian concerns, including subsidiaries, controlled companies, and unincorporated branches in all lines of business. There were 1,722 such concerns in the manufacturing industries, of which 1,402 were controlled from the United States, 274 from the United Kingdom, and 46 from other countries.

In order that the Canadian economy may derive the greatest benefit from industry controlled beyond its borders, it is hoped that there will be increasing recognition on the part of such enterprises that good public relations makes it advantageous to

   (1) invite the participation of Canadian equity capital in the Canadian entity
   (2) widen Canadian representation on their boards of directors
   (3) progressively increase the Canadian content of their products
   (4) carry out a measure of product development, engineering and research in Canada
   (5) provide for greater participation in export markets
   (6) in the case of resource developments, carry out the processing of the product in Canada to the fullest practical content.

The Association does not, however, favour legislative compulsion to to bring about these ends.[10]

If barriers erected by American business enterprises against local participation could bring about such vigorous opposition by responsible groups in Canada, one could well understand the harsher de-

[10]*Representations of the Canadian Manufacturers' Association to the Royal Commission on Canada's Economic Prospects* (Dec. 1955), p. 9. See also Gordon Hudson, "Foreign Control of Canadian Business," Parts I and II, *Business Quarterly*, Vol. XXII, No. 3 (Fall, 1947), and No. 4 (Winter 1957); John Manning, "American Investment in Canada," *Colorado Quarterly*, Vol. VI, No. 2 (Autumn 1957); Irving Brecher and S. S. Reisman, *Canada–United States Economic Relations* (Ottawa: Royal Commission on Canada's Economic Prospects, 1957); and George Mowbray, "Little Canadianism and American Capital," *Queen's Quarterly*, Vol. 65, No. 1 (Spring 1958).

nunciation — and countermeasures — undertaken by those governments which must deal with much less politically enlightened and
economically sophisticated electorates than does the Canadian government. Quite unlike most Canadians, the ordinary folk in many un-
developed countries started from a point of heavy nationalistic bias
against the West in general and private business in particular.
Could any sensitive person then claim that encouragement of local
partnership made no difference?

It is interesting to note one final point regarding management
demand for control of foreign subsidiaries. It seemed odd that many
of the companies demanding control via ownership were, nonetheless,
turning over effective management of their foreign plants to local
executives. Such practice logically vitiated — or at least substantially
weakened — many arguments against local participation, such as
quality control, dishonesty of local partners, and secrecy of processes.
One thus suspected a high degree of rationalization by some managements in explaining their policies in respect to the extent of ownership
required for favorable action on overseas projects.

Desire for Majority Foreign Equity Interest   A number of firms in
the survey either insisted on taking a minority equity in foreign
ventures or were willing to accept a minority position even though it
might not be forced by government regulation.

Two large hotel companies, for example, sought opportunities to
go into foreign hotel ventures on a minority basis, though accompanied by management contracts. Minimum requirements for a
foreign project that might be approved by the board of one were: (1)
majority interest or management control; (2) a 15-to-20-percent
return or better on invested capital; and (3) adequate local financing.
Management had refused to consider projects requiring any substantial investment by the company itself. The reasons were explained by an executive thus, "It is hard to be on both sides of the
fence — that is, both part owner and the man who works for the
owner." The company simply did not have enough money available
to go in on a majority basis. Consequently, participation had to be on
a minority basis. Management felt that it was best in any event to
have local interest in a hotel; it was somewhat less of a drain on the
local economy and hence the enterprise was less vulnerable politically.

In discussing the willingness of their firm to go into minority
partnership with a Turkish group, executives of one company explained that they were actively avoiding majority interest for they

did not wish to be responsible for financing the venture. The company had gone into the Turkish venture on the basis of a management contract valid for ten years (with an option for extension) and a 20-percent interest in the company (in return for patent rights and trademarks). In respect to a possible conflict of interest, a board member explained that it had been agreed that his company would bill parts to the Turkish company at a standard price charged all distributors. Management of the Turkish company was free to buy from any source desired; it was not obligated to buy from its United States associate. It was obligated, however, to produce a machine of a design approved by the American company, and certain parts for the approved machine were manufactured only by the United States firm. The latter also received profit on the sale of parts to its Turkish associate and, in addition, secured a 2-percent royalty on sales. Eventually, it would gain further income from the repatriation of profits or dividends. Despite many problems, the American management seemed reasonably well pleased with the relationship it enjoyed with its Turkish associates.

In another case it appeared that if Company *J* went into an Indian manufacturing venture, as was likely, it would insist on a minority position. The member of management chiefly concerned with investigating the proposal expressed no fear of being pushed out by a majority Indian group. Management sought a minority position so that it could limit its investment to used machinery. It did desire some participation in ownership in order to have a voice in management.

A motor vehicle manufacturer had been involved in a Belgian enterprise since early 1956, an enterprise controlled and owned by Belgian interests. The American firm had only a small interest in the company, an interest received in return for patents, drawings, and technical assistance. One reason for going into this venture was the management opinion that there was a European market for certain models of its vehicles. Perhaps the trade agreements that Belgium had with other European countries could be annexed to permit the export of some of the Belgian-made vehicles into these other countries. In order to induce the Belgian government to seek such annexation to present trade agreements, management felt compelled to satisfy the Belgian government that the vehicles contained a substantial percentage of Belgian content. Inasmuch as the company manufacturing these vehicles was in fact a Belgian company with little foreign capital investment, the charge could not be made that it was a foreign manufacturer. Hence, its political position vis-a-vis the Belgian government was stronger.

In sharp contrast with two important competitors, management control of Company X's foreign ventures, with but one exception, was held by the group domiciled in the country of investment. In addition, X had fifteen-year to twenty-year technical assistance contracts with all of its foreign associates. The company president observed that if an American company really assisted a foreign enterprise in terms of research and new products, there was no reason to fear that the foreign associate would draw away. In two instances, technical assistance contracts in which X had been participating had run out, and in both the foreign company had approached X before the expiration of the original contract for extension of the agreements. The president commented, "It all depends on the kind of job one does." This company had had no trouble in plowing back profits into foreign business operations. The avoidance of conflict over the use of profits depended on the choice of local partners, the president felt. Management also tried to choose businessmen, instead of promoters, on whom to base its foreign ventures. It wanted the range of interest held in foreign associates to run between 20 percent and 49 percent. The firm decided it was definite policy to stay clear of majority interest. The president acknowledged that there were two schools of thought in the United States business community with respect to the optimum percentage of equity one should hold in foreign ventures, but the key to the matter was the character of the people with whom one associated abroad.

Why was minority interest in foreign ventures deemed desirable by another management? Because each national market constituted but a small segment of its total business, and management wanted to conduct business in many different countries in order to gain protection through spread. It could not do so on the basis of its own capital. In each foreign agreement there was a provision that in event of sale of stock, the United States firm had the right of first refusal.

Flexibility in Regard to Foreign Equity Interest   Another group of companies pursued flexible policies in that their managements were willing to enter into either 100-percent-owned subsidiaries, majority-controlled subsidiaries, minority interests, or contractual relationships, depending upon the circumstances of the particular country or particular project in question.

A prime example of such flexibility of policy was that of a large chemical company. Its foreign interests went from 2-percent to 100-percent ownership. "We feel that it is best to have either a minority interest *or* a controlling interest," one executive commented. The firm had a number of fifty-fifty interests abroad, and in some instances problems had arisen in reaching decisions. As to the fears voiced by some managements in regard to minority interests, fears which had to do with loss of markets and control over patents and processes, the executive merely commented, "Hogwash." His firm had never permitted a person or firm to use a company mark outside the country of manufacture unless the United States company controlled the company involved. The restriction would not, of course, prevent such a company from exporting, but it could stop it from using the United States marks in other markets. "We feel that a foreign company should develop a mark of its own; it is in its best interest to do so," the executive explained. "If our marks were ever taken away from it, it would be left without any marks of its own." The board chairman had directed that whenever the company took a minority interest in a foreign enterprise, the contract with that enterprise should be so written that the interest of the United States firm could not be watered down by an increased capitalization by the foreign owners. It was admitted that such a provision was really an impossible one to work out. "If I were a majority interest," one executive observed, "I would object to being bound by an agreement with a minority interest to the effect that I couldn't increase the capitalization of the company without the approval of the minority interest." The company had encountered difficulty in Spain, Italy, and Japan in maintaining its equity. In one instance management had used know-how royalties to purchase additional stock, as well as the foreign currency proceeds from the local sale of American-made products. In another case dividends from its minority stockholdings had been ploughed back into the foreign enterprise. Although the problem of maintaining equity in foreign companies in which minority interest was held could be a very real one, there were, nonetheless, ways of meeting this difficulty by an ingenious and interested management.

The Celanese Corporation of America was another company with a flexible policy regarding joint ventures. A general policy of the company has been to become part of the countries in which it is active rather than merely to repatriate profits. Therefore, management has been very much interested in securing local partners, although admittedly a joint enterprise can be loaded with problems. In a public statement, a vice president of the Celanese Corporation of America had this to say:

> I have a strong opinion that every company establishing a manufacturing facility in Mexico, or anywhere else for that matter, should organize it as a venture jointly owned with local capital. In the first place, the capital is available. In the second place, it becomes possible to stimulate national pride when selling the product. Local partners will help one avoid mistakes and handle local problems better than he. An affiliated company is not likely to become a political target whereas a foreign subsidiary may become fair game for anyone.
>
> Moreover, some of the most successful ventures in Mexico all seem to be jointly owned. The largest is Celanese Mexicana, a company of considerable dispersion and diversification. Others are Industria Electrica de Mexico, the large Westinghouse affiliate; Telefonoa de Mexico, owned by International Telephone & Telegraph, the Swedish Ericson Company, and Mexican interests; the tire companies — Goodrich-Euzkadi, General-Pope, and Goodyear-Oxo; the steel company La Consolidada; Pepsi-Cola de Mexico; Compania Mexicana de Aviacon, owned by Mexican capital and Pan American Airways.
>
> There may be some questions as to whether a foreign company should enter Mexico or any other Latin American country on a financially equal basis or in a minority position. My company has done all three. Over the years, I think the attitude has developed that the position of stock ownership should reflect the contribution made by the respective partners. There may also be the feeling that if you don't get along with your associates it doesn't make much difference what proportion of the stock you own. As a matter of fact, Celanese Corporation of America, after originally owning a majority of the common shares of Celanese Mexicana, allowed its holding to decline to a minority position when new issues of shares were made. To me that seems significant of the company's confidence in its Mexican associates.[11]

The president of the Celanese Corporation of America, Harold Blancke, spoke on this same subject before the Empire Club of Canada in November 1951. In part he said:

> This point brings up another fundamental policy. We desire joint ownership with local citizens of these affiliated companies. It is a part of our philosophy that modern industry, international in scope should be composed of local units in each country where it has interests.

[11]Emery N. Cleaves, "Economic Climate for Manufacturing in Mexico," before the Conference on Business and Industrial Opportunities in Mexico (East Lansing: Michigan State University, Feb. 2, 1957), pp. 12–18.

Although industrialization is growing, at different rates, in every country in the world, only a few countries have the natural resources to provide the basic materials for industry. Local people must participate in the exploitation of the natural resources which they own. They must participate in development of their own markets. And we are happy to share in the opportunities of the local people in each country where we are invited.

It is unsound to permit local industrial problems to become foreign problems. Such a situation is entirely unnecessary. It is logical for people to want to share directly in the prosperity of the local enterprises with which they are familiar and in which, on a local basis, they take pride.

The president of another corporation stated that he endeavored to keep each investment abroad as low as possible. The one thing "we have to offer" is know-how, in return for which it may be possible to secure some interest in a foreign company. "We'll take a chance on a small equity. We have no particular qualms on joint ventures," he went on to explain. "If the operation were a big one, we'd probably want a majority interest, but where we are going into a relatively small market, it is somewhat different." In any event, the company tried to employ local management personnel. In justifying this attitude, he said, "No New York lawyer would try a case in Illinois without getting local talent to help him."

An executive of a large concern explained that the general philosophy of his company was that American firms should go into joint ventures abroad. He mentioned his firm's Mexican investment where the Mexican partners were adamant that they had to have a 50-per-cent interest. The Mexicans were likewise negotiating with another American company, which insisted on 51 percent for itself. Because of this insistence the other company lost out, and the Mexicans joined his firm in a trial venture. Management felt that it had to get along with its foreign partners whether it had a 40-percent, 50-percent, or 60-percent interest. The vice president observed, "Absolute control is not so important. You must develop a feeling of mutuality with your foreign partners." As to the security of product and processes if the company were to go in with a foreign partner on a basis permitting something less than absolute control, the vice president pointed out that his firm's Mexican partners were just as jealous of their methods as the Americans were of theirs. Also, an ex-employee of the company might start up in competition right here in the United States. An American company had no certainty that its employees who knew its processes and products would not go to another company or organize one of their own. There was no greater danger abroad.

Choice of Foreign Partners There is a further policy question concerning the identity of the foreign partners. A problem confronting many American managements and bearing very heavily on their decision as to whether or not to go abroad in respect to specific projects is related to this matter, for in a number of instances the prospective foreign partner is a governmental agency. Although in some cases such an arrangement seemed to cause no particular concern, many American managements appeared to oppose vigorously the idea of going into partnership with agencies of foreign governments. As suggested earlier, where an enterprise would be a net consumer of services or products coming out of the public sector, a mixed venture might be the most appropriate form of organization. No management related these factors.

The reaction of one management to the idea of a mixed enterprise in India was voiced by a vice president of foreign operations. In such ventures there was inclined to be a lack of common interest. "I know of no case where a government has been proud of making profit. Governments are much more interested in producing cheaply." It is pointed out that this view was not universally valid; for example, the publication by the Turkish Government of profits realized by Turkish state economic enterprises. There was reason to believe that profits claimed were, in fact, exaggerated for political purposes.

Commenting on a hypothetical situation in which his company was asked to cooperate with an agency of the Turkish government in developing a particular industry in Turkey, an executive stated, "We'd say the hell with it. That is not our idea of free enterprise." A comment from an official in another company was, "We are a business, not a government agency." A large international company reported a policy of shying away from government enterprise as part of a more general policy of doing everything possible to be non-political. Not only did it disassociate itself with particular political groups, it also avoided such politically vulnerable commodities as newsprint. An executive of yet another corporation commented that his company would never think of going into a mixed venture. He added, "You cannot find one case in the world where government operations are not more inefficient than private. Mixed companies almost always lead to conflict and to the influx of political pressure in the business operation." The reader will note that here were voiced various expressions of the doctrinaire, free enterprise approach.

It might be appropriate to point out that in comparing the efficiency of government operations with private operations it was necessary to specify which government operation where and which private operation where; a general statement was meaningless in this context. Government operations did exist which were more efficient than some private operations. Insofar as the influx of political pressure into business operations was concerned, such pressure was not unknown within wholly private business. The generalization that mixed companies almost always led to conflict was one which would be difficult to support on the basis of available evidence. The experience of mixed ventures in Turkey, for example, tended to support the contrary. In any event, for a variety of reasons, one could anticipate very active and substantial government participation in economic affairs in the underdeveloped countries. To refuse to associate with such state economic enterprise was perhaps to close one's eyes to reality and to admit the inability of private enterprise to cope with that reality.

The top management of one large chemical company reflected an awareness of this reality when the president declared in a public statement that:

> The Indians suggested we go into partnership with a government-owned corporation to produce a long list of needed ... [products]. In view of the realities of the situation, we agreed to consider this proposal, even though it meant indirect partnership with Socialism. Our refusal to be rigid and our willingness to look at India's problems from the Indian point of view have, I believe, been major contributing factors in stalling the Russian offensive [to participate in this particular industry in India] for almost two years.

The executive went on to explain that in the end the Indian proposal proved impractical "mainly because we thought there would be too many basic conflicts of interest in a partnership with a government agency in such a broad enterprise." (The management of the international subsidiary company apparently disagreed sharply with the management of the parent company on this point.) The president continued, "But we were able to offer them a creative alternative ... we are now helping Indians build what will probably be the most modern ... plant in the world." The new plant was to be owned by an agency of the Indian government. The United States firm had obligated itself to build the plant, supply engineering assistance, and train Indian technicians in company know-how. Also, the American management had assisted the Indians in securing an Export-Import Bank loan for the purchase of machinery. In return, the company was to receive a modest fee (2½ percent on domestic sales and 5 percent on export sales). The president continued:

> We will be criticized . . . because we are helping build a . . . plant in the public sector. If it succeeds — and we are doing our best to make it a success — won't this encourage the Indians to produce more . . . [products] in the public sector?
>
> We took a long, hard look at this question before we made our decision. It is not easy for a believer in private enterprise to swallow a Socialist deal. There are several reasons why we did it.
>
> *First, this is the way the Indians wanted it.* They made this perfectly clear to us after we had done our best to dissuade them. We finally concluded that, if we really meant to help the Indians, we would have to help them in the way they wanted to be helped. To have insisted that we do it our way or not at all would have been transparently arrogant, a quality the Asians find less than endearing. . . .
>
> *Second, by revising our plan, we forestalled the Russians,* who, in the midst of our negotiations, offered the Indians a $20 million, 40-year loan at the incredibly low rate of 2 percent to finance several basic units for . . . industry. . . .
>
> *Third, our willingness to be flexible enough to adapt our resources to their needs* undoubtedly helped make . . . [*our company*] *seem a reasonable company with which to do business in the private sector.* The fact is, we now will build a private sector . . . plant. There is, therefore, a possibility that what started out to be a government-owned industry may end up being mostly in the private sector. This will probably hinge on whether we and the other producers do a good job in India.[12]

One management observed that there were two sides to its minority partnership with an agency of the Turkish government. At times, the American management had wished it were operating a completely private company, but on other occasions, such as when a million-dollar allocation of foreign exchange was received (the manager of another United States enterprise in Turkey — wholly private — was complaining at the same time that he could not get $30,000), management was content to be involved with an official agency. A further advantage in joining an agency of the Turkish government in such an enterprise, an executive explained, lay in the fact that if a strictly

[12]Italics are not in the original.

private competing company were to come into Turkey, the Turkish government, because of its interest in the mixed enterprise, would probably subsidize the latter so that it would be able to compete more effectively. And perhaps a private competitor would not be permitted to set up shop at all.

Another management reported no particular objections to mixed ventures. In Mexico the company's local partner was a semigovernmental agency. When queried about the possible penetration of political influence by reason of this association, an executive observed that generally the company secured a special management contract or management control by the American company was specified in the original contract. He remarked pointedly that political influence in business was "not exactly unknown in the United States."

Several mixed ventures have attracted international attention. E. A. Bayne, Iranian specialist for the American Universities Field Staff, reported on the agreement between the Iranian National Oil Company and the Italian government-owned Ente Nazionale Idrocaburi (ENI).

> The formula, which provides in accordance with Iranian law for a 50-50 division of oil profits from a given production, has the further feature of making the production company in Iran half Iranian and half Italian. The result, at least theoretically, is that Iran would be receiving 75 per cent of the profit, while other agreements in the Middle East are restricted to the 50-50 formula. American diplomatic pressure was obviously [used] ... to prevent the institution of a new formula, unfavorable to the West, that might upset existing agreements, elsewhere in the region. Now, American oil men are less concerned, and have pointed out to the Iranians that the agreement also provides for the repayment to Italians of development costs which United States companies normally absorb, and that in terms of quick return as cash bonuses which American and other companies would be willing and able to pay, the formula is not as attractive as it looks.[13]

The point was, of course, that the international ownership concept had substantial psychological advantages over a mere split in profits. (In this case the venture was not a true mixed venture, for *both* partners were agencies of their respective governments. But if ENI were private, the situation would remain essentially the same.)

Another mixed venture in Middle Eastern oil involved work on a

[13]E. A. Bayne, *His Excellency* (New York: American Universities Field Staff, Nov. 1957), p. 8.

projected pipeline paralleling the Suez Canal. Various Egyptian agencies, including the Suez Canal Authority and the Economic Organization, were slated to contribute 51 percent of the capital, the remaining 49 percent to be subscribed by private foreign firms. (The Egyptian government was to receive 50 percent of the gross revenue of the company which, with all its installations, would become Egyptian property after twelve years from the date operations started.)[14]

In June 1958 three similar ventures were reported. A concession for forty-four and one-half years was granted by Kuwait and Saudi Arabia to the newly formed Japanese oil concern, Arabia Oil, for offshore oil exploration and development. (Both governments were involved, for the concession lay off the coast of the Neutral Zone over which both exercised equal and undivided sovereignty.) Under the agreement, each government was authorized to purchase 10 percent of the shares of the company at face value, *once oil was found*. In addition, each was to receive a stipulated percentage of the net profits of the company.[15]

In Indonesia in 1958 United States and Canadian oil interests were reported to be seeking formation of a company in association with the Indonesian government for the production of oil in Sumatra. The United States–Canadian offer was on the basis of a 50-percent interest for the government and a 50-percent interest for themselves, organized as Asamera Oil (Indonesia) Ltd., a registered Canadian company. The joint company would pay 52 percent of its profits to the Indonesian government. It was also agreed that Asamera would sell its share in the mixed Indonesian company to the Indonesian government at the end of thirty years.[16]

On June 29, 1958, the Iranian Lower House ratified a contract for a mixed venture to be undertaken by the National Iranian Oil Company and Sapphire Petroleum, Ltd., a Canadian concern.[17] Apparently, this last was a fifty-fifty proposition, with 75 percent of all profits going to the Iranian organization.

In private conversation in the same year a number of American oil men admitted the long-run inevitability of joint ventures — mixed or otherwise — in exploiting foreign oil concessions. A major problem seemed to be in inducing local participants to share in the

[14]As reported in *International Financial News Survey* (Nov. 8, 1957), p. 156.
[15]*International Financial News Survey* (June 13, 1958), p. 389.
[16]*New York Times* (June 23, 1958).
[17]*Ibid.* (June 30, 1958).

initial risk of exploration. The United States companies objected — and with some reason — to giving local interest the right to buy in after oil was found, particularly if the purchase price of the stock was fixed at the start.[18]

A mixed venture was organized in 1958 to construct a hydro-electric project in Brazil, the largest ever undertaken in Latin America. It was likewise the first in which private companies had joined official Brazilian agencies in a major power development. Common stock, representing 50 percent of the equity capital, was held by the Brazilian government, by the state of Sao Paulo, and by CEMIG, a corporation owned by the state of Minas Gerais. The greater part of the preferred stock was held by private companies — 51 percent by the Sao Paulo Light Company, an affiliate of the Brazilian Traction, Light and Power Company of Canada, and 9 percent by Companhia Paulista de Forca e Luz, an affiliate of the American and Foreign Power Company. The World Bank made the enterprise possible by a $73-million loan to the joint enterprise, known as Central Electrica de Furnas, S.A.[19]

A variation on the mixed venture is a venture in which the participants are a foreign company and a local labor union or federation. In Cuba two unions had invested portions of their retirement funds in joint ventures with foreign companies, thereby "making possible the largest and most luxurious hotel in Cuba and a multi-million dollar bagasse by-product plant."[20] In Turkey the government-administered Labor Pension Fund had constituted an important source of capital for projects in which foreign capital had participated. But few managements seemed alive to the possibility of such local participation.

For a variety of reasons, the role of government in the economic life of an underdeveloped country has been by necessity very much greater than that of the United States government in American industry. In order to demonstrate the effectiveness of private business and private management — not to mention the possibility of doing business at all in a given country — it frequently has been necessary

[18]Perhaps this is not an insurmountable obstacle. The General American Oil Company negotiated an agreement with the Spanish government for the exploration and exploitation of ports of the Spanish Sahara under which the Spaniards were to put up half the exploration cost in return for half of any production (in kind) after a 10-percent royalty. See *Forbes* (Oct. 15, 1958).

[19]Press Release No. 558 (Oct. 3, 1958), International Bank for Reconstruction and Development.

[20]Newman, *op. cit.*, p. 11.

for both local and foreign business groups to enter into mixed ventures with government agencies. The fact that relatively few American firms included in the author's survey seemed willing to entertain any consideration of mixed ventures revealed substantial prejudice. Granted, there were undoubtedly many solid objections to the mixed venture, but to dismiss all such ventures without analysis, to lump all governments and all public agencies together, hardly seemed a rational business approach. Nonetheless, the survey indicated that a major breakthrough in this area might be under way. Old doctrinaire prejudice was being shed by some American businessmen as they moved into mixed ventures.

Sharing Technical Information and Skills   Another form of management participation is the sharing of technical information, technical skills, and management talent with a foreign business group. Such intangible assets, as well as patents and trademarks, may in some instances be capitalized and form part of a contribution to an international joint venture. Or, even if not, if the "investing" firm enters a contractual relationship with a foreign concern in which payment is contingent upon sales or profits of the enterprise, such a relationship may constitute a joint venture if the risk is in fact shared to any significant degree by the investor. Not infrequently, it was found in the survey conducted by the author, the initial ownership share held by an American firm in a foreign enterprise had been received in payment for intangible assets. Later, in an attempt to build up equity, the American partner had often contributed tangible assets.

Management reaction to sharing its intangible assets varied greatly. A tire and rubber company had not given any technical assistance or license agreements for tire manufacture abroad because it did not wish to relinquish any of its production techniques or formulas. Such a fear obviously rested upon a lack of confidence in prospective foreign business associates. Not surprisingly, such a policy was linked to a parallel policy of not going into foreign enterprises other than those 100-percent owned by the parent company. Another management feared that by giving know-how to foreign groups it might in effect be transmitting these processes to the company's competitors in the United States. This was the alleged reason the company did enter a Dutch project. The same executive added, "What is to prevent one of their engineers one day from coming over here looking for a job."

One might observe that it would be even easier for an *American* employee to shift his allegiance to a competing American firm.

Even those processes and products of a patentable nature were held to constitute a real problem in respect to adequate international protection. One management met this problem, at least tentatively, by selecting twenty-one countries, the firm's important markets, and applying for patents in all twenty-one. It was estimated that the total cost of such coverage would probably be about $25,000. Theoretically, someone might still purchase or build machines of the type developed and used by the corporation in producing its principal product, set them up in some small market, and produce for sale in the United States in competition with the United States firm. The products involved — pressed-pulp packaging materials — were bulky and light weight, and consequently rather expensive to ship any distance. Nonetheless, because the machinery was better covered by patents than was the product, there was no reason why a producer outside the United States could not ship into the United States the same sort of packaging material that the American firm was manufacturing, provided the other firm operated the machines in an area where the patents were unprotected.

An executive of Company *M* recounted that when his firm had refused to go into an English venture, the English company had proceeded to manufacture parts for its machines without the approval of the United States management. Granted, the English company could not sell these parts under *M*'s name, but they could sell them *specifically for use* in *M* machines. A similar situation was that reported by the Caterpillar Tractor Company shortly after World War II when there appeared in various markets substantial quantities of spurious Caterpillar parts, parts produced without Caterpillar approval. So long as the parts were not labeled "Caterpillar," but only advertised as fitting Caterpillar products, there was no legal recourse.

The management of a well-known processed-food manufacturing firm confessed that it was in difficulty in Brazil in respect to trademark protection. A few years before, various officers of the company had agreed that the company should protect its trademarks in countries where it might become active in the foreseeable future. The sales director then proceeded to try to protect the company's trademarks but learned that someone else had already registered them in Brazil. This fact stimulated the firm's executive committee to approve a much broadened program of trademark protection. It was estimated that the company had spent some $20,000 or more implementing this program. As an example of the difficulties involved, the case was cited of an Australian firm which had copied the company's advertising, as well as its product. One executive observed, "They've got it covered. We can't protect it because we don't ship regularly to Australia." As implied in this last statement, there were some markets — notably the Commonwealth countries — in which it was necessary to supply the market in order to maintain effective protection.

In a magazine article Peter G. Schmitt, Director of Associated Companies for Westinghouse Electric International Corporation, wrote:

> It is not enough to accept the opportunities of the moment. The operator in the world market must interpret the forces and trends at work in all areas of the world toward some logical end result. As an illustration of the importance of acquiring a mastery of global changes, I might mention that at one time, for purposes of patent application, we divided the world into "a," "b" and "c" areas, consisting of so-called primary countries, such as those of Western Europe, which had highly developed economies and industrial systems; secondary countries which had developed their industries, transportation systems and economics to a lesser extent but which were showing signs of dynamism and progress; and finally, those countries which had not yet become part of the movement toward general industrialization.
>
> In general, patent applications were filed in the "a" area since it was there that we required the greatest protection for our basic technical discoveries. But we no longer follow this simple general practice because the distinction between areas "a" and "b" has broken down under the impact of industrial advancement.[21]

In general, in view of the reported difficulty of protecting patents and trademarks in many underdeveloped countries, it seemed that maximum protection was afforded the owner by his production within these countries to the extent economically feasible, or by his licensing a local producer to do so. So long as the patent or mark owner provided some form of continuing service of value, there was a motive for the foreign firm (and its government) to observe proprietary interests.

[21]Peter G. Schmitt, "Licensing Arrangements vs. Branch Operations," *Export Trade and Shipper* (Apr. 22, 1957), p. 5.

Conclusion   Quite apart from all of the business consideration involved, it appeared that the American managements included in the survey seldom recognized the fact that under some circumstances joint ventures were very much in the interest of the host society. Reference is made to such factors as those suggested by the following questions.

1. Is the degree of ownership by the American firm limited to the foreign exchange components of the initial investment? More? Less? (If the American firm is capitalizing what might be available within the local economy, it may be vulnerable.)
2. Is the enterprise, by its nature, politically vulnerable (that is, basic industry, defense industry, monopolistic industry, politically important consumer industry, service industry, public utilities, agriculture)?
3. Is the American firm's contribution (skills, know-how, research, new capital, market organization, and so forth) to the host country via its foreign enterprise a continuing one?
4. What is the net contribution the American firm would make to the host country (in terms of net value added, balance of payments, national revenue, allocation of local resources, and innovation) if its relationship to its local associated enterprise were different? Now? Twenty years from now?
   a. Joint venture?
   b. Minority equity?
   c. Debt (rather than equity)?
   d. Contractual (managerial, license, technical assistance) arrangements?
   e. A combination?

Security of a firm's overseas assets, one might suggest, could be associated closely with management sensitivity to this facet of international business organization. Rigidities of policy in regard to structure of association with local interests limited the range of alternatives seriously considered by managements of investing companies and hence their ability to use the criteria developed in Chapters 2 and 3.

Factors seriously limiting American managerial freedom in this area — but rarely mentioned — are contained in these United States legal restrictions.

1. For a United States parent firm to be able to deduct from its United States tax liability foreign taxes paid by associated firms abroad, the parent must own at least 10 percent of the equity of the foreign concern. (Foreign taxes paid by a subsidiary of a subsidiary can be used as deductions by the United States parent only if the first subsidiary has at least a 50-percent interest in the second subsidiary.)

2. Participation of a foreign or United States competitor in a joint venture abroad — even though on a minority basis — may make a United States firm liable to United States antitrust prosecution if the two companies enter into any sort of restrictive agreements, including the allocation of territories.

3. A foreign subsidiary of a United States parent must be 100-percent owned if it is to benefit from the AID-administered investment guaranties program. (At the time of the author's 1956–1959 survey, *no* foreign subsidiaries could qualify. This innovation was enacted in 1961.)

4. United States restrictions on trade (for example, with the Soviet bloc, Communist China, Cuba) apply to foreign-based firms controlled by U.S. nationals.

One further point should be mentioned:

Where tax treatment of dividends paid to non-residents (*e.g.,* a parent company in the United States) is significantly different from that accorded dividends to local nationals, joint ownership of an enterprise by an American company and a foreign partner may result in basic disagreements on dividend policy. In such cases it is normally prudent for the American company to retain full ownership of the subsidiary company, or at least to hold clear majority control, in order to maintain flexibility with respect to dividends.[22]

Growth Policies

A management's attitude toward growth can be critical in determining its attitude toward a foreign project. For example, one company had never seriously considered producing abroad, largely because of a general policy not to expand. The managements of numerous smaller companies, particularly those privately owned, seemed hesitant about seeking external financing — hence a policy of non-expansion, which applied to foreign ventures as well as domestic.

[22]*Market Europe* (New York: Morgan Guaranty Trust Company, 1961), p. 55.

Therefore, they did not seek to satisfy the needs of the developing countries, whatever the profit potential or political pressures.

Diversification   The extent of a firm's foreign operations — that is, *geographical diversification* — is in a sense an insurance. Failure of one particular enterprise may not be of critical importance. Also, with multiple undertakings abroad, a company may find use for nearly all types of foreign exchange; hence the risk of nonconvertability of foreign exchanges is minimized. In addition, the firm may be in a position to exploit fully comparative factor price advantages so as to enhance its competitive position. The point is that in some cases it might be important that a company making its initial move abroad expand into other foreign areas as rapidly as possible in order to minimize the risk of loss or competitive disadvantage. If the company has a general history or policy contrary to rapid expansion, it might well hesitate to move abroad at all.

The choice of foreign projects and their structure is likewise related to a management's attitude toward *product diversification*. One management, in the survey, had been interested primarily in developing new product lines and had been seeking opportunities for acquiring companies in the United States, the availability of which was an active competitor for capital against foreign ventures. The president observed, "If we came up with a European venture and then had an acquisition available to use here, we might throw over the European." The chairman of the board of another firm stated, of a board decision not to go into a Brazilian manufacturing operation, "Our Board only last week reached the conclusion that our efforts and our money could be better spent on further diversification in this country than in additional manufacturing abroad, and we have, therefore, definitely tabled any plans for a foreign operation."

Several executives commented on the difficulty faced in diversifying into products related to those with which the company has been traditionally associated; by so doing they might move into competition with either important suppliers or customers. Some managements apparently felt strongly that they should remain in the same line of business with which they had been identified. Therefore, they were more inclined to seek geographical diversification rather than product diversification. An executive of one such company stated, "We wish to stay in the business we know best." Further expansion of his company's business in the United States was somewhat doubtful in that no easy growth in established lines seemed likely. And if the firm diversified into related products, it would find itself competing with important customers. But foreign interest was beginning to appear in management.

One large cement corporation had not invested any new dollars abroad since 1931, primarily because of the chronic inflationary situation in the area of its chief interest. Another reason for noninvestment appeared to be the conservative attitude of management toward product diversification. A key executive pointed out that although he believed in diversification in certain situations, diversification often went too far. He added, "We do one thing only and that is to produce and sell cement. We have gone into no allied businesses." He implied that this specialization was an advantage in doing business abroad in that the countries in which his company operated plants had a certain common denominator, and the company had people who were "profoundly well informed on developments in ... [this particular area] as they affect our particular business." Obviously in such companies, the range of projects considered was limited in that industry and geographical criteria were controlling, not the sort of criteria suggested in Chapters 2 and 3.

Integration   The key to the expansion of one large company both within the United States and abroad had been its policy of integration at every stage, from the processing of raw cotton to the production of consumer goods utilizing cottonseed oil. Thus, the company had expanded gradually in the United States from ginning to oil refining and finally to the manufacture of margarine, shortening, and salad oil. Though company development abroad tended to follow a similar evolution, it first entered the consumer products field in these countries. For example, in Brazil the company produced insecticides, and then proceeded into the purchase of coffee and the manufacture of the fertilizer. Generally, the reasons for spreading into these seemingly unrelated fields were to protect investment in cotton. Thus, fertilizer and insecticide production was undertaken in order to insure the quality of the cotton crops financed by the company. In other words, there was a predisposition toward such projects, however they and alternative projects might measure up under the criteria suggested in the preceding chapter.

For another firm, one of the problems holding back foreign expansion was alleged to be the difficulty of finding locations abroad where at least minimum manufacturing services were available. An executive observed, "When a valve on one of our machines breaks down, we want to be able to run down the street to a machine shop and have it repaired. We do not wish to have to maintain our own shops." The company manufactured film in the United States but subcontracted the manufacture of its cameras, the principal product with which it was identified. Hence, when it came to developing its camera and special film abroad, there was a further difficulty in that the company had to provide manufacturing facilities for both camera and film, which it did not do in this country. (Management had decided *as a matter of policy* that the company should exploit its own patents rather than license other producers.) The absence of manufacturing services abroad, plus the fact that the company's production was not integrated in the United States but would necessarily have to be abroad in view of company policy, constituted two facets of the problem of integration as it bore on the selection and structuring of foreign projects. What was not realized at the time was that a policy devised for the domestic market was not necessarily a valid policy elsewhere.

A machine tool builder pointed out that his company, although manufacturing a very high percentage of their own production machinery, did not manufacture bearings, belts, motors, pumps, switch gear, and other electrical items. Nor did the company have its own foundry. Management had found it easier to purchase from specialty foundries. The firm had sixteen to eighteen foundries working for it, many of them specializing in particular types of castings. The company had six or eight men circulating among these foundries to make certain that the products came up to the company's standards. He observed that there was always a question in overseas areas whether or not adequate foundry facilities were available. In other words, the firm's domestic policy against more vertical integration had been transferred overseas without challenge, thereby severely limiting the firm's horizon and making the application of general, "national interest criteria" impossible.

Product and Process Design Policy

The degree of company flexibility in terms of product and process design can greatly affect the selection and structuring of foreign projects. For example, an executive stationed in India for many years commented that generally speaking United States companies were based primarily on the North American customer and had very little concern for customers elsewhere. Concrete evidence of such disregard was the poor job United States firms had done in helping set up worldwide standards. "United States industry has not even taken the trouble — or spent the money — to have its 1,700 national standards translated for use in foreign countries," the president of the American Standards Association is reported to have said. "It is no coincidence that American industries doing the largest export business — the electrical and motion picture industries, for example — are the ones that have helped develop international standards."[23]

Such a pronouncement of general disinterest in the foreign customer would seem to be a safe generalization, although there appeared to be a tendency on the part of at least some managements to study more carefully the requirements of foreign markets and to modify their American-oriented products accordingly.

It was difficult to pin down situations in which the intransigence of a company management in respect to modifying its product for foreign manufacture had been, for instance, the critical factor in rejection of a foreign investment project. Nonetheless, the necessity for redesign, added to other obstacles, could block foreign involvement; time and effort and expense were considered too great. The export manager of one large corporation observed that a major bottleneck to foreign investment was the *inflexibility* of its engineering department.

Directly related to willingness to modify product design was the problem of quality.

The fact that quality was not an absolute value, but was related to use, was realized by only a handful of managements.

The experience of one corporation in Africa was relevant.

The local African government had been buying from the corporation hand-operated dusters for use in distributing pesticides in the cotton fields. The dusters were loaned to individual Negro farmers. The duster supplied by the corporation was a finely machined device requiring regular oiling and good care. But the fact that this duster turned more easily than any other duster on the market was relatively unimportant to the native farmers. Furthermore, the requirement for careful oiling and care simply meant that in a relatively short time the machines froze up and broke. The result? The local government went back to an older type French duster which was heavy, turned with difficulty, and gave a

[23]*Time* (June 30, 1958), p. 74.

poorer distribution of dust, but which lasted longer in that it required less care and lubrication.

From the point of view of the small Negro cotton farmer, the quality of the French dusters was more appropriate than that of the American dusters. In this relative sense, the quality of the French machine was superior.

This same view was reflected in a remark by the director of the international division of a large company to the effect that Europe could produce anything more cheaply and better than the United States. By "better" he meant *better relative to the demands of the foreign market.* He admitted that many American-made products were much better than their foreign counterparts in an absolute sense, but that this superiority in quality was too expensive to be "within the circle of demand" of many foreign markets. For example, his company manufactured one item with an average life of thirty-five years. The trouble was that many people abroad could not afford to pay for a device lasting that long, and they were not impressed.

Another way of looking at quality was to consider that the additional cost of a highly durable product represented an added investment. If the cost of capital were relatively high, as it was in many of the underdeveloped countries, it might not be economically feasible to purchase the more durable or higher-quality product of the developed nation.

As a matter of policy, an internationally minded management examined deliberately and systematically the products it intended to market within Country X from the point of view of the environment of Country X. It made no assumptions about the validity of an American-oriented product. Major environmental factors considered in relation to the design of a given product were:

Environmental Factor	*Design Change*
Level of technical skills	Product simplification
Level of labor cost	Automation or manualization of product
Level of literacy	Remarking and simplification of product
Level of income	Quality and price change
Level of interest rates	Quality and price change (Investment in high quality might not be financially desirable.)

Environmental Factor	Design Change
Level of maintenance	Change in tolerances
Climatic differences	Product adaption
Isolation (heavy repair difficult and expensive)	Product simplification and reliability improvement
Differences in standards	Recalibration of product and resizing
Availability of other products	Greater or lesser product integration
Availability of materials	Change in product structure and fuel
Power availability	Resizing of product
Special conditions	Product redesign or invention

The author's survey likewise demonstrated that there was a singular inflexibility on the part of a substantial number of American companies in their *productive processes*. A member of the export division of an electrical appliance company observed that he had designed a plant for Chile which the company's engineering department had estimated at $190,000. He added, "I had it down to about $40,000." He then went on to explain that, of course, his experience in manufacturing was about thirty years behind him, but perhaps that was why he could think in terms other than the most modern manufacturing innovations.

A tractor company executive spelled out another difficulty: "We know how to make 10,000 tractors a year, but not 500. In Mexico we are doing things by hand that we'd never do here." In planning the Mexican assembly layout, the vice president had asked the company engineering group for a "low-cost assembly line." The engineers evolved a line costing $175,000 — to build sixteen tractors a day. The engineers planned on a paint room, a drying room, and other elaborate installations which were taken more or less for granted as part of any American assembly line. Besides other changes, the vice president ordered the use of a tent for a paint room and a hand sprayer. The result was that the $50,000 investment in paint facilities was reduced to $750, and the over-all cost for the assembly line from $175,000 to $29,000. The vice president added, "Our people simply can't think in these terms."

Flexibility of product and process design was reflected in this description of the General Electric and Kelvinator plants in Mexico:

An half-hour drive from the city limits stands the new General Electric Plant, employing nearly 800 people of whom only six are Americans, and giving the surface impression that it is the perfect model of a modern plant. And it is as modern as the plant will let it be. All G.E. products turned out by this plant have been redesigned, although the casual observer might miss the differences. Some of the differences are to make the product more salable in Mexico. Most of the differences are to adapt the product to manufacture on general purpose machines. This one G.E. plant turns out a dozen product lines: a few for industry, like transformers; most for consumers, like radios, refrigerators, irons, and television sets, which they assemble, using imported parts in Mexican cabinets. Each of the dozen products turned out in this one plant has a separate plant setup in the United States.

The nearby Kelvinator plant, controlled by Mexican capital, worked under similar limitations. Doors for their refrigerators require a stamping press of a size and capacity too great for their Mexican operations. So unfinished steel refrigerator doors are shipped in from Detroit and piled roof high. The stamping and the cutting of the rest of the box is done on a press setup for several dies, which require operations by two crews. This is a far cry from recommended Detroit production practice, but it is a way of getting the most out of an expensive machine in an as yet limited market.[24]

Few company managements, included in the author's survey, could visualize manufacturing facilities of this sort. An executive of one of the large automotive companies summarized the trouble encountered in many of foreign markets thus, "If we put our international company in, we must conform to certain standards. We can't do business in mud-huts. . . . It is difficult for us to be small." This, then, is a factor making it difficult for some companies to respond positively to the generally narrower markets of the emerging nations.

Likewise, few firms could visualize products other than those being manufactured domestically. When the possibility of making older, simpler type machine tools in such places as Brazil was suggested to a manufacturer, it was observed that United States companies in Brazil would constitute an important market for any tools manufactured there. These companies were accustomed to United States tools and would want the same as those produced in the United States. Management had once talked of taking an obsolete model machine tool to China. (This discussion took place before the Communist take-over.) It developed that the Chinese were reluctant to accept older machines. The company president added that there was a

[24]Richardson Wood and Virginia Keyser, *Sears, Roebuck de Mexico, S.A.* (Washington: *National Planning Association*, 1953) p. 6–7.

natural reluctance for anyone to admit that they were not capable of assimilating and using the latest model machines. The firm did not undertake production in China.   Two points should be made at this juncture: (1) United States companies operating in Brazil might not have a free choice in demanding the latest model machines when it came to foreign exchange allocation and import permit, particularly if acceptable machines were available — and presumably more economic machines, given Brazilian conditions.   (2) In many of the developing nations machine tools of other than the latest models were being manufactured.

The management of one relatively small company operating in the foreign field believed that its big advantage lay in the very fact of its smallness, which gave it *flexibility to operate on a custom basis.*   For instance, the truck division of the company produced only on order. It worked from certain basic models, but for each there were a number of possible modifications.   The export director of the company explained that the truck division "offered" the greatest line of optional equipment of any manufacturer of trucks in the world.   This truck had been strong in the Middle East precisely because the customer could order what he wanted.   Company engineers had designed two special models for the Middle East, one feature being doors that opened from the front so as to give the driver a maximum amount of air (a desirable feature in the high temperatures of the Middle Eastern desert countries).   The vehicle to be produced in the company's Turkish plant was to incorporate several special features, including four-wheel drive, five-speed transmissions (instead of four), an extra large radiator and fan (because of the high elevations at which many of these vehicles were to be operated), increased size of wheels and reinforced frames (because of poor roads).   Ford, Chrysler, and General Motors officials admitted that it would be exceedingly difficult for them to design special vehicles for different areas of the world, in part because of the enormous size of these corporations and their fundamental reliance on the American market.   One of the three, nonetheless, seemed to be changing its policy in this regard.   A member of the export division of this corporation said, "We believe the world demand for cars will be larger by 1975 than is the North American market.   Also, we believe the demand will be for a car we are not now producing."   He then went on to point out that most of the world is just on the verge of coming into the model "T" stage, not the

Cadillac. He declared, "We are definitely and irrevocably committed to foreign expansion." The inference was a line of special vehicles.

Virtually every management, other than those already heavily involved in foreign manufacturing, commented about the difficulty of going abroad because of the small national markets. However, it seems that the real difficulty in many cases did not lie in the small national market, but rather in the inflexibility of the company itself in terms of product, manufacturing processes, and organization. Therefore, the range of choices in respect to overseas ventures, and their structure, was severely limited. Consequently, the firm was necessarily less responsive to what the national interests of the host society might demand; hence, the risk factor was blown up unnecessarily. The result was management refusal to give serious consideration to overseas projects.

Extraordinary flexibility in process design was reflected in a public statement by the vice president and general manager of the International Business Machines World Trade Corporation.

> When we decided to expand our production abroad, we knew that manufacturing for our type of equipment would be prohibitively costly unless we could make one item in one place and supply from there to all countries. Could this be done? Let me illustrate this problem by referring to a single one of our products — the IBM electric typewriter. Our sales outside the United States until 1950 were trifling; yet we were certain that there was a big market. To tool and equip a factory to manufacture electric typewriters costs a great deal of money — several million dollars. Suppose we made them in England and supplied the rest of the world from there? That would be fine — except that many countries had their own typewriter industries and imports would surely be restricted or prohibited.[25]

In order to resolve this difficulty IBM established what is called the "interchange plan." The vice president explained, "Under this plan we divide the manufacture of the typewriter among nine countries — the United Kingdom, Sweden, Switzerland, The Netherlands, Belgium, France, Germany, Italy, and Canada. Each company makes the total over-all requirements for certain parts and supplies them to all countries." He went on to say, "We are just now develop-

[25]*International Management Association Special Report No. 1* (New York: American Management Association, Jan. 1957), pp. 14–15.

ing an interchange for manufacturing a complete line of our products among a group of Latin American countries. We are confident this program will enable all countries in Latin America to use our equipment and services more freely, thereby contributing to an increase in employment and in economic development."[26]

It is not being suggested that all companies either could or should go into all markets, but it did appear that a good deal of the talk about the small national market, the inappropriateness of specific products to foreign markets, and the difficulty of maintaining quality in these markets was sheer rationalization arising out of a lack of imagination, initiative, and effort on the part of management. Given this inflexibility, management had no way of knowing whether it was maximizing long-run return on investment or whether its products and processes were designed for maximum benefit to the host society in terms suggested in Chapter 3. Few managements seemed to be aware that a plant was a complex of processes, many of which could take place apart from the others. Those electronic firms that were exporting materials for labor intensive processing and then importing the resulting components for domestic installation had learned to separate processes. Everyone gained in the long run. But rare flexibility of process design — and perhaps product design as well — was required.

Investment Policies

In addition to the foregoing elements of policy inflexibility, there are also those relating to internationalization, regional specialization, size, and the investment of "new" dollars. Finally, the absence of any policy guide lines or criteria can likewise constitute a limitation on the range of management choice and, hence, its ability to use national interest criteria.

Internationalization   It is worthwhile to consider the definition of company policy offered by various executives in explaining the rejection or acceptance of specific foreign projects. Many companies had laid down general policies, such as that given in the 1955 annual report of the American Optical Company: "We are following a course [that is, a policy] of securing additional coverage by manufacturing in foreign countries where this could be done to advantage." In another case, as a result of a special study authorized by the board of

[26]*Ibid.*, pp. 14–15.

directors, management determined to become international and there-upon set up a committee to explore actively foreign opportunities. Several executives in another company said that in their opinion there had been an unwritten policy in the corporation to the effect that it should not invest abroad. The corporation, given an intervening change in management and a report on the company's international position by an outside consultant, later became "irrevocably committed" to foreign expansion. The financial director of a chemical company observed that an important element in the consideration of such projects as those proposed in Brazil and Colombia had been the underlying policy of the company to be international. "We want to be an international company," he said.

Such policy positions obviously related to a management's willingness to consider overseas projects, whatever the criteria of choice among them might be.

An implicit policy not to invest capital and time of company personnel in foreign enterprises was reflected in the extreme caution of some concerns, which caution could be measured by the offers made to foreign groups by these firms. In some cases foreign investment projects failed simply because the American company involved offered too little. An example was one management which had been approached by the Indian government to undertake an enterprise in India. The product involved was eighth or ninth on the Indian list of dollar imports, hence the official interest in stimulating local production. At the start, the Indians indicated acceptability of any kind of proposition: the American company could either establish a plant itself or, if necessary, the Indian government or private Indian groups would participate. If the company wished to furnish only know-how, that too would be acceptable; the capital could be found in India, either private or public. Although there was some doubt as to the availability in India of the materials necessary in the processes involved, a member of top management visited New Delhi to discuss the proposal. He indicated that the company would go ahead if the Indian government were willing to put up 60 percent of the capital as a long-term loan to be secured by a mortgage on the physical assets of the Indian subsidiary. The American company and/or its associates would put up 40 percent of the capital as equity. The Indian company was to be wholly controlled by the American group. The Indian government refused this offer; it was no longer willing to loan the necessary capital. Perhaps under these circumstances the expectation that the Indian government would put up the majority of the capital but relinquish management control to a foreign concern was unreasonable, perhaps not. In any event, the offer of the American company was turned down because it was found inadequate by the Indians.

Again in reference to an Indian project, one corporation really rejected a project by offering much less than that required. The initial proposal called for about a $7 million investment by the American firm for a 49-percent share in the business. Inasmuch as the company indicated that it was prepared to risk only one-half million dollars in India and would expect to get its money out within two years, the proposal did not get very far. In making such a counter-proposal to the Indians, it seemed likely that management anticipated rejection.

The rather unattractive offers — unattractive from the viewpoint of the foreign interest — that one corporation had been making in connection with a number of foreign hotels was clearly a function of the over-all conservatism and caution of management. Unconsciously, management anticipated rejection of its offers and the stringent terms that it would impose. For example, an official of the corporation told the Consul General of Israel in New York that the basis for negotiation for an Israeli hotel would be as follows: (1) his company would have a twenty-year management contract and an option for renewal for another ten years; (2) the Israeli government or owners of the hotel would provide all of the financial requirements, including the furniture, furnishings, fixtures, inventory, and working capital; (3) the company would receive one third of the operating profit and would not be required to compensate the Israeli government or the owners for any operating loss. Nothing happened. Again, negotiations by the same firm with the owners of a hotel in Peru broke down because management offered to purchase the hotel at a price considered "entirely out of the question" by the owners. On at least one occasion negotiations by the firm on a Turkish hotel project collapsed because it offered too little. In going through the file of correspondence and comments on the Turkish project, one received the distinct impression that at no time did management anticipate acceptance of its conditions by the Turkish group. Hence, it seemed reasonable to conclude that the conservative offers made by the company really added up to management rejection of the idea of going into Turkey.

The impression such experiences left was that managements with a real desire to go into foreign manufacturing or other associations with foreign groups made more reasonable offers and closed deals much more quickly than did managements which were really fundamentally opposed to the investment of time and money outside of the United States. Some managements, which were basically foreign-oriented, moved quickly and decisively when the opportunity to buy or invest advantageously abroad arose. Other managements considered and reconsidered for years as opportunities slipped by. No investment criteria at all seemed to be used — whether defined by company policy, business interest (that is, profit), or national interest. That these three factors should be mutually dependent was wholly irrelevant in such situations.

Regional Specialization Several corporation executives cited policies of regional specialization. Companies were simply not interested in anything outside a particular region, an example being one management's rejection of a Turkish project because it was outside the Western Hemisphere. Other managements reported interest in only certain industries or types of industry (basic industry, intermediate industry, essential industry, and so forth).

Although some companies did thus limit themselves policywise to certain industries and to specific regions, others limited themselves to the number of ventures per country in order to achieve spread, the advantages of which have already been discussed. A hotel corporation executive reported that during one year his company had had the opportunity of buying some 150 hotels abroad. However, company policy was to have only one hotel venture per country for the time being. Such a policy obviously placed a major obstacle in the way of any project calling for involvement in a second hotel within a single country, even though such might be in the interests of all concerned.

Project Size Some companies exhibited fixed policies relative to the size of enterprises with which they would become associated. One corporation rejected any thought of going into a Turkish wolfram development because tungsten had a relatively small development potential. As a matter of policy, the company was not interested in small proposals; neither management nor technicians had time to develop small mining ventures. Hence, most small projects suggested to the company were rejected out of hand, regardless of the interests that might be served by participation. Yet, experience would indicate that those projects least vulnerable to political risk are very frequently the smaller ones.

"New" Dollars A general policy of one company was not to invest any new dollars into Latin America, only to plow back sufficient earnings in South American projects to retain the relative position of each existing plant in its market. Robert Barlow and Ira Wender reported that a number of companies had exhibited this "race track philosophy,"[27] namely that of investing in foreign ventures only local earnings and not any "new" dollars, just as a race track addict was more inclined to reinvest his winnings in new bets than in pulling additional dollars out of his pocket. The managements of some companies thus seemed to possess an unconscious feeling that foreign earnings held abroad were somehow of a different quality than dollar resources. Of course, difficulty in repatriating earnings from many parts of the world gave some logic to this differentiation. Nonetheless, the distinction seemed to be a controlling one for a number of companies. For example, the vice president of one company admitted that there was a problem in respect to the availability of dollars for investment abroad. Company policy at the moment was not to put any more dollars overseas, but to let the foreign companies generate earnings and capital for additional foreign undertakings. He said, "There is passive understanding that we will send no more dollars abroad." Such a policy controls the timing of overseas investment and limits the degree of involvement, thereby creating rigidities in policy unrelated either to business criteria or to national interest criteria.

Lack of Policy

In answer to a question whether his company had an over-all policy in respect to foreign investment, an executive in a large, diversified firm replied in the negative. The company looked at each particular situation or proposal on its own merit. For a company with few foreign interests and opportunities, such a lack of policy might be no handicap. But, if a large foreign-oriented corporation lacked a policy or policies in reference to foreign investment, it could be a serious matter for top management.

An executive in one such firm explained that historically his company had gone into projects without thinking through company policy and objectives. However, it had undertaken a serious and costly project to analyze what the company was doing abroad, what its

[27]E. R. Barlow and Ira T. Wender, *Foreign Investment and Taxation* (Englewood Cliffs, N. J.: Prentice-Hall, Inc., 1955).

strength and weaknesses were, and what it should be doing. It was almost a foregone conclusion that the company should concentrate in Latin America. The study resulted in a definitive statement of company policy and objectives and made recommendations for investment by industry and by country. Prior studies made in this field had related to specific proposals as they had arisen, and, hence, had been on a piecemeal basis. Future proposals which might have some hope of favorable action by the company would have to come within the framework of this plan. A company executive pointed out that in the past management had had a "terrific burden" because of the lack of definition of the nature and objectives of the company's business. Consequently, many problems and decisions had come up to top management and had burdened it to the point of rendering the decision-making process exceedingly difficult.

An opportunity to do something outside the present plan, executives noted, would have to be exceptionally attractive and, in any case, would necessitate a re-examination of the company's basic policy. Two examples were given as projects rejected because they did not fall in with company policy, as specified in the plan. There was a chewing gum proposal in Colombia in 1956. The proposition was rejected on the ground that such a venture was not basic enough to the economy of Colombia, nor was the industry large enough in volume to merit the effort and attention that could be involved. One executive explained, *"that the company should not be in any business abroad that could be run just as well by local nationals."* Further, management was committed to expanding on a "line of endeavor concept." By this phrase was meant *concentration on intermediate industries*, particularly in the chemical and paper field. In answer to a question as to whether or not the company would be interested in an iron and steel development in Colombia, an executive said that it probably would not because this industry did not have the characteristics of an intermediate industry. Also, "We would not be making any significant contribution; anyone can buy a steel plant and run it." Here was a situation in which explicit company policy had been decisive in the rejection of specific foreign investment projects.

One of this company's overseas ventures, made after the determination of company policy, namely, oil exploration in Africa, seemed to be somewhat outside of the company's own criteria in terms of regional specialization as well as disinclination to go into mining enterprises. (Certainly oil exploration and production was not an intermediate industry.) However, as one company executive explained, the decision was in line with the policy that the company should interest itself in proposals in respect to activity in underdeveloped areas which might help *solve the foreign exchange problems* of these areas and where the economics of the project provided justification. He said, "We feel that it is all right for the company to be in mining in a minor way, but major mining enterprises would not fit the image of the company we are trying to create." He explained that the earnings of mining companies were somewhat discounted in the United States financial community, although admittedly mining was important to many countries in solving foreign exchange problems. The point of view of management was that major mining projects were better undertaken by the companies committed to mining. Company policy was that the firm should not be much more than a grub-staker in respect to mining. One company executive admitted, however, that if the African oil venture worked out, the company could find itself in the oil industry in a very major way. (It then developed that the project had come about, in part at least, from a very close friendship between a member of the top management of the company and that of its partner in Africa, an American oil company.)

Despite the hesitation and uncertainties, this company had moved far in the direction of identifying its business interest with the interests of the host societies.

Conclusion

In these several respects then — ownership, growth, product and process design, and investment — company policy might either (1) arbitrarily limit the range of management choice in respect to selection of overseas projects and their structure, (2) set no limit on the range of choice, or (3) establish limitations that are reasonable within the context of company resources and competency on the one hand and the economic and political interests of the host countries on the other. The first two types of policy discourage the use of the criteria developed in Chapter 3.

In general, firms would be well advised to hold to no fixed policies in regard to what they will or will not do overseas *except those dictated by the resources and competency available to the firm.* (In this regard, management should make certain that its assessment is not colored by implicit policies.)   Within the area thus defined (in regard to process, product, and geographical region), management should utilize both business interest (profit) and national interest criteria.   Each project satisfying these criteria (projects in which the business and national interest criteria produce coincidental values) should then be studied in reference to the most appropriate structure.

However, the problem does not end there, for the ability to render decisions in this manner — and to service an overseas involvement — is related to the domestic structure of the firm.   The mere statement of an appropriate policy is not enough.

Environmental Dimensions of
the Firm: Company Structure

Company policy is only one of a firm's environmental factors defining the geographical and functional horizons of a management, and hence, of its ability to seek out and implement overseas projects in the manner suggested in preceding chapters. It is necessary to look further at the barriers to companies, and to the likelihood of their acting internationally in the way recommended.

A second set of critical factors determining a firm's international activity is its structural dimensions — as measured by its financial position, personnel situation, formal organization, and decision-making mechanism. To what extent do these aspects encourage or discourage the applications of the national interest criteria developed in Chapters 2 and 3? And what have been the distinguishing structural characteristics of firms with long success records in international business? This chapter is addressed to these queries.

Financial Position

Given the frequency with which financial considerations were mentioned in conversations with company officials in the author's 1956–1959 study, one judged that such matters were in the forefront of management's thoughts.

A scholarly study of domestic investment decisions concludes:

By far the most outstanding aspect of the direct inquiries is their virtual unanimity in finding that internal liquidity considerations and a strong preference for internal financing are prime factors in determining the volume of investments. . . . These attitudes can be explained in terms of three main causes: (1) the disadvantages that arise when a firm extends

192

its external debt position; (2) historical events and institutional adjustments which have made outside funds difficult and expensive to obtain; and (3) the hierarchical structure and motivations of corporate management which make outside financing asymmetrically risky for the established or "in" group. . . . If a debt-financed project backfires and ends in bankruptcy or substantial loss, the managerial group could readily lose everything, that is, their jobs in connection with the corporation.[1]

The authors explained that "for any but the better-known stocks [the equity market] . . . has, for some time, been a relatively expensive method of raising capital."[2] This same study continues:

> Where access to outside funds which seem to really count, that is, in rapidly growing industries, the small firms have used or have been able to obtain substantially less outside money than their large competitors. Furthermore, there is fairly clear evidence that small firms' investment plans are more sensitive to levels of liquidity flow and less sensitive to capacity utilization than those of the large firms.[3]

Although the sheer size of company and its cash position might have much to do with the way in which management looked at foreign projects, nonetheless size — as an isolated factor — appeared only in the rare instance as a critical factor to the rejection of foreign proposals (7 out of 172 firms in the 1956–1959 survey). Too many small companies had operated successfully abroad. But there was one risk for a small company that was considerably greater than for a large corporation, namely, the ability of the latter to self-insure through dispersion of investment.

A small company, given its limited resources and the difficulty often encountered in raising outside capital, may find it necessary to expand more slowly, whether in the United States or abroad. This is particularly true abroad inasmuch as capital is admittedly more difficult to secure for foreign expansion than for domestic — unless, that is, the firm is willing either to accept local participation, to pay relatively high interest rates for local loan capital, or to expand via the route of contracted services. For a certain period of time, then, the foreign interest of a small company might be limited to one or two national areas. At the same time, a large corporation could expand into perhaps a dozen or more national areas. The very

---

[1] John R. Meyer and Edward Kuh, *The Investment Decision* (Cambridge: Harvard University Press, 1957), pp. 17–19.

[2] *Ibid.*, p. 19.

[3] *Ibid.*, p. 161.

breadth of this investment is in a sense an insurance against the loss of individual enterprises. Thus, the risk is somewhat reduced.

The minimum size of an economically feasible industrial unit is the same for the large corporation as for the small — unless management inflexibility is such in the large corporation as to discourage any modification in processes, products, and policies. It was true, for example, that in the case of a grain-milling elevator project in Israel the cost would have been roughly the same whether Firm X or its giant competitor were to undertake it. The national market was given, likewise, the economically feasible minimum size of operation. This meant that any given investment abroad constituted a substantially larger share of the total assets of a small company than of a large company.

On the other hand, this observation is not true for every industry. Many statements by management about minimum plant size, one might suggest, are largely a function of inflexibilities vis-a-vis plant and process design and, to a lesser extent, product design. Also, few managements analyzed projects in terms of processes rather than plants. Finally, many executives in larger companies seemed to feel that they could not afford to be interested in small projects abroad; too much time and effort was demanded relative to the return which could be reasonably expected. Some or all of these inflexibilities might reflect sound business judgment under certain circumstances, but they did limit the horizon of decision.

Rather than a firm's financial position being controlling in respect to foreign involvement, much depended on management policy regarding debt and equity financing, growth expectations, standards of "worthwhileness," attitudes toward participation in joint ventures and/or contractual arrangements abroad, and flexibility of plant, process, and product design. The treasurer of one company, when asked about the effect of a tight money market in the United States on foreign investment, replied that money was always available for sound propositions. It was not infrequently pointed out in those companies heavily committed to overseas production that foreign expansion often required less cash investment than comparable domestic development. A few companies had parlayed returns from various forms of contractual relationships (license, technical assistance, management, marketing, etc.) into large equity holdings in important foreign firms. If one is worried about liquidity but has valuable special skills, foreign markets might be very alluring —

assuming that management is able and willing to undertake continuing obligation to foreign interests. In this latter respect, personnel and organizational factors — as well as policy considerations — are perhaps controlling.

Personnel Situation

Adequacy of personnel for staffing overseas facilities was mentioned frequently by company executives as bearing on foreign investment decisions, both in relation to the initial commitment and the manner in which the projects were structured. Some observed that there was a fundamental difference in the manner in which a government agency and a private firm planned foreign projects. A government agency, it was said, tended to plan a project first and then hire outsiders to administer the project, whereas a company was inclined to ascertain first the availability of personnel within the company and then plan the project around those individuals. This generalization might not be a safe one, but it was certainly true that few companies seemed to invest in manufacturing facilities abroad in the absence of any personal interest on the part of key personnel within the company. But the existence of such persons did not necessarily mean that they could or would be pried loose to manage or to otherwise service the new foreign enterprise. The tendency was increasingly for foreign plants of American companies to be operated and managed almost entirely by foreign nationals. Many managements reported a decrease in the number of Americans employed per plant overseas.

One management insisted that it had never faced a personnel problem in regard to its overseas activities since no overseas plant was managed by United States personnel. A few Americans might be attached to a foreign enterprise for a brief time, but generally foreign personnel were brought to the United States and given training, including management training. Another company had set up the headquarters of an international company in Switzerland, one reason for which was the possibility of attracting European management personnel at half the price of American personnel. Still another company had established industrial research laboratories in Europe, in part because it could hire European technicians and scientists for so much less than comparable American personnel. (It might be possible in certain areas to use blocked funds for research purposes through the establishment of research laboratories in the areas involved.) As an executive in a large chemical company pointed out, the higher level of United States living made foreign service somewhat less attractive to American personnel. The premium one had to pay Americans to go abroad was held to be "exorbitant." His firm's policy was to utilize local personnel to the maximum extent. The difficulty was that the shortage of engineers and qualified technical personnel was a world-wide one.

The vice president of Company *X* had faced something of a problem in securing an adequate manager for an Argentine subsidiary. To send a man down from the United States would have cost between $15,000 and $18,000 a year, which was felt unwarranted, to run a $100,000 business. However, technically qualified management personnel were very scarce in Argentina. This executive devised the scheme of recruiting a man in Spain, what one might call "off-shore" recruitment.

In recruiting engineers for its Cuban venture, the international division of another company visited United States engineering schools to interview students of Cuban origin, thereby lining up several Cuban engineers for responsible jobs in the projected Cuban plant.

Nonetheless, many managements reported considerable difficulty in securing personnel for overseas assignments. A multitude of examples could be cited.

The board chairman of an industrial products company explained that it was almost policy that if his firm went abroad at all, it would purchase a growing plant and not attempt to start from scratch. If management had to send out key personnel to oversee the construction and inauguration of a foreign plant, which would do only a fraction of the business that one of the company's three United States plants did, how did one rationalize their absence? The chairman recounted that several years before there had been an Indian proposition. The company had dismissed the idea, but not so their chief British competitor who proceeded to build a plant in India on a fee basis. The chairman obviously felt that this would not have been worthwhile from the standpoint of his firm and he wondered why the British had been willing to commit personnel and effort to such a project. Later, the man responsible for developing the Indian project undertaken by the British company, when told of comments made by the United States management relative to the work load involved in foreign projects, observed, "Water always looks cold to a nonswimmer." He explained that for the Indian project, on which he himself had been employed, he had brought to Britain two Indians and trained them in what they must do. In India the British firm provided the works and sales managers; that was all. The opportunity to go to India was offered to people in the parent company, particularly to junior engineers, some of whom seized on this opportunity as a method of advancing themselves more quickly than would otherwise have been the case. In referring to a projected Brazilian operation, this Briton said that in order to get it started he would be inclined to give the key jobs to foremen and others who had not had the opportunity to go up in the parent operation. "All you need is enthusiasm. They will be talking all their lives about when they set up the assembly line in Brazil." He went on to say that when the plant was operating, then it should be visited by some fairly high-ranking officials of the parent. "Over all this," he added, "you must have someone who is competent and whose interest is in foreign business."

Clearly, there were a number of approaches to the problem of securing adequate personnel. One suspected that not infrequently when managements specified that the shortage of personnel was a critical reason for rejecting an otherwise reasonable foreign project, in fact they were perhaps concealing their true motive in refusing to go abroad. Although the board chairman for a chemical corporation pointed out that it was difficult enough to get personnel to move from Massachusetts to Ohio, let alone to go abroad, he admitted that the tax advantages enjoyed by Americans living abroad in some areas was an inducement not present in a move to Ohio. After all, tax exemption from the United States income tax for those earning up to $20,000 a year after eighteen months of foreign residence (or an exemption of $30,000 a year after the third year if one qualified as a *bona-fide* foreign resident) might represent a substantial increase in net income to the individual.

The fact that so few managements seemed to have knowledge of and to have used the facilities of the Institute of International Education constituted added evidence that many of those managements rejecting foreign projects on the grounds of inadequate personnel made virtually no attempt to find a way around this barrier. The Institute maintains an index of internationally trained persons situated overseas and in the United States. Several corporations with international operations had found this index helpful in locating United States–trained personnel who might be recruited abroad, and American citizens with personnel knowledge and experience of other countries. The Institute reported:

> This service, for example, located Venezuelans who studied chemical engineering in the United States for the E.I. du Pont de Nemours and Company; for the Standard-Vacuum Oil Company, Pakistanis who had studied business administration; and Americans who speak Japanese, Portuguese, or Hindustani for various corporations.

In reference to the conflict between domestic and overseas business on an operational level, and also to the conflict between the export and manufacturing-oriented points of view, some managements had found it to the advantage of all concerned to institute a system of interdepartmental credits for services rendered to the international division, or foreign subsidiary, or associated enterprise. Under such a system the department or division releasing personnel for overseas assignments received credit in its profit and loss statements for the persons concerned (salary plus some negotiated amount). This device tended to break through management resistance at the divisional or departmental level to the release of such personnel. That so few companies had utilized a system of this kind gave added force to the suspicion that many of the comments about the personnel shortages and the unwillingness of operating personnel to go abroad or of their manager's reluctance to release them, were perhaps more rationalization than fact.

Formal Organization

The manner in which a company was structured relative to export, foreign operations, and research bore very heavily on the way in which management reacted to foreign projects. Whether or not a company entered into production abroad was very often not determined by systematic survey of the advantages to the company, to say nothing of a systematic survey based on a dispassionate consideration of the possible reactions of the host country.

Centralization of International Business   An excellent example of how structure affected a firm's foreign dealings was the difference in the manner in which Corporations *A* and *B*, both large chemical producers, handled the foreign ends of their respective businesses.

The latter had taken no steps to manufacture abroad except in Canada; Corporation *A* had production facilities around the world. The president of *B*'s international corporation explained the difference between these two similar companies. Company *A* had entered the English market when his own firm was thoroughly preoccupied in the United States. Also at that time *A* had been (and still was) more heavily weighted toward end products and specialty products than *B* was. But more significant, the president went on to say, "We had a completely decentralized setup. No one except the management of the dye division had a stake abroad. And, unfortunately, the least dynamic part of the business was precisely that part of the business." Until 1956 apparently no one in the company had looked abroad. "We were too busy with domestic expansion." According to company executives, this absence of attention to foreign markets was primarily a matter of organization. Each of the seven operating divisions had had their own export departments, and exports for any one of them had not amounted to more than perhaps 5 percent of their respective sales. Hence, no one department was particularly interested in foreign business. But, in 1956 an international company was set up as part of a general centralization program initiated by the company's head office. The man spearheading the centralization move took the view that the export business was no one's business when left to the different divisions. He felt that foreign business warranted the special attention of full-time people. Prior to the establishment of the international company there had been no formalized exploration of what the company wanted to do abroad. But now, as one executive stated, "Our thinking in the international division is 100% abroad." Meanwhile, Corporation *A* had been working for several years through an international division which enjoyed the same status within the company as the domestic operating divisions.

An executive of a Boston company gave, as one of the two principal reasons his firm had not been interested in foreign investment, the highly centralized type of management in the company. A twenty-one-man board of executives, each one of whom was headquartered in Boston, really ran the business. "They're the real managers. We don't delegate authority to branch managers, say even in Hartford. . . . We tried to expand into upstate New York and got into a management problem just that far away," an executive explained.

The management of a large industrial equipment company had

been considering a proposal to channel all foreign sales through its international company, but, as the chairman of the board pointed out, "We have been operating on a divisional basis. With our variety of product, I doubt if they should be centralized." The executive assistant to the president pointed out that one of the manufacturing divisions did most of the export business of the entire corporation. He added, "It doesn't make much sense to force them to do business through the international company." (The international company was a wholly owned subsidiary of the parent corporation.) The firm was trying out the idea of having all its European subsidiaries report to the international company, but this was a very recent proposition. Proposals calling for foreign investment or licensing went to the division managers, who examined them first and then approached top management for eventual board approval. Other than for Brazil and Turkey, no proposals had been made to top management to engage in foreign manufacture. The head of the international company, headquartered in New York, spoke vigorously in favor of an integrated international company. He said very emphatically that there were advantages from every aspect in complete integration of the international company and added that jealousy was one reason for the continued separation among the divisions of various foreign activities.

In discussing the problem of decentralization versus centralization in foreign business, the assistant to a division president of a chemical corporation pointed out that while he had been in the New York office of the parent corporation people very frequently had come to him in respect to various foreign projects. Part of his job had been to steer these people to the right persons within the company, not an easy task since thirteen different company offices were involved in overseas development at the time. In early 1957 each division was still operating with almost complete autonomy in the foreign field in respect to both exports and investments. The trouble was that the company had grown through the acquisition of other companies, and there was a strong vested interest in maintaining the independence of each division, which in the past had been a separate company. Hence, it was very difficult to coordinate investment and to establish diversified enterprises abroad. For instance, while on a Mexican survey mission for his own division, one executive for Company *C* had written a report on the possibility of developing a peroxide plant in Mexico. The opportunities looked good, but the division manufacturing peroxide would have nothing to do with it. The mere idea that someone from another division had made a report on one of their products generated resistance. The same executive knew that still another division had been interested in the possibility of producing pesticide sprayers in Turkey. But other than an exchange of information, this Turkish project had not been coordinated at all with his own division's Turkish interest in regard to a related product. In a company that had grown through the acquisition of other companies, it often happened that the company ended up with an internal board of directors, each member with a vested interest in a particular division. In Company *C*, two division managements had voiced strong objections to combining overseas responsibilities — apparently out of fear that they would lose control over their respective foreign enterprises. A proposed international division, upon which a new executive vice president of the corporation was working, would have both export and management responsibilities, but there seemed little likelihood of its rapid organization. In fact, an international division appeared some two years later, but with only limited responsibility.

Reducing Resistance to Foreign Business   There were devices to cut through intracompany obstacles. The international division of a chemical corporation gave the operating divisions statistical credit for income generated out of the latter's international participation. For example, for the export of fertilizer, the international division tabulated the sale, as did the division manufacturing the fertilizer. The treasurer of the international division explained, "We had to do that to stop the squabbling that arose over the release of a big chunk of the business [that is, export] of each division." He was referring to the centralization of all the exports and foreign activities of the company in the international division.

A second chemical company had a similar mechanism whereby an operating division (that is, the people who made the effort in relationship to an overseas development) actually received financial credit for the success of the operation. For example, if the international division sold know-how for $200,000 plus the out-of-pocket overhead expense, the company might take $200,000 in equity in the foreign concern. This equity, although turned over to the company's Panamanian subsidiary, was, at the same time, credited to — say — the plastics division of the parent company. An identical amount was entered as a debit in an "executive and administrative account."

If the foreign company then made a profit, it paid a dividend to the parent. The portion of the plastics division product against total sales was calculated, and that percentage of the dividend was credited back to the plastics division. The same was true of royalties. These profits went into the plastics division's profit and loss statement. Inasmuch as a plastics division manager was judged in part on the rate of return that his division was able to secure on investment, this return from a foreign project could be important to him personally. An executive in the international division commented, "It is remarkable how these people change." He was referring to their change in attitude from one of opposition to foreign investment to enthusiastic support after instituting such a credit policy.

It seems that, in the absence of some type of interdepartmental credit system, the hostilities attending attempted diversion of company personnel and effort into overseas projects, particularly on the operating division level, can readily constitute the critical factor defeating foreign projects or in severely limiting the range of possible ways of associating the firm with them. Under such circumstances, a firm cannot respond fully to the political and economic interests of the host society.

Delegation of Authority   Centralization of *all* authority in the home office represents a failure to delegate authority to a specialized subordinate management. Such usurpation of authority had in the past been an important reason one large corporation found itself well behind its principal competitors in manufacturing and assembling abroad. Until 1955 management had been very much a one-man affair dependent largely upon the president, during whose latter years — although "past his peak" — continued to exercise complete control over "everything from design up and down." Hence, no one else in the company could take any initiative in developing the foreign end of the business.

It appears generally true that in companies which have internationally minded presidents or board chairmen the international corporation or division sometimes does not enjoy the autonomy or authority that would enable it to pursue long-range planning on a truly responsible basis,[4] one dimension of which is the minimization of political vulnerability.

[4] A point made independently by Prescott Crafts, Vice President of the First National Bank of Boston, in a seminar at the Massachusetts Institute of Technology, Dec. 4, 1962.

One reason for delegating authority to specific individuals or groups within a company to handle foreign business relates to *the matter of work load and initiative.* For example, two executives of the international division of Company *M* agreed that it was not until 1955 when the international division had been set up that an internal environment had been created within the company favorable to the consideration of foreign investment projects. One can not expect busy people to push new activities which merely added to their own work load. The recognition of this fact, indeed, was apparently one of the major reasons for forming the new division. The president of a technical products company reported that in the past he personally had handled all exports and studies of possible foreign ventures. He estimated that about 50 percent of his time had been devoted to these matters, which he felt to be too large a share to be so allotted.

An executive in an electrical appliance manufacturing company explained that he had been the principal man charged with the investigation and negotiation of licenses abroad. He added that if more than two or three such agreements were actually negotiated, it would be more than he personally could handle. The supervision of these international negotiations was a job assigned in addition to the executive's other tasks, and consequently it was only natural that he did not press too hard in the international direction; such activity on his part would only add to his other responsibilities.

Assignment of Responsibility In addition to the problem of work load, the matter of responsibility arose in some companies.

In not a few corporations there was literally no one responsible for developing the foreign phase of the business, work load or no work load. One firm's international sales had grown prior to World War II very gradually on the basis of unsolicited orders. After World War II the corporation developed a new line of machinery and was the first in production with it, hence giving it a competitive advantage. The demand for new machines was met quite rapidly, "and that was that." Sale of these machines then fell off, and though it needed additional sales desperately, management had no policy of promoting any products abroad. In 1956, for the first time, an executive was put in charge of the foreign business — that is, made responsible for the profit and loss on the foreign business.

In another corporation, even within a single division, there seemed to be no clear-cut responsibility for follow-up on foreign projects. For instance, foreign operations were not the principal responsibility of the assistant to the division president; he interested himself in them largely because of a personal inclination to do so. No one was pushing him in this direction, and the division export director did not seem to be particularly interested in following through anything other than export sales. As a result, whenever the assistant went off to survey a specific foreign project, such as in Colombia or Mexico, correspondence relating to other foreign projects, such as that in Turkey, had to await his return or, barring that, be answered by someone else who was not familiar with the line of thinking that had been pursued. It thus proved impossible to follow through at the time and in the manner called for. As a result, management no doubt passed up opportunities for profitable ventures abroad. The Turkish project was a case in point, in that correspondence had continued over three years between the company's Turkish distributor and the division management in New York. In the files were frantic letters from the Turkish distributor pleading with the company to answer his last letter, which indicated that an opportunity was perhaps slipping by.

Another example was the one-man effort in a hotel corporation to investigate adequately projects suggested to the company. Because of the "shotgun" approach with which the corporation began investigation of overseas opportunities and the fact that the responsibility for investigation was entirely in the hands of a single man, who had other important duties within the corporation, follow-through was slow and often inadequate. Potentially important letters from foreign interests remained in the head office for weeks without answer while the one man responsible was traveling off in another direction investigating projects elsewhere.

Within a large chemical company export sale and the development and management of foreign manufacturing and licensing ventures were located in two different divisions of the company. The company's export manager, headquartered in New York, had virtually nothing to do with these latter activities. (When his attention was drawn to a news item in the house organ to the effect that the manager of the company's patent development department had been in Europe to carry out negotiations for licensing and patent rights in Germany, Holland, France, and England, the export manager admitted that he had heard nothing about this trip.) He observed that perhaps the critical factor in the apparent reluctance by management to manufacture abroad lay in the fact that there was no group in the company specifically assigned the task of developing foreign projects. Although both the president of the company and one of the vice presidents were personally interested in foreign development, they were primarily concerned with other matters, and the development of foreign manufacturing was simply one more item added to their work load. The export manager agreed that the critical factor was perhaps organizational. He expressed quite strong feelings that all foreign business — export, licensing, and foreign manufacturing — should be centralized. On the other hand, there was a real problem in this regard inasmuch as the company's foreign operations were not really large enough to justify the full-time employment of the type of people required.

Choice of International Management It is not easy to locate competent individuals to head international divisions or corporations. The president of one corporation had looked for three years for someone who had lived and worked abroad and was capable of heading an international subsidiary. The executive vice president of another company stated that management had been looking for some time for a man to head up the export and foreign division of the business. Until that time the various divisions had had their own separate export businesses because the company had grown through mergers. But this decentralized control had become an inefficient and ineffective way of conducting foreign business. Management resolved to place all of its export business, as well as management of its foreign enterprises, under one head in an international division. However, it had been unable to find an individual to take charge.

Simply appointing the man who had been in the export end of the business to take over the leadership of an international division is not always an effective solution. There is such a thing as being sales-oriented in respect to foreign business, which is quite unlike being manufacturing- or licensing-oriented. Ideally, a company should have a man in charge who could look at foreign markets from all points of view and determine the best way in which to conduct business in each market and to make such decisions in a disinterested manner. One management explained its reluctance to invest capital in certain countries in terms of its dislike of taking over operations from distributors who had invested considerable time and money in the local promotion of company products. It is suggested that this explanation was rationalization. There are many ways in which licensing and manufacturing activities could have been conducted to the mutual profit of both company and ex-distributor. It seemed more likely that such a statement simply revealed export-orientation.

A number of companies in the survey indicated that conflict existed between sales people and those attempting to promote foreign manufacturing or licensing enterprises. In some cases, of course, the issue was so clear that conflict was ruled out. For example, in one company there was no opposition to foreign manufacturing by the sales staff because the alternatives were all too obvious; the company either manufactured in the market to which it was exporting or lost the market entirely. It was reported that the resident sales supervisors abroad of one corporation very seldom suggested investment in local manufacturing; their concern was almost entirely with sales. Company executives did admit that there was some basis for conflict in that not infrequently these resident sales supervisors felt they had built up a market through technical assistance and their own efforts, a market which would be destroyed for them if the overseas division were to build a local plant. By way of contrast, the salesmen for another company had been delegated the authority by management to investigate local markets and to suggest how best the company might conduct its business in these markets up to and including licensing and local manufacturing.

The export mentality was perfectly reflected in comments made by the general manager of the international division of a large company, a company which had been almost exclusively concerned with exports. The general manager was frankly against foreign investment. "I have seen too much of it and seen what has happened." When further exports became impossible, he favored licensing in lieu of direct investment, although his company had entered into only two foreign licensing agreements, one in Mexico and one in Italy. Some foreign groups had tried to induce management to invest abroad, but the manager had resisted all such moves by informing these groups that management was not interested. Thus, none of these proposals had been scrutinized with any care.

Some managements do recognize the importance of having full-time, internationally oriented executives to present the case for foreign business. A vice president of the international division of the Minneapolis-Honeywell Regulator Company at a session of the American Management Association stated:

> By 1946, the world was again at peace and our farsighted president, H. W. Sweatt, established a separate international division designed to fight the battle of our subsidiaries and distributors against the domes-

tically oriented home office, to get the special equipment we needed for these overseas markets, and to provide our growing overseas organization with a sympathetic and understanding group in the United States that would act as liaison with the various factories and top management. . . . The next step, and by far the most important, is one to which most companies are driven; I refer to the first venture in overseas manufacture.[5]

These two developments — the organization of an international division and the first direct investment in overseas manufacturing — were closely related. Perhaps the immediate reasons this company decided in favor of foreign manufacturing were other than the organizational structure of the company, but it seemed safe to speculate that in the absence of an international division, and the vested interest in international business such a division represented, the company might not have undertaken manufacturing abroad at all.

It was no coincidence that the companies in the author's study which had established a reputation for their ability in building and managing successful foreign enterprise followed a general pattern, organizationally. *First*, there was delegation of authority to a group beneath that of top management for the initiation of overseas projects. *Second*, there was definite responsibility lodged at some point within the company for the promotion of foreign business and for its success. *Third*, all foreign activities of the business (exports, licensing, assembling, manufacturing) were centralized in one division or a single subsidiary company, thereby avoiding orientation in one specific direction, for example, exports at the expense of foreign manufacturing. *Fourth*, responsibility in respect to foreign development was delegated to executives with no other tasks. A profit-maximizing management desired the existence of a group or an individual within the company (or available to the company) whose full-time job it was to study and develop foreign projects and argue for them as alternatives to domestic opportunities. *Only in this way* could management be reasonably confident that its capital resources were flowing into those projects most profitable from the company's point of view Necessarily included in that profit calculation was security of assets or market position, which — to a very substantial extent — was a function of management sensitivity and response to the interests of the host nations.

[5]International Management Association, *Special Report No. 1* (New York: American Management Association, 1957), p. 41.

The Decision-Making Mechanism

Company policy and structure conditions the decision-making mechanism, but it neither determines nor describes it. The manner in which decisions are reached influences what a management does overseas and is therefore relevant to the organizational requirements for the application of the criteria developed in Chapter 3.

The decision-making mechanism resolves itself into four stages — (1) the build-up of pressure on management and the stimulation of management interest in an overseas project, (2) the decision to commit company time and personnel to serious investigation, (3) analysis and reporting, and (4) the investment decision itself.

Stimulation of Interest   Pressure leading to serious thought about the wisdom of producing in a particular foreign market frequently comes from individuals so close to the firm — and so important to it — that management feels compelled to manifest some positive response to proposals suggested by them. Such pressure could become compelling. A company president put it, "When roots are deep in a country, such as [ours] in Brazil and Australia, it means that the company comes under considerable pressure from its own people in these countries to assemble or manufacture locally." Management then could not fail to reflect very soberly upon the possibilities of local production. Cases were reported in which chronic pressure from a company's distributor abroad had virtually forced management to make a serious investigation of foreign manufacturing or similar ventures, in part to make peace with the distributor. For example, the Turkish distributor of one firm for several years had kept up a constant stream of letters to the company pleading with it to give serious attention to the proposition of manufacturing in Turkey. It became awkward not to make an investigation.

Also contributory to many decisions to investigate was the confidence management had in the source of the proposal. Asked why it was that his company had given serious consideration to certain countries in Latin America and not others, a chemical company executive replied that a lot depended on the confidence one had in the people with whom one talked. The general manager of another corporation indicated that an Indian proposal had not been examined seriously, one reason being that management had little confidence in the man trying to promote the project. In the case of a venture in Pakistan, the confidence felt in the company's proposed Pakistani partner was one of the principal reasons why management had taken serious interest. A spokesman for an electrical appliance manufacturing firm went even further when he said, "We would have to have known the proposed [foreign] associate for many years. If a stranger came to us, he would probably never get a contract."

The regard in which a foreign group or individual approaching an American company with a foreign project was held could be critical in determining whether or not management decided to make a serious examination of the proposal. In certain cases proposals had been dismissed summarily simply because of adverse management reaction to the proponents. The initial approach was particularly important inasmuch as it seemed generally true that a foreign business group was received in an American company at a much higher level than would have been a comparable American business group. Frequently, foreign businessmen were received directly by the president of a large American corporation rather than by a lower-level executive. Although rarely expressed, many American managements seemed to feel that international good will and courtesy dictated that foreign businessmen be received at the highest possible level. Hence, one suspected, the initial approach by a foreign business group, and the management response generated thereby, could be controlling.

The author's 1956–1959 study provided adequate basis for the following generalizations relating to the initiation of interest in an overseas project by an American company.

First, the most important agencies by which management was drawn initially to foreign projects were foreign business groups and a company's own foreign representatives. *Second*, the most salient reasons inducing a company to give serious thought to a foreign project were the threatened loss of a present or potential market, need for resources, the degree of confidence in (and relationship to) the person or persons initiating the project, and company policy. *Third*, the most important source of information used in evaluating proposals to determine whether or not they merited serious consideration was "general knowledge," which was doubtless a result of general company environment and past exposure to foreign experience. Information sources of secondary import were reports emanating from the company's exporters and distributors, general legal firms (that is, those not specializing in private international law), and banks, plus a generalized view of the experience of other American companies in the country being considered. *Fourth*, the controlling variable was the presence in management, at a sufficiently high level, of someone inclined to be responsive to foreign projects and with the time to devote to discussing them. Multiplying the value of this variable were two others: the degree to which screening criteria had been formulated by the firm, and the presentation of adequate project prospectuses by the external agency. *Fifth*, the level within the company on which the decision was made to commit company time and money in serious investigation varied considerably. Where such decisions were made on a level lower than top management, a decision to investigate was perhaps more likely to rest on at least an attempt to look at the objective facts and relate them to the interests of the firm.

All of this reduced to the fact that the initiation of serious investigation of specific foreign markets or foreign projects was rarely based on really reasoned business considerations. A reasoned business approach at this level of decision would have called for periodic global surveys of all markets in which the company was able to sell, a time-consuming and expensive exercise. Except for three or four of the largest corporations included in the survey, plus one or two smaller firms, management had not undertaken organized and objective, country-by-country surveys to set up criteria for use in the selection of those projects meriting serious consideration. In at least one case management had skipped this level of decision entirely and had gone immediately into the investigation of *all* projects submitted. Time and staff had not permitted adequate follow-up on many, some of which might have been productive, because of the large number presented for consideration as the company's general interest in foreign expansion became known. Until management made a country-by-country survey of those business conditions relating to the specific industry in which the company was operating, it was difficult to see how it could sift investment projects suggested to it on a really sound basis.

To an extraordinary degree, the absence of effective communication was thus blocking consideration of overseas opportunities, let alone their measurement in terms of local political interests.

Decision to Investigate Of almost equal importance to the decision to commit company resources to a continuing riskful venture overseas is the decision to give serious thought and consideration to a foreign project. This decision is equivalent to a declaration of intent. For a firm that has never before concerned itself with foreign opportunities, it represents an important psychological breakthrough. Once the company commits time and money and personnel to serious investigation, it is likely that sufficient momentum will develop within the company to take it abroad, either in reference to the particular project which stimulated the investigation in the first instance or in reference to some other which had come up by reason of the investigation. The author's study revealed only three firms with only one foreign enterprise. There seemed good reason why this course of events tended to be general. A serious study presumed the build-up of a certain amount of vested interest in international business on the part of someone within management. It seemed unlikely that an individual or group which had prepared a detailed study of a particular project and recommended action to top management lost all interest once its findings were committed to paper. The individual or individuals working up a foreign project abroad might anticipate roles in its eventual fruition, perhaps by being named as officers in the foreign business to be established. Some managements deliberately included in foreign survey teams the individual most likely to manage an overseas venture if such were created. Thus, as investigation proceeded, certain individuals became identified with the foreign interests of the company and knowledgeable of the same. It was then in their personal interest to push development in that direction. Of course, this procedure did not occur so frequently for large corporations that already had extensive foreign interests and possessed specialized research or survey groups to examine foreign investment proposals.

It was apparent that the decision to give systematic thought to a foreign investment project to which management attention had been drawn could come at almost any level — from that of the development group or territorial manager within the international company or division up to and including the board of directors and chairman. It was difficult to generalize in respect to the level of decision. But it appeared that for those companies in which the decision to investigate might be made at a level below that of the executive committee or the president, there was somewhat more likelihood that a go-ahead verdict might be given. If a company employed specialists in foreign business, as some did within their international branch or subsidiary, it would seem sound practice to give these specialists authority to select for study those projects which seemed most reasonable to them, rather than referring the matter to executive committee or board level.

When management did decide to investigate a foreign proposition, what in fact did it commit — and how did it proceed? There was no set formula among the firms studied: the plan of study and analysis varied greatly from company to company. In fact, the very difference could be significant in determining whether or not investment took place.

The least investigation undertaken before making a definite offer to a foreign group was that reported by a New York machinery manufacturer. As a result of an approach by a Turkish promoter in New York, management offered to supply a certain amount of surplus machinery to his Turkish principals and participate in a joint Turkish enterprise. In studying the proposal and in making the offer, no one in the company visited Turkey nor talked with the prospective partners. An extreme case in the other direction was the time-consuming and expensive consideration of an undertaking in Venezuela by one large corporation, of which an executive commented, "We have been talking about Venezuela for seven years. This is the fifth staff report, including field trips, that has been made."

No generalization could be made in respect to the company status of persons involved in on-the-spot studies of foreign investment projects. In one instance, the analysis might be undertaken by the board chairman and in another, by a young assistant to the president, or, yet again, by a team on which were included some fairly low-level management representatives.

In only one instance was a *formal* report prepared by a corporation president who had been involved personally in a foreign survey. In most such situations where chairmen and presidents had been responsible for making foreign surveys there was either no formal written report at all, or a very sketchy one. If a survey were undertaken at a lower level, it was common to present a formal and fairly detailed report of findings and comments. Other than in the very smallest companies, such a procedure would seem to be valuable in terms of generalizing the experience that a few have had. In analyzing foreign situations and reporting on foreign events, it is surely useful to record observations and comments contemporarily rather than to permit the passage of time and the intervention of other incidents to warp memory and recollection. One suspected that some top executives of the survey's firms had given personal attention to a foreign investment project whereas they would not have done so for a comparable project in the United States. (Perhaps the lure of foreign travel was an inducement for some presidents and board members to usurp legitimate functions of staff or of company management.)

It would seem sound practice, when investigating a foreign project, to include as one member of the team, if not as its chief, the man designated by management to head or to participate in the foreign venture if such were to become reality. The membership of such an individual on a survey team might be the source of some bias if he were keen on creating such a position abroad for himself. In some companies it might be one path by which promotion could be accelerated. It is equally true that the personal bias of one who knows that he might be assigned to the overseas project that he is investigating might oppose a favorable recommendation. Personal problems involved in prolonged foreign residence could be such as to make an individual very reluctant to create a foreign demand for his services. Possible causes of bias in an overseas investigation might be such considerations as appropriate schooling for children, the reaction of one man's wife, the ownership of an attractive residence in an American community, differences in language and religion (consequently a feeling of not belonging), and the nonavailability of goods and services to which one was accustomed. The possibility of uncompensated bias is, in fact, one very good reason for not sending abroad on an important survey mission a single individual, be he board chairman or what. Collective assessment and evaluation by a group, some members of which are known not to be slated for assignment in developing the project were it to materialize, seems the more reliable approach. Yet, dispatch abroad of a survey team is an expensive business.

Although the more adequate surveys and analyses are perhaps those compiled by teams drawn from management below the top level, it, nonetheless, remains true that it might well be critical in the investment decision to have either the chairman or the president himself look over the project on the spot. The vice president of one company observed that a turning point in his firm's Brazilian project had come when he persuaded his president to visit Brazil. He added that in many companies it was difficult to get top management to look directly at foreign projects in that the foreign market was rarely large enough, as measured against total market, to warrant such personal attention. The most effective procedure appeared to be a careful study by a group of lower-management status and then a quick on-the-spot review by a high-level member of management, perhaps the president or the chairman.

The decision to give serious consideration to an investment project abroad is a decision not to be taken lightly inasmuch as such an investigation might require much time and effort by key personnel, plus cash investments, and, in some cases, investment in goods as well. The author's study suggested that many overseas proposals broke down at this level, as a result of management's unwillingness to commit adequate resources and personnel to do an effective job of analyzing projects. Obviously, more time and effort was required in the analysis of a foreign project than in the analysis of a comparable project within the United States, where the staff specialists of the home office were immediately available. The seriousness in which this decision to investigate was held was reflected in the fact that a great many managements did not undertake investigation of foreign projects until clearance had been secured from either the board of directors or top management. Managements requiring such high-level clearance were much less inclined to act on specific proposals than would otherwise have been the case, and hence, less likely to bring to light the foreign project that would be most advantageous from the point of view of the company and of the host country.

In recognition of this problem in mid-1962 the Agency for International Development (AID) undertook a program to finance 50 percent of the costs of surveying overseas projects incurred by private United States firms. If, as a result of such a study, a firm participates in the project under consideration, it is expected to repay AID. If it does not go into the venture, the firm is obligated to turn over to AID the survey report, which then becomes the property of the United States government.[6]

Analysis and Reporting The actual decision-making process begins with the preparation of a formal report or authoritative opinion. Cases could be cited in which a corporation president had made the on-the-spot survey himself and compiled a rough statement of his travels and observations. More frequently, however, such studies were compiled by survey teams drawn from various departments and from various levels of management. These statements often consisted of detailed analysis of the general economic and political climate as well as of a specific project and an evaluation of the same. Seldom

[6]*International Commerce* (Washington: U.S. Department of Commerce, July 16, 1962), p. 43.

were consultants or the foreign employees of a company called in to do this job. In some instances no management report was prepared at all.

Although it seemed true that in most of the larger companies with foreign interests detailed management studies of foreign projects were worked up prior to a decision, many exceptions were noted. In the case of one investment in Pakistan, only a very brief management statement was prepared, most of the presentation to the board of directors being made orally by the vice president in charge of the operating division most concerned. Although a paper company had made serious investigation of investment proposals in Cuba, South Africa, and the Philippine Islands, apparently no comprehensive management reports had been prepared on any of these projects. The president of another company, commenting on the nonavailability of any written reports on the company's Australian and Brazilian ventures, explained that there was not much documentation — not more than a paragraph or so in the minutes of the board of directors' meeting referring to these proposals. A presentation to the management committee studying foreign investment proposals within one of the pharmaceutical companies was a brief, six- or eight-page, type-written document presenting only the bare facts, plus estimates of the capital needed for machinery and facilities, together with estimates of potential sales. The board chairman of an appliance company stated:

> There was no formal management report on the Colombian situation. Our top management here are a pretty closely knit group, meeting about every two weeks so that the heads of the different divisions — sales, engineering, manufacturing, and so forth — know what each other is doing. The Colombian situation was discussed with these people, but not in the form of a written report. The same thing was true when the matter was taken up with our board of directors. The report was verbal and the minutes simply indicate that I was authorized to go ahead with the venture after discussion with the board.

Despite the wide and varied investigation by one corporation into foreign hotel properties — from the point of view of both management contracting and investment — the files disclosed no management analysis of the various projects under consideration. The main work seemed to have been carried on by conversations between the company official assigned the task of investigating these projects and the president of the corporation.

In a number of instances where no or very sketchy statements were prepared, one suspected that management would have been somewhat dismayed if it were aware how thin and uncertain the information was upon which it acted. A formal, rigorous analysis committed to writing before reaching a decision was more likely to expose the thinness and uncertainty than conversation. Certainly, the type of analysis suggested in Chapter 3 as essential requires many calculations and close analysis. There is no substitute for "pencil-pushing," even if the author were the only reader. (This discussion is not concerned with the many technical reports that follow a "go" decision.)

Apart from the degree of formality in which foreign investment projects and climates were studied by various managements, there also was a striking difference in whether a company approached foreign investment on a project-by-project basis, or on a global or national basis.

The larger corporations with research departments or groups within their international division or subsidiaries tended to maintain a continuous examination of markets on a global basis, constantly subjecting them to critical examination from the point of view of improving the company's position in them — up to and including the alternative of establishing manufacturing facilities. Other companies looked primarily at national markets in which some crisis had arisen. In the latter approach, national investment climates were not necessarily weighed one against the other, but various alternatives within a national market *might* be considered. However, for many firms, particularly the smaller ones, the experience was very different. In these firms management considered overseas projects only as they were brought to management's attention and as management interest was aroused. There were no systematic surveys. How management reacted to a project located in a particular national market was in large measure a function of both "general knowledge" and "impression" of that particular investment climate — or of management reaction to the proponent of the project — not the result of any objective and detailed study. Under such circumstances the approach to international business urged in Chapter 3 is obviously impossible.

Decision   Final decision on a foreign project may come on any of three levels: (1) the board of directors, (2) top management of the parent company, or (3) top management of the international division or subsidiary holding company.

Most foreign projects considered by the firms in the 1956–1959 survey were *rejected* at the top-management level, with or without knowledge of such rejection on the part of the board of directors. In most instances *positive* action on significant foreign undertakings demanded approval by the parent company's board before company resources could be committed. In some firms, such decisions were decentralized on the basis of size of investment. In a few cases decisions as to specific foreign projects were decentralized through the budgetary process, certain funds being earmarked for foreign development in designated geographical areas. Infrequently did the managements of international divisions or subsidiary international companies have authority to commit company funds to any major project without clearance from the parent company, except for indirect investment via contracted services. This distinction did not seem entirely reasonable. Under only unusual circumstances did a management make a negative recommendation to its board. And, it was quite apparent that the known attitudes of board members were of very great importance in shaping management recommendations to the board and offers to potential foreign associates. This feedback was peculiarly important because of the greater concern shown at board level for overseas projects than for comparable domestic projects. Since solid financial and business analysis was difficult for many overseas ventures, personal opinion — and emotion — had a correspondingly greater weight in decision-making. Anticipated rejection by the board undoubtedly restrained some managements from making proposals, particularly in the foreign area. It also seemed apparent that, faced with a potentially hostile board, management might have recourse to several devices to secure at least board acquiescence if not enthusiastic approval for foreign endeavors — such devices as the employment of international business specialists to present the case, inducement for board members to travel, participation in international business conferences, and the like. But the use of such devices implied a more than casually interested management.

It should be emphasized that approval of a firm's first foreign project was a singularly important event in the evolution of a purely domestic firm into an international organization. It was interesting to note that the individual or group making a final decision in this area was rarely knowledgeable of international business. And rarely were they internationally oriented. Often, responsibility for decision fell on those with heavy work loads, or with only casual interest in the matter at hand. Unfortunately, foreign business proposals were peculiarly vulnerable to emotional and unreasoned reactions, particularly by those with neither the time nor inclination to study such proposals in detail and with objectivity — such as the usual board member.

The decision-making mechanism is strongly conditioned by a firm's financial position, personnel situation, and formal organization. Undue financial or personnel restrictions, or organizational inertia or conflict, heavily influence the decision-making process. Generally, the decision-making mechanism in internationally oriented firms was such as to facilitate careful study of alternative overseas proposals and thoughtful decision, within policy limits, by individuals experienced in, and knowledgeable of, foreign opportunities and problems. In the absence of such a mechanism, it is difficult to see how a management could select those overseas projects in which the area of common interest between business and national objectives might be the greatest.

▶ ▶ ▶ ▶ **6**

The Time Dimension:
Outlook for the Future

Precisely because the policies and organizational devices suggested in the preceding pages have been practiced by only a few Western firms, our "collective capitalism" is not meaningful to most non-Westerners. That is, most firms seem to have been unable to internalize the criteria suggested in Chapters 2 and 3. Company policy and structure have been too domestically oriented, too inflexible. The result has been that in non-Western eyes Western business has not adequately related its ideas and institutions to non-Western hopes and problems. It has become quite apparent that the concept of a professionally managed, socially responsible capitalism founded on widely dispersed ownership, voluntary labor, and production for mass consumption has failed to fuel the explosive development errupting in nation after nation as economic incentives become effective and levels of political expectation rise. Indeed, many persons seem convinced that private business, by its very nature, cannot live in these explosive developmental situations. This failure plus the enormous residue of antibusiness attitude inherited from the past eras seem to have turned the ideological tide generally against the West in Asia and Africa, and perhaps in Latin America as well. Words alone, or even sympathetic visitors, one suspects, will not reverse the drift. After all, the Soviet Union appears to be moving ahead at a catch-up rate of development, while business-based societies *outside the Western industrial community* seem to be running far behind. The Soviet Communist appears to offer hope; the West, perpetual inferiority.

A very much greater flow of private capital[1] into the underdeveloped nations is urgently needed. An adequate flow of government

[1]Private capital includes technical skills, managerial abilities and know-how, as well as money and machines.

loans and grants cannot be anticipated, nor do recipient nations wish to be subjected to political influence implicit in government-to-government aid. If the over-all shortage of capital (as defined) is such that these peoples feel compelled to use totalitarian controls and ideologies to sustain their national development, then the image of Western business — and private business generally — will become even less appealing, hostilities will become more intense, markets will be lost, and profits will shrink accordingly. The private business concept, however defined, will have been found inadequate and irrelevant, and all will be the losers. R. L. Bruckberger observes in his *Image of America:*

> I am deeply convinced that if America does not do what is up to America to do, and do it quickly, the world is very close to being lost. By the world I mean this world, man's world with his individual and concrete liberties, his life on earth, a human life worthy of being lived.[2]

What has been done here is simply the extension of the time and geographical dimension of profit determination. Profits (and assets) may be here today and gone tomorrow — and so may Bruckberger's world of man. It would seem that there is a horrible urgency in making Western economic concept internationally viable if man's dignity is to be preserved — and incidentally, a profitable private business.

On what many would call a more "hard-headed level," the point has been made by numerous internationally minded executives that in certain industries in ten or twenty years only those firms organized internationally will survive. In these industries the competitive advantages to be gained from international integration of resources, production facilities, and/or markets are such as to doom the isolationist firm. One suspects that a growing proportion of the present "foreign" competition, both within the American market and without, stems from overseas plants in which American companies hold a financial interest either as licensor and/or stockholder.[3] (No wonder that a liberal trade program has gained adherents.) A truly international firm processes or manufactures any place in the world where the

[2]R. L. Bruckberger, *Image of America* (New York: Viking Press Inc., 1959), p. 270.

[3]An example: during the first half of 1959, 28 percent of all United States automobile imports were products of foreign subsidiaries of American companies. (*New York Times*, Jan. 28, 1960).

Another case: a large percentage of textile imports from Hong Kong is a product of American enterprise.

peculiar mix of productive factors provides some advantage. By the same token, it will sell out of, and into, any national market, taking full advantage of more rapid delivery, lower shipping charges, orders against softer currency, international exchange transactions, bilateral trade agreements, and triangular trade deals. It may manufacture part *A* in one country, part *B* in another, part *C* in another, exchange all three and assemble the final product in all three countries. The firm thereby gains the competitive advantage derived from official support and a larger market — indeed, a common market for the product involved but not for competing products. It may move depreciated machinery, which is obsolete in relation to the size and nature of demand in Country *X* out of that country and into Country *Y*, where the machinery may have many years of productive competitive life left.

Whatever the justification one may use for stepping up the flow of skills and capital into the underdeveloped countries, it is basic that building mutual interest between the developed nations and the developing nations within the context of international business is a vital national interest.

The conclusion may be drawn on the basis of this study that it is theoretically possible for a Western private business firm to operate successfully in the international field. That is, it is possible to establish a substantial area of common interest between itself and the developing societies of Asia, Africa, and Latin America. Behind that finding, however, it is necessary to maintain one important variable constant — the assumption of favorable governmental policies on the part of the home government. This assumption is a dubious one and should be more carefully studied. What concerns the author particularly is the attitude reflected in United States governmental policy and acts via-a-vis private international business. In September 1962 a distinguished business spokesman declared:

[I have] . . . very deep concern about the relations between United States Government and United States industry in the international field. It is a truism to say that the Government's influence on private international business is great and growing, and that the Government must rely on business for accomplishments crucial to our national welfare and indeed survival. Yet the evidence is clear that where there should be understanding between them, there is suspicion; where there should be communication, there is a wall of silence. . . .

Both in the Congress and in the Administration, there is a basic ignorance of the motivations, the nature and the results of direct private foreign investment. For a number of bureaucrats and Congressmen, such investment is an instrument of exploitation, a form of business imperialism.[4]

He added, "Every day we get new examples of how this frame of mind hurts business — and the nation." He cited the 1962 tax law as it related to foreign-source income, the antitrust law and policy, the inadequateness of export credit, and the cases of active discouragement by government officials of private foreign projects. Unfortunately, he observed, the other side is equally at fault: "Business in general has exhibited very little understanding and active support of United States foreign economic policy goals."

One suspects that any pronouncements to non-Western societies on political and economic liberalism, constitutional government and the like, will be largely ineffective, as likewise will be the insistence on the creation of political-economic climates favorable to private business *as a pre-condition* for Western investment. But the liberal concept can be actively encouraged and nourished by means of international, socially responsible business enterprise that is built solidly upon international cooperation, mutuality of interest, and enlightened management dedicated to the ultimate realization of liberal ideals. It seems inevitable that international economic integration, satisfactory investment climates, and constitutional governments will follow. It will take a long time before these developments will demonstrate their desirability and efficacy. These concepts can be transmitted most effectively by socially responsible business enterprise — *not* by military pacts, political alliances, official representation, nor the Voice of America, all of which are really agents of nationalism.

It is useful to bear in mind that in all probability international business of the future will consist primarily of international federations of locally owned firms, to which the central organization will sell research findings, technical assistance, debt capital, and access to international marketing organizations (including international transport, brand names, distribution networks, and so forth). The central organization itself is likely to be owned by nationals of many different states.[5] As ownership and operation broaden geographically, the

[4]Elliott Haynes, Executive Vice President and Director of Business International, Inc., and Editor of *Business International*.

[5]A point made by Frederic O. Donner (chairman of General Motors), in an address, "The World-Wide Corporation in a Modern Economy," delivered to the

rationale that would require the central body to register as a legal entity under the laws of any *one* national state appreciably weakens, and the argument for the recognition of private, internationally chartered corporations becomes compelling.

One can predict with some confidence that in the last decades of the twentieth century, Western business will constitute a powerful pressure in the direction of *internationalizing* the process of political socialization, through the institutional relationships it creates and the flow of communication inherent in them. Even Communist societies may be included, for the private ownership of the actual machines of production is not a necessary prerequisite in this relationship. In many countries joint public-private ownership of large sectors of production is already occurring, and in some of these situations private Western enterprise is participating in the manner suggested above.

It is relevant to point out that a number of foreseeable technical developments will likewise push in the direction of *international* — rather than national — development. Reference is made to such innovations as submarine mining, weather control, supersonic transport flight, world-wide television networks, arctic exploitation, and the like. An authoritative study on this subject concluded:

> Current concepts of national sovereignty are not well suited to the orderly regulation of these advances nor to their development for maximum utility with minimum conflict. Policy planners will find it increasingly necessary to explore new types of supranational organization.[6]

Already, certain leaders within the international business field are transcending national frontiers in their willingness to undertake anything, anywhere, in association with anybody, so long as it promises a reasonable long-run return. By legally elevating the transmission of those business services suggested here to the international level, the business organizations involved would be, at least in part, insulated from use by nationalist political authorities to further the ambitions of

8th International Congress of Accountants, New York, Sept. 27, 1962 (privately printed). In this speech he was echoing a privately circulated proposal made by R. K. Evans, a former vice president of General Motors, in 1956 entitled, "For Peace's Sake, Let the World Have Free Enterprise" (typed manuscript).

[6] *Possible Nonmilitary Scientific Developments and Their Potential Impact on Foreign Policy Problems of the United States* (prepared by the Stanford Research Institute, for the Comm. on Foreign Relations, S., 86th Cong., 1st Sess., Sept. 1959), p. 1.

any state against another. One can sense that already there exists an international business community, the members of which have ceased being emotionally committed to the perpetuation of particular cultures and value systems. This community has members in both developed and underdeveloped worlds.

The significance of this development may be enormous. Political scientist Hans J. Morganthau once wrote, "When the national state will have been replaced by another mode of organization, foreign policy must then protect the interest in survival of that new organization." He then suggested that such organization come into existence only by conquest or by "consent based upon the mutual recognition of the national interests of the nations concerned."

The author suggests that there is perhaps a third path which has been largely overlooked — specifically, the expansion of internationally constituted private groups (that is, business) whose mutual interests are contrary to the continued existence of national sovereignty as presently constituted. One can look forward perhaps to the day when these groups will become so large and powerful as to have a significant impact on national foreign policy itself. It is also conceivable that they will of themselves create a supranational interest possessed of not insignificant power. "Foreign policy must then protect the interest in survival of that new organization."[7]

The distinguishing characteristic of the international business approach to international relations is that it envisages institutional, functional, nonpolitical, multinational relationships that are conducive to the weaving of an ever larger fabric of common interest and loyalty, thereby eroding the concept of national sovereignty and conflicting national interests. In the end it is possible even to imagine the appearances of privately owned supranational corporations, registered, controlled, and taxed by an international organization, perhaps some agency of the United Nations or International Bank.[8] But, there is a long road to travel. International business needs a theory, a unifying purpose, and internationally competent managements to give it reality. It is hoped that this study contributes to bringing that reality closer.

[7]Morganthau's comment on these two paragraphs: "What you say about the problem of national sovereignty is entirely correct." (personal letter)

[8]Insofar as is known by the author, this idea was first suggested by Eugene Staley in his *War and the Private Investor* (New York: Doubleday & Company, Inc., 1935).

▶ ▶ ▶ ▶   **Bibliography**

Books and Brochures

Abegglen, James C., *The Japanese Factory* (New York: The Free Press of Glencoe, 1958).

Allen, G. C., and Audrey G. Donnithorne, *Western Enterprise in Far Eastern Economic Development* (New York: The Macmillan Company, 1954).

———— and ————, *Western Enterprise in Indonesia and Malaya* (London: George Allen & Unwin, Ltd., 1957).

Barlow, E. R., and Ira T. Wender, *Foreign Investment and Taxation* (Englewood Cliffs, N. J.: Prentice-Hall, Inc., 1955).

Beard, Miriam, *A History of Business* (Ann Arbor, Mich.: University of Michigan Press, 1962).

Bell, Laird, *Technical Cooperation in Latin America* (Washington, D. C.: National Planning Association, 1956).

Blaisdell, D. C., *European Financial Control in the Ottoman Empire* (New York: Columbia University Press, 1929).

Breecher, Irving, and S. S. Reisman, *Canada–United States Economic Relations* (Ottawa: Royal Commission on Canada's Economic Prospects, 1957).

Brierly, J. L., *The Law of Nations* (New York: Oxford University Press, 1959).

Bruckberger, R. L., *Image of America* (New York: The Viking Press, Inc., 1959).

Bryce, M. C., *Industrial Development: A Guide for Accelerating Economic Growth* (New York: McGraw-Hill Book Company, Inc., 1960).

225

Chenery, Hollis B., George E. Brandow, and Edwin J. Cohn, *Turkish Investment and Economic Development* (Ankara: U.S. Operations Mission to Turkey, 1953).

Chicago Research Center in Economic Development and Cultural Change, *United States Business and Labor in Latin America* (Washington, D.C.: United States Senate, Committee on Foreign Relations, 86th Cong., 2d Sess., January 1960).

Clemens, Samuel, *Roughing It* (Hartford, Conn.: American Publishing Company, 1872).

Davis, K. G., *The Royal African Company* (London: Longmans, Green & Co., Ltd., 1957).

Domke, Martin (ed.), *International Trade Arbitration* (New York: American Arbitration Association, 1958).

Donner, Frederic G., "The World-wide Corporation in a Modern Economy," speech delivered to the Eighth International Congress of Accountants, New York, September 27, 1962 (privately printed).

Evans, R. K., *For Peace's Sake, Let the World Have Free Enterprise* (privately printed, 1956).

Fayerweather, John, *Facts and Fallacies of International Business* New York: Holt, Rinehart and Winston, Inc., 1962).

Fforde, J. S., *An International Trade in Managerial Skills* (Oxford: Basil Blackwell and Mott, Ltd., 1957).

Fleming, H. M., *States, Contracts, and Progress* (Dobbs Ferry, N.Y.: Oceana Publications, Inc., 1956).

Ford, A. W., *The Anglo-Iranian Oil Dispute of 1951–'52* (Berkeley, Calif.: University of California Press, 1954).

Friedman, W. G., and George Kalmanoff, *Joint International Business Ventures* (New York: Columbia University Press, 1961).

Furnivall, J. S., *Colonial Policy and Practise: A Comparative Study of Burma and Netherlands Indies* (New York: Cambridge University Press, 1948).

Gilbert, M., *Comparative National Products and Price Levels: A Study of Western Europe and the United States* (Paris: OEEC, 1958).

——— and I. B. Kravis, *An International Comparison of National Products and the Purchasing Power of Currencies* (Paris: OEEC, 1954).

Gras, N. S. B., and H. M. Larson, *Casebook on American Business History* (New York: Appleton-Century-Crofts, 1939).

Hagen, Everett E., *On the Theory of Social Change* (Homewood, Illinois: Dorsey Press, 1962).

Hall, D. G. E., *Burma* (London: Hutchinson & Co. (Publishers), Ltd., 1956).

Huang, T. T. Y., *The Doctrine of Rebus Sic Stantibus in International Law* (Shanghai: Comacrib Press, 1935).

International Management Association Report No. 1 (New York: American Management Association, 1957).

Jenks, L. H., *The Migration of British Capital to 1875* (New York: Alfred A. Knopf, Inc., 1938).

Kalmanoff, George, *Joint International Business Venture in Colombia* (New York: Columbia University, 1957, mimeograph only).

Kent, J., *Commentaries on American Law* (Boston: Little, Brown & Company, 1873).

Knox, E. R. (ed.), *South Pacific Enterprise* (Sydney: Angus & Robertson, 1956).

Kuebler, Jeanne, *Protection of Investment in Backward Countries* (Washington, D. C.: Editorial Research Record Reports, Vol. II, No. 2, July 11, 1962).

Lerner, Daniel, *The Passing of Traditional Society* (New York: The Free Press of Glencoe, 1958).

Lillich, Richard B., *International Claims: Their Adjudication by National Commissions* (Binghamton, N. Y.: Syracuse University Press, 1962).

Meyer, John R., and Edwin Kuh, *The Investment Decision* (Cambridge, Mass.: Harvard University Press, 1957).

Michener, James A., *Hawaii* (New York: Random House, Inc., 1959).

Mitchell, J. D. B., *The Contracts of Public Authorities* (London: London School of Economics, 1934).

Morganthau, Hans, *Politics among Nations* (New York: Alfred A. Knopf, Inc., 1950).

Myrdal, G., *An International Economy* (New York: Harper & Row, Publishers, 1956).

Norman, E. H., *Japan's Emergence as a Modern State* (New York: Institute of Pacific Relations, 1940).

O'Connell, D. P., *The Law of State Succession* (New York: Cambridge University Press, 1956).

Powdermaker, Hortense, *Copper Town: Changing Africa — The Human Situation in the Rhodesian Copperbelt* (New York: Harper & Row, Publishers, 1962).

Representations to the Royal Commission on Canada's Economic Prospects (Canadian Manufacturers' Association, December 1955).

Robinson, Richard D., *Cases in International Business* (New York: Holt, Rinehart and Winston, Inc., 1962).

Samuelson, Paul A., *Economics*, 4th ed. (New York: McGraw-Hill Book Company, Inc., 1958).

Staley, Eugene, *War and the Private Investor* (New York: Doubleday & Company, Inc., 1935).

Stanford Research Institute, *Possible Nonmilitary Scientific Developments and Their Potential Impact on Policy Problems of the United States* (Washington, D. C.: Government Printing Office, 1959).

Stirling, Paul, *Social Structure of Turkish Peasant Communities* (Oxford University, unpublished Ph. D. dissertation, 1951).

Tinbergen, Jan, *The Design of Development* (Baltimore: The Johns Hopkins Press, 1958).

U.S. Department of Commerce, *U.S. Business Investment in Foreign Countries* (Washington: Government Printing Office, 1960).

U.S. House of Representatives, Committee on Foreign Affairs, 80th Cong., 2d Sess., Subcommittee print, *The International Trade Organization* (Washington, D. C.: Government Printing Office, 1948).

————, Committee on Ways and Means, Subcommittee on Foreign Trade Policy, 85th Cong., 2d Sess., *Private Foreign Investment* (Washington, D. C.: Government Printing Office, 1958).

Ware, Edith E., *Business and Politics in the Far East* (New Haven, Conn.: Yale University Press, 1932).

Williams, Mary W., *The People and Politics of Latin America* (Boston: Ginn & Company, 1944).

Williston, S., *A Treatise on the Law of Contracts* (New York: Baker, Voorhis & Co., 1936).

Wilson, Charles, *Empire in Green and Gold* (New York: Holt, Rinehart and Winston, Inc., 1947).

————, *The History of Unilever* (London: Cassell & Co., Ltd., 1954).

Wright, Quincy, *The Study of International Relations* (New York: Appleton-Century-Crofts, 1955).

Articles, Chapters, Addresses

Almond, Gabriel A., "A Functional Approach to Comparative Politics," *The Politics of Developing Areas* (Princeton, N. J.: Princeton University Press, 1960).

Anonymous, "The Fetish of Impossibility in the Law of Contracts," *Columbia Law Review*, Vol. 53 (1953).

Bayne, E. A., "His Excellency" (New York: American Universities Field Staff, November 1957).

Becker, A. S., "Comparison of United States and USSR National Output: Some Rules of the Game," *World Politics*, Vol. xiii, No. 1 (October 1960).

Braucher, R., "The Renegotiation Act of 1951," *Harvard Law Review*, Vol. 66 (1952).

Brierly, J. L., "The Judicial Settlement of International Disputes," *Journal of the British Institute of International Affairs*, Vol. 4 (1954).

Brown, W. O., and H. Lewis, "Racial Situations and Issues in Africa," *The United States and Africa* (New York: American Assembly, Columbia University, 1958).

Carlson, K. S., "Concession Agreement and Nationalization," *American Journal of International Law*, Vol. 52 (1958).

Cheng, B., "Expropriation in International Law," *The Solicitor*, Vol. 21 (1954).

Cleaves, Emery N., "Economic Climate for Manufacturing in Mexico," address given before Conference on Business and Industrial Opportunities in Mexico, Michigan State University (February 2, 1957).

Coleman, James S., "The Character and Viability of African Political Systems," *The United States and Africa* (New York: The American Assembly, Columbia University, 1958).

Coon, C. S., "Operation Bultiste: Promoting Industrial Development in Saudi Arabia," *Hands Across the Frontier* (Ithaca, N. Y.: Cornell University Press, 1955).

Fachiri, A. P., "Expropriation and International Law," *British Yearbook of International Law*, Vol. 6 (1925).

Fensterstock, H. W., "The Rationale of Renegotiation," *Federal Bar Journal*, Vol. 16 (1956).

Friedman, W., "Some Impacts of Social Organizations on International Law," *American Journal of International Law*, Vol. 50 (1956).

Galenson, Walter, and Harvey Lubenstein, "Investment Criteria: Productivity and Economic Development," *Quarterly Journal of Economics*, Vol. LXIX (August 1955).

Garner, J. W., "The Doctrine of Rebus Sic Stantibus and the Termination of Treaties," *American Journal of International Law*, Vol. 21 (1927).

Goldschmidt, Walter, "Culture and Changing Values in Africa," *The United States and Africa* (New York: American Assembly, Columbia University, 1958).

Gordon, W. C., "International Investments: Process and Nature," in P. D. Zook, *Economic Development and International Trade* (Dallas, Tex.: Southern Methodist University Press, 1959).

Hill, C., "The Doctrine of Rebus Sic Stantibus in International Law," *University of Missouri Studies*, Vol. 9 (1934).

Huang, T. F., "Some International and Legal Aspects of the Suez Canal Question," *American Journal of International Law*, Vol. 5 (1957).

Hudson, Gordon, "Foreign Control of Canadian Business," *Business Quarterly*, Vol. XXII, No. 3 (Fall 1947) and No. 4 (Winter 1957).

Hyde, J. N., "Permanent Sovereignty over Natural Wealth and Resources," *American Journal of International Law*, Vol. 50 (1956).

International Chamber of Commerce, United States Council, "Economic Issues at the Fifteenth General Assembly of the United Nations," *Notes on International Economic Issues*, Vol. 57 (1961).

Jacobsson, Per, "Address," *International Financial News*, Vol. xiv, No. 37 (September 21, 1962).

Kamarck, Andrew M., "The African Economy and International Trade," *The United States and Africa* (New York: The American Assembly, Columbia University, 1958).

Kessler, Frederick, "Contracts of Adhesion: Some Thoughts about Freedom of Contract," *Columbia Law Review*, Vol. 43 (1943).

Kunz, J. L., "The Mexican Expropriations," *New York University Law Quarterly Review*, Vol. 17 (1940).

Leontief, W., "Factor Proportions and the Structure of American Trade: Further Theoretical and Empirical Analysis," *Review of Economics and Statistics*, Vol. xxxviii, No. 4 (November 1956).

Lippitt, R., N. Polansky, and S. Rosen, "The Dynamics of Power," *Human Relations*, Vol. 5, No. 1 (1952), pp. 44–50.

Llewellyn, K. N., "What Price Contract? An Essay on Perspectives," *Yale Law Review*, Vol. 40 (1931).

Lombardini, Siro, "Quantitative Analysis in the Determination of the Efficiency of Investment in Underdeveloped Areas," *International Economic Papers No. 9* (New York: The Macmillan Company, 1959).

Machlup, F., "Equilibrium and Disequilibrium," *Economic Journal*, Vol. LXVIII (March 1958).

Manning, John, "American Investment in Canada," *Colorado Quarterly*, Vol. VI, No. 2 (Autumn 1957).

Martin, Harold H., "The Oil of the Arab World," *Saturday Evening Post* (February 17, 1962).

Matthews, Herbert L., "Diplomatic Relations," *The United States and Latin America* (New York: American Assembly, Columbia University, 1959).

Means, Gardiner C., "Collective Capitalism and Economic Theory," *Science*, Vol. 126, No. 3268 (August 16, 1957).

Miller, A. S., "Foreign Trade and the 'Security State': A Study in Conflicting National Policies," *Journal of Public Law*, Vol. 7 (1958).

——, "Government Contract and Social Control: A Preliminary Inquiry," *Virginia Law Review*, Vol. 41 (1955).

Mowbray, George, "Little Canadianism and American Capital," *Queen's Quarterly*, Vol. 65, No. 1, (Spring, 1958).

Neumark, Daniel S., "The Character and Potential of African Economies," *The United States and Africa* (New York: American Assembly, Columbia University, 1958).

Nolte, Richard H., "A Tale of Three Cities III (continued): Jedda and the Oil Company" (New York: American Universities Field Staff, Inc., 1958).

Nove, A., "The United States National Income A La Russe," *Economica*, Vol. 23 (1956).

Ohman, O. A., "Search for a Managerial Philosophy," *Harvard Business Review*, Vol. 35, No. 5 (September–October 1957), p. 44.

Owen, A., "Implied Terms in Contrast," *Law Journal*, Vol. 102 (1952).

Presthus, Robert V., "Authority in Organization," *Public Administration Review*, Vol. XX, No. 2 (Spring 1960).

Pye, Lucian W., "The Politics of Southeast Asia," *The Politics of Developing Areas* (Princeton, N. J.: Princeton University Press, 1960).

Robinson, Richard D., "Conflicting Interests in International Business," *Boston University Business Review*, Vol. 7 (Spring 1960).

——, "The Challenge of the Underdeveloped National Market," *Journal of Marketing*, Vol. 25, No. 6 (October 1961).

Rottschaefer, H., *The Constitution and Socio-Economic Change* (Ann Arbor, Mich.: University of Michigan, 1948).

Schmitt, Peter G., "Licensing Arrangements vs. Branch Operations," *Export Trade and Shipper* (April 22, 1957).

Samore, W., "The New International Law of Alejandro Alvarez," *American Journal of International Law*, Vol. 32 (1958).

Schultz, Theodore W., "Capital Formation by Education," A. E. R. Paper No. 5807, rev. (February 4, 1960, typed manuscript).

Silvert, Kal H., "Political Change in Latin America," *The United States and Latin America* (New York: The American Assembly, Columbia University, 1959).

Skinner, C. W., "Management Problems Slow Progress Abroad," *Virginia Law Review*, Vol. xii, No. 23, (April 22, 1958).

U.S. State Department, *The Suez Canal Problem* (Washington, D. C.: Government Printing Office, 1956).

Verzijil, J. H. W., "Western Influence on the Foundations of International Law," *International Relations*, Vol. 1 (1955).

Vorys, Karl von, "Some Political Incentives for Economic Development in India, Pakistan, Burma, and Ceylon," *The Western Political Quarterly*, Vol. xi, No. 4 (December 1959).

Wienshienk, R., and F. Feldman, "The Current Challenge of Military Contract Termination," *Harvard Law Review*, Vol. 66 (1952).

Weiner, Myron, "The Politics of South Asia," *The Politics of Developing Areas* (Princeton, N. J.: Princeton University Press, 1960).

Westinghouse Electric Corporation, "Memorandum on the Buy American Act" (February 16, 1955).

Legal Cases

Anglo-Iranian Oil Company, *International Court of Justice Reports*, 1952.

Barber v. Connolly, 113 U.S. 27 (1884).

City of Vernon v. Los Angeles, 45 Cal.2d 710, 290 P.2d 841 (1955).

Czechoslovakia v. Radio Corp. of America, *American Journal of International Law*, Vol. 30 (1936).

East New York Sav. Bank v. Hahn, 326 U.S. 230 (1945).

Martini Case, *American Journal of International Law*, Vol. 25 (1931).

Hebbia v. New York, 291 U.S. 502 (1934).

O'Grady v. M. Saper, Ltd., 3 All England Law Reports 527 (1940).

Ohio Life Ins. Co. v. Debolt, 16 Howard 428 (1853).

Pennsylvania Coal Co. v. Mahon, 393 U.S. 414 (1922).

Radio Corp. of America v. China, *American Journal of International Law*, Vol. 30 (1936).

Rederiaktiebolaget Amphritite v. The King, 3 K.B. 500 (1921).
Robert E. Brown Claim, *British Yearbook of International Law*, 1924.
United States v. Bethlehem Steel Corp., 315 U.S. 289 (1942).
United States v. Corliss Steam-Engine Co., 91 U.S. 321 (1876).

Laws, Resolutions, Aide-Memoire

Draft Bill on Foreign Investment, Official translation (Djakarta: Government of Indonesia, June 27, 1957).
Foreign Aid Act of June, 1962, United States Congress Public Law 87–565 (1962).
Government of Bolivia, "Executive Decree of 13 March 1937," *Annuario Administrativo de 1937*, translation in *United States Foreign Relations*, Vol. 5 (1937).
Government of Guatemala, "Aide-Memoire," delivered by the Ambassador of Guatemala to the U.S. Department of State (June, 26, 1953).
Resolution 625, Supplement No. 20, United Nations General Assembly Official Records, 7th Sess. (A/2361) (1952).
Resolution 626, Supplement No. 20, United Nations General Assembly Official Records, 7th Sess. (A/2311) (1952).
Sugar Act, United States Congress Public Law 87–535 (1962).
U.S. State Department, "Note from the Secretary of State to the Mexican Ambassador in Washington, 22 August 1938," *United States Foreign Relations*, Vol. 5 (1938).

Business Case Studies

Geiger, Theodore, *The Case Study of TWA's Service to Ethiopia* (Washington, D. C.: National Planning Association, 1959).
May, Stacy, and Gato Plaza, *The Case Study of the United Fruit Company in Latin America* (Washington, D. C.: National Planning Association, 1958).
Robinson, Richard D., "Merck & Co., Inc., in India," Harvard Graduate School of Business Administration, 1959 business cases ICR 183 and 184.
———, "W. R. Grace & Company: Foreign Investment," Harvard Graduate School of Business Administration, 1959 business case ICR 167.

Thornburg, Max, "The Anglo-Iranian Oil Company," Harvard Graduate School of Business Administration, 1959 business case ICR 217.

Wood, Richardson, and Virginia Keyser, *Sears, Roebuck de Mexico, S.A.* (Washington, D. C.: National Planning Association, 1953).

▶ ▶ ▶ ▶

Index

Chemical industry (*Cont.*)
  organization of firm, 198–199, 200,
    201–202, 204
  personnel, 197, 198
Chenery, Hollis, B., 108–109, 110
Chettiars, 17
Child, Josial, 5
Chile, 180
China, extraterritorial rights in, 70
  investment in, 181–182
  nationalism in, 32
  penetration by Western enterprise,
    in Commercial Era, 10–11, 12
    in Concessionary Era, 26, 28,
      29–30
    in Exploitative Era, 18, 20–22, 23
    in National Era, 30, 32
  Radio Corporation of America, dis-
    pute with, 59–61
China, Communist, 36, 174
Chinese, in Hawaii, 16
  in Hong Kong, 18
  in Java, 18
  in Malaya, 18
Christian expansionism, 5, 16
Chrysler Corporation, 182
City of Vernon v. Los Angeles, 67
  (n.70)
Claims commissions, 98
Cleaves, Emery N., 87, 162
Coercion, defined, 79–80
  lack of alternatives, flowing from,
    71, 72–73, 79
  redefined, 91–92
  tests, 82
  unequal power, flowing from, 79–80,
    89, 93
  See also Duress
Cold War, 33, 34, 91, 165
Collective capitalism, 219
Colombia, conquest of, 6
  interest in, 215
  investment in, 185, 189, 204
  joint ventures in, 153, 155
  Spanish in, 6
Colonial Sugar Refining Company, 20
Colonialism, in Africa, 7, 15, 27
  Belgians, 27

Colonialism (*Cont.*)
  British, 5, 6, 7–8, 9, 20, 27
  in Burma, 20
  coercion, and law on, 80–81
  in Congo, 27
  Dutch, 7, 9
  emerges from charted companies,
    14–16
  in India, 56, 7–8
  in Latin America, 6, 15
  in North America, 6, 15
  as origin of injury to state, 91
  post-revolutionary effect of, 127–128
  pressure against, 26
  pressure for, 11–12, 13–15
  in Southeast Asia, 7, 15
  Spanish, 4–5, 6
  state succession, and law on, 76–77,
    82
  termination of, 32–34
Columbus, Christopher, 3
Commercial Era, 2, 3–14, 39
Commodities, elasticity of supply and
  demand, 116
Communication, intrafirm, 30, 137–
  138, 138–139, 140
Communications, in Africa, 27
  in China, 12, 20–21
  International Telephone and Tele-
    graph Company, 85, 162
  in Japan, 23
  political vulnerability of, 141, 142
  Radio Corporation of America: in
    Czechoslovakia, 58–61; in China,
    59–60
  Western penetration via, 9, 12, 14,
    20–21, 27, 39
  See also Air transport; Railways;
    Suez Canal
Compania Mexicana de Aviacon, 162
Company environment, authority in,
  202–203, 207
  centralization of function, 198–201,
    202, 205–207
  conflict within, 198, 201–202, 205–
    206
  financial position, 192–195
  formal organization, 198–208

Decision-making within the firm (*Cont.*)

decision to investigate, 210–214
delegation of, 202–203
final, 216–218
level of, 210, 212, 213, 214
mechanism for, 208–218
ramifications of, 218
stimulation of interest by, 208–210
usurpation of authority for, 213
Discrimination against alien business,
codes to prevent, 54
in United States, 47, 52
in West, 52
Diversification, of economy, 101, 116, 117
of the firm, 175
geographical, 175, 193–194
by product, 175–176
and joint ventures, 160
Dominican Republic, 30
Donnithorne, Audrey G., 11 (n.29), 12 (n.34), 17 (n.41), 20 (n.51), 21 (n.52–57), 22 (n.58–60), 23 (n.62), 34 (n.80)
Drug industry, 137–138, 141, 142, 151–152
Dualism, economic, 101
du Pont de Nemours and Company, 198
Duress (*see* Coercion)
Dutch East India Company, 7, 9, 18

Economic development, (*see* Economic growth)
Economic growth, definition, 100 (n.1), 102, 122 (n.26)
geographical dispersion of, 129–130
goals of, 122 (n.26), 128
innovation and, 102
measurement of, 103–104
national objective, as, 100, 101
and political modernization, 41
psychological compulsion for, 128–129
role of ideology in, 128–129
sacrifice of consumption for, 129
structural imbalance and, 101–102

Economic growth (*Cont.*)
and Western enterprise, 219–220
Ecuador, 37–38
Education, and allocation effect, 125
capital intensity of, 123–124 (n.32)
as net value added, 106–107
sponsored by Western enterprise, 30
training local management, 30–31
See also Skills, international transmission of
Egalitarianism, idea of, 1
Egypt, Anglo-French-Israeli attack, 91
Aswan Dam, 91
civilized, recognized as, 52
in Concessionary Era, 26
development, 129
mixed ventures in, 168
Suez Canal, 33, 48, 91, 130
Suez pipeline project, 168
Eisenhower, Dwight D., 64
Electrical appliance industry, 19, 172, 180–181, 203
Elite, concern with natural growth, 121–122
discounts future consumption, 122
emphasis on economic growth, xi, 122–123, 124
future role of, 124
traditional, displaced, 9–10
weakened, 17
England (*see* United Kingdom)
Ente Nazionale Idrocaburi, 167
Equity (*see* Joint ventures; Mixed ventures; Ownership policies and foreign investment)
Ericson Company, 162
Ethiopia, 28
Europe, research laboratories in, 195
Exploitative Era, 2, 14–32, 39
Explosives, 142
Export-Import Bank, 166
Exporting, organizational implications, 200–205
orientation toward, 199, 205–206
See also Trading
Expropriation, Anglo-Iranian Oil Company, 33, 37, 55, 130
Brazilian Telephone, 85